CORE JSP

ISBN 0-13-088248-8

PRENTICE HALL PTR CORE SERIES

Core PHP Programming, 2/e, Atkinson

Core Python Programming, Chun

Core Visual Basic 5, Cornell & Jezak

Core Java Media Framework, Decarmo

Core Jini,* Edwards

Core Servlets and JavaServer Pages,* Hall

Core Web Programming, 2/e,* Hall

Core JSP, Hougland & Tavistock

Core Visual C++ 6, Klander

Core CSS, Schengili-Roberts

Core C++: A Software Engineering Approach, Shtern

Core Java Web Server, Taylor & Kimmet

Core Java Foundation Classes, Topley

Core Swing: Advanced Programming, Topley

Core Web3D, Walsh & Bourges-Sévenier

**Sun Microsystems Press titles*

CORE JSP

DAMON HOUGLAND
AARON TAVISTOCK

Prentice Hall PTR, Upper Saddle River, NJ 07458
www.prenhall.com

Library of Congress Cataloging-in-Publication Data

CIP data available

Production Supervisor: Wil Mara
Acquisitions Editor: Karen McLean
Technical Editor: Carl Burnham
Editorial Assistant: Rick Winkler
Marketing Manager: Kate Hargett
Manufacturing Manager: Alexis Heydt
Cover Designer: Talar Agasyan
Cover Design Direction: Jerry Votta
Art Director: Gail Cocker-Bogusz
Series Design: Meg VanArsdale
Composition: Alexis Heydt

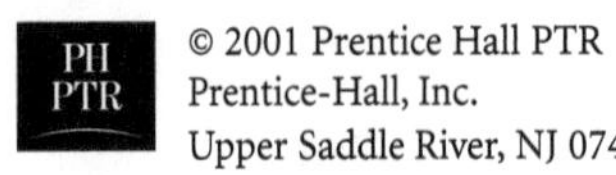

Prentice-Hall, Inc.
Upper Saddle River, NJ 07458

The publisher offers discounts on this book when ordered in bulk quantities. For more information contact: Corporate Sales Department, Prentice Hall PTR, One Lake Street, Upper Saddle River, NJ 07458. Phone: 800-382-3419; FAX: 201-236-7141; E-mail: corpsales@prenhall.com

Printed in the United States of America

10 9 8 7 6 5 4 3 2

ISBN 0-13-088248-8

Prentice-Hall International (UK) Limited, *London*
Prentice-Hall of Australia Pty. Limited, *Sydney*
Prentice-Hall Canada Inc., *Toronto*
Prentice-Hall Hispanoamericana, S.A., *Mexico*
Prentice-Hall of India Private Limited, *New Delhi*
Prentice-Hall of Japan, Inc., *Tokyo*
Pearson Education Asia Pte. Ltd.
Editora Prentice-Hall do Brasil, Ltda., *Rio de Janeiro*

Contents

Foreword

In recent years, a large amount of software development activity has migrated from the client to the server. The client-centric model, in which a client executes complex programs to visualize and manipulate data, is no longer considered appropriate for the majority of enterprise applications. The principal reason is deployment—it is a significant hassle to deploy client programs onto a large number of desktops, and to redeploy them whenever the application changes. Instead, applications are redesigned to use a web browser as a "terminal". The application itself resides on the server, formatting data for the user as web pages and processing the responses that the user fills into web forms.

If you set out to develop a web application, you need to choose a technology that has several important characteristics. You need to generate large amounts of dynamic HTML conveniently. You require access to databases and other services. The technology must provide an architectural foundation for performance and stability. Finally, you must be able to partition your program logic in a way that allows for future growth and maintainability.

The first web applications used the CGI (Common Gateway Interface) mechanism and a collection of server-side scripts, typically written in Perl, but occasionally in C, Python, PHP or other languages. There are numerous problems with this approach. The CGI mechanism does not scale well since every web request spawns a new server process. Communication between processes—for example, to share resources such as database connections—is extremely awkward to program. And finally, exotic programming languages may have their charm but they lack the ability to do the "heavy lifting". Features such as database access or security are typically not part of the language but supplied by a non-standard third-party library. That puts the programmer at the mercy of not only the implementors of the language itself but also the providers of various third-party libraries.

Java programmers have enjoyed the power of servlets for some time, which solves many of these problems. Servlets are programmed in Java, a language that is widely supported. Java has built-in features for database access, networking, multithreading, security, and so on. Each servlet executes in its own thread, thus avoiding the cost of generating server processes. Servlets can easily share resources such as session state and database connections. The principal disadvantage of servlets is that it is plainly tedious to generate HTML. All HTML must be generated programmatically, by statements that print all the text and tags. In particular, that means that the pages are generated by programmers. We all know what can happen when programmers try their hand at web design.

An increasingly popular approach in recent years has been the use of web server scripting languages such as Netscape LiveWire and Microsoft ASP (Active Server Pages). With these systems, a programmer embeds code snippets into web pages. The pages themselves can be professionally designed by a web designer. The web server executes the code snippets when serving the page, inserting the HTML that results from the execution of each snippet. The advantage of this approach—and the reason for its popularity—is that you can get simple results very quickly. But what looks like fun and great productivity early on turns out to be a maintenance nightmare later. When you intermingle the presentation (the static parts of the HTML pages) and the business logic (the code snippets), it becomes very difficult to change either when the need arises. Web designers will not know how how to move the code around when redesigning the pages. This makes any redesign a costly affair involving frequent interaction between programmers and web designers. Finally, keep in mind that you are tied into a particular web server. For example, if you develop your application in ASP and later want to use Apache instead of Microsoft IIS, you are stuck.

The JSP technology that is the topic of this book overcomes these issues. JSP has the same advantages as servlets—in fact, JSP pages *are* servlets. You use the full power of the Java language, and not some scripting language, to implement your business logic. By using beans, XML transformations, and tag libraries, JSP lets you separate the presentation logic and business logic. For example, in a well-structured JSP application, you can have the same business logic with multiple interfaces, giving your users the choice to use a regular web browsers or a mobile phones that uses WAP (the wireless access protocol).

This book teaches you how to build robust and scalable web applications with JSP. It covers the JSP syntax, the features that JSP inherits from servlets such as session management, the interaction between servlets and beans, a number of useful Java topics such as JDBC (Java Database Connectivity) and XML. Finally, and most importantly, you will learn about application partitioning and deployment—these subjects make all the difference between a quick hack and a robust application that will withstand the test of time.

Unlike other books, this book takes a properly JSP-centric approach, in accordance with the recommendations that Sun Microsystems makes in their Java Enterprise blueprints. This is very appropriate and a major strength. Where other books start out with servlets and discuss JSP as a second method for web programming, this book shows you why JSP pages have a higher position in the food chain. A JSP page can do everything a servlet can, but where you have to do a lot of tedious programming and organizing when you use servlets, JSP has higher level capabilities that let you focus on your business problems instead.

In the spirit of the Core series, this book contains is plenty of real-world advice that you won't find in the online documentation. The authors don't dwell on tedious syntax and boring minutiae. Unlike so many computer book authors, they have done the hard work and separated the wheat from the chaff. You won't waste time studying features that you won't use, but you will find good coverage of those subjects that you actually need when building real applications. I am confident you will find this Core book truly useful. I hope you enjoy it and have the opportunity to use it for building great web applications.

Cay Horstmann
San Jose, August 2000

Acknowledgments

This book wouldn't exist if it were not for the multitude of supportive people that have helped us throughout the process.

Our first praise must go to our editor, Karen McLean, for putting up with our endless barrage of questions and keeping us on course. Without her help we would have been endlessly lost, trying to figure out what actually goes into creating a book.

Of course our reviewers, Cay Horstmann, Carl Burnham, and Glenn Kimball, deserve a special round of applause as well. Their sharp eyes and bountiful comments helped us smooth the book into the more readable text that you see today.

Finally and maybe most important, we'd like to thank the entire Java and JSP community. Java, Java Servlets, and JavaServer Pages are evolving and growing into a powerful force primarily because of the drive of countless individuals who dedicate their time to make them better. These technologies are a flagship for the power of communities and open standards.

From Aaron

When I first committed to writing this book, I knew I was expecting a little one. She has very quickly become the most important thing in my life. Undoubtedly, my strongest drive to complete this book was so that I could spend more time with her. Zella Arden Tavistock-Thaman is my most important dedication.

I also want to voice my profound appreciation for the patience and understanding that Zella's mom has given me. Raquella Thaman has been supportive and helpful throughout the long weekends and nights, all the while helping me keep track of the important things going on in the world around me. I don't think I can truly state my love and appreciation for you, Raqui.

Then there is the whole Tavistock family. To my parents, Daniel and Marjorie Tavistock, for always being there and being supportive. To my sisters for putting up with me as a big brother and letting me rile up all the nieces and nephews.

Of course, I also had a great coauthor. We each have our own set of skills that seem to compliment the other's and yet we work in similar ways to get to an end-goal. It has been good to work with a talented and driven person like Damon.

It was hard work, fun, and its finally finished... thank you everyone!

From Damon

For putting up with all of the long hours, weekends at the computer, and 3 A.M. writing sessions, I dedicate my efforts toward this book to my wonderful wife Julie Hougland. Without her constant support and encouragement this book would never have been completed. She is the sensation of joy I feel when I awake every morning, and the warm, comfortable feeling of contentment when I close my eyes at night.

I also want to thank my best friend, my daughter Abigail Nora Hougland, and my hope for the future, my little son Gibson Charles Hougland. Their smiles and laughs remind me what life is all about. Their curious eyes and warm embraces make my life full.

Special thanks goes to my parents, Christine and Bill Gollery, as well as my sister Jamie Thomas. Thank you for always being there with your support and love. I owe the success and happiness I have in life to the foundation you created, nurtured, and still care for.

I want to thank my Grandparents, Jack and Barbara Wells. Nana, you built my self-confidence by telling me I could succeed. You always encouraged me to learn and do more. Papa, you are my role model. The quiet way you are always there for the entire family. You always led by example, taking care of us whenever anything was wrong and always making us feel special. You have built a large and loving family.

Thanks to my aunt Paula Wells, whose experience, advice, and encouragement helped us from concept to appendix. Your guidance made this book possible.

And I won't forget my coauthor Aaron, for sticking with me from my crazy idea for a book to the final pages. It has been a long road, and I wouldn't have gone down it with anyone else. Thanks!

INTRODUCTION

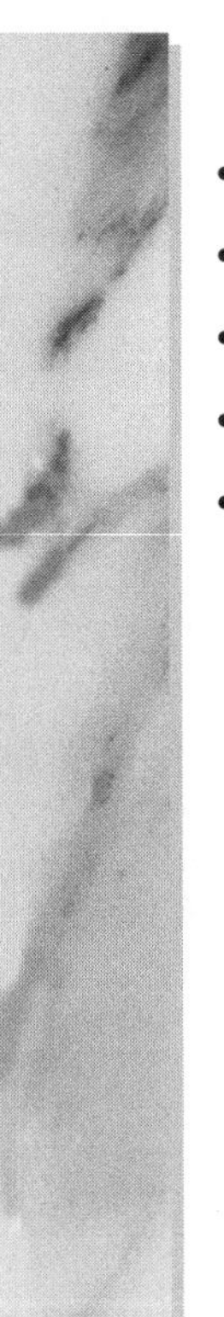

Topics in this Chapter:

- A History of the Web
- JavaServer Pages
- The Power of Java
- A Simple JSP
- Understanding HTTP

Chapter 1

In today's environment, dynamic content is critical to the success of any Web site. Users want and need very specific information tailored to their situation. As the Web becomes a standard platform for enterprise computing and e-commerce, Web development steadily gets more complex. Web servers are becoming Web application servers. Complex databases and applications are turning up all over the Internet. Content providers want a solution that is easy to create and quick to market, yet powerful and flexible.

JavaServer Pages (JSP) is an exciting new technology that provides powerful and efficient creation of dynamic content. JSP is a presentation layer technology that allows static Web content to be mixed with Java code. JSP allows the use of standard HTML, but adds the power and flexibility of the Java programming language.

JSP does not modify static data, so page layout and "look-and-feel" can continue to be designed with current methods. This allows for a clear separation between the page design and the application. JSP also enables Web applications to be broken down into separate components. This allows HTML and design to be done without much knowledge of the Java code that is generating the dynamic data. Businesses will no longer have to hunt down the rare software developer who understands graphic design, layout, application programming, and software design.

As the name implies, JSP uses the Java programming language for creating dynamic content. Java's object-oriented design, platform independence, and protected-memory model allow for rapid application development. Built-in networking and enterprise Application Programming Interfaces (APIs) make Java an ideal language for designing client-server applications. In addition, Java allows for extremely efficient code reuse by supporting the JavaBean and Enterprise JavaBean component models.

1.1 A History of the Web

To understand the power of JSP pages, one must first take a look at the past approaches to creating Web pages.

Static Pages

With a static Web page, the client requests a Web page from the server and the server responds by sending back the requested file to the client. The client receives an exact replica of the page that exists on the server (See Figure 1–1).

Traditional Web pages are static and unchanging. Under normal conditions they will always remain the same. Requests from multiple clients for the same static page should all receive the same results.

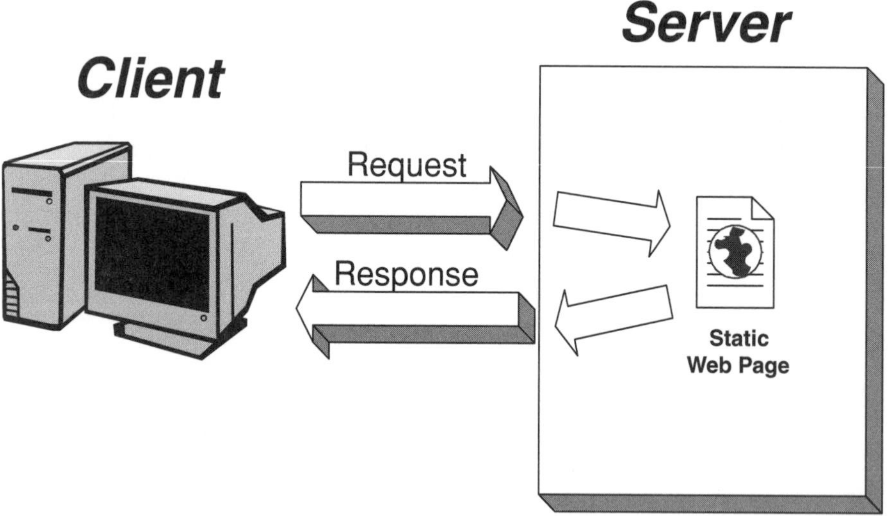

Figure 1–1 Standard HTML Document

Dynamic Pages

Since the earliest days of HTML there has been a need for handling data dynamically. It may have started out as simple as providing a feedback form. Today's Web site requires a lot more than static content and a feedback form. Dynamic data is important to everything on the Web, from online banking to playing games.

The definition of dynamic content is Web pages that are created at the time they are requested, changing content based on specified criteria. For example, a Web page that displays the current time is dynamic because its content changes to reflect the current time. Dynamic pages are generated by an application on the server, receiving input from the client, and responding appropriately (See Figure 1–2).

There have been several methods of generating dynamic data used over the years. Understanding the other approaches and their strengths and weaknesses helps to understand JSP pages.

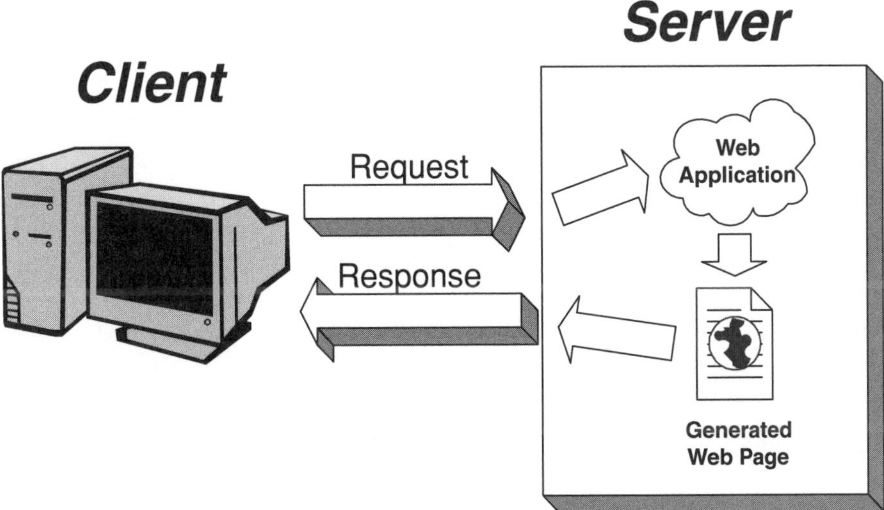

Figure 1–2 Dynamic HTML Document

Common Gateway Interface

The Common Gateway Interface (CGI) is probably the most prolific form of Web application in use today. Designed early on in the Web-server era, CGI allows requests to be sent to an external program. These external programs could be written in just about any programming language—most commonly C, C++, Perl, and Python.

While CGI is a solution for creating dynamic content on the Web, it has several facets that make it very inefficient. CGI programs typically use a large amount of system resources; not just CPU usage, but also large amounts of memory. For each request sent to a CGI program, the Web server loads, runs, and unloads the entire CGI. CGI programs are independent from the Web server and cannot write to the Web server's logs or find out about the capabilities of the server. Additionally, CGI pages are often not readily portable to other platforms.

Since the implementation of CGI programs, several vendors have created unique approaches to working around its inherent limitations. FastCGI, created by Open Market, is a CGI alternative that creates a single persistent process for each CGI request. While this helps, there is still one process for each CGI program, and further resources are consumed if that process needs to launch an interpreter such as Perl. To find out more about FastCGI visit the Fast Engine Web site at: *http://www.fastengines.com/*.

Another method of increasing CGI performance was embedding an interpreter into the Web server. This allows the Web server to precompile and prefork the CGI. It also allows for native API hooks into the Web server. The largest limitation associated with these approaches is that they are tied to a very specific language, platform, and Web server. Some examples of this include mod_perl for the Apache Web server and PerlEx by ActiveState for the Microsoft Internet Information Server. To get more information on mod_perl go to the Perl/Apache Web site at *http://perl.apache.org/*. Find out more about PerlEx by visiting Active State's Web site at: *http://www.activestate.com/plex/*.

While all of these attempts to overcome the limitations of CGI programs have improved their performance, the limitations of the CGI process itself is responsible for most of the system's drawbacks.

Server APIs

Another method for creating dynamic Web applications is Web-server specific APIs. Netscape provides the Web Application Interface or WAI (formerly NSAPI) for its server suite, and Microsoft provides ISAPI for its Internet Information Server. The Apache Web server has a module-based programming interface that allows modules to be loaded within the httpd executable.

All of the server APIs offer tremendous speed and resource gains by integrating tightly with the native Web server. Unfortunately, this also creates a solution limited to a particular platform and Web server. Additionally, server API extensions can create several security issues. Since the API extension runs as a part of the Web server itself, a problem with the extension could cause the Web server to crash.

Client-side Scripting Solutions

These are a class of Web development in which the code is pushed to the user and run on the user's machine. These can be very useful tools for developing dynamic content; however, they have severe limitations.

The client needs to support the scripting language in exactly the ways expected. Differences between the way that Microsoft's Internet Explorer and Netscape's Navigator interpret a client-side script can make a dramatic difference in what is seen in the client's browser.

VBScript is one example of a client-side scripting language. VBScript is based on Microsoft Visual Basic. It is currently only supported on Microsoft Internet Explorer.

JavaScript, also known as JScript and ECMAScript, plays an important role in creating dynamic Web applications running completely on the client. The European Computer Manufacturer's Association has recently standardized JavaScript by combining the popular versions created by Netscape and Microsoft (ECMA-262).

JavaScript is limited to the Web browsers that support the language; Netscape and Opera Web browsers both support JavaScript directly, while Microsoft supports a version of the JavaScript standard called JScript. JavaScript plays a very different role than JSP pages, but the two languages can be used together to create some amazing results. An excellent source for more information on JavaScript is Janice Winsor and Brian Freeman's *Jumping JavaScript* (Pearson Technical Reference/Prentice Hall, 1998).

Server-side Scripting Solutions

There are several common scripting solutions to create Web applications. These are scripts that are run on the server before the page is sent to the user.

Netscape's server-side scripting solution is called Server Side JavaScript (SSJS). In SSJS, JavaScript is executed on the server to modify HTML pages, and scripts are precompiled to improve server performance. SSJS is available on several different versions of Netscape Web Servers. To learn more about SSJS go to: *http://developer.netscape.com/tech/javascript/ssjs/ssjs.html*.

Microsoft servers offer Active Server Pages (ASP). ASP pages are very similar to JSP pages. ASP allows developers to embed VBScript or JScript code directly into a Web page. ASP pages have to be compiled every time they are run, mirroring one of the major drawbacks of CGI scripts. ASP is only available to developers running Microsoft's Internet Information Server 3.0 or above.

By far the biggest drawback of the major scripting solutions is their proprietary nature. All of the solutions discussed are dependent on either certain Web servers or specific vendors.

Java Servlets

Java Servlets are a powerful alternative to CGI programs and scripting languages. Servlets are extremely similar to the proprietary server APIs, but since they are written in the Java programming language they can be easily ported to any environment that supports the Servlet API. Since they run in the Java Virtual Machine, they bypass the security problems that affect the server APIs.

Servlets are run inside a Servlet engine. Each individual Servlet is run as a thread inside the Web server process. This is a much more efficient solution than multiple server processes implemented by CGI programs. By running in threads Servlets are also very scaleable, and since they are a part of the Web server process themselves they can interact closely with the Web server.

Servlets are extremely powerful replacements for CGI programs. They can be used to extend to any type of server imaginable. The built-in thread and security support make Servlets a robust tool for extending a server service.

All major Web servers now support Servlets. The major drawback of using Java Servlets is in their power. The Java programming language is at once both powerful and complicated, and learning Java is a formidable task for the average Web developer.

1.2 JavaServer Pages

JSP is an extremely powerful choice for Web development. JSP is a technology using server-side scripting that is actually translated into Servlets and compiled before they are run. This gives developers a scripting interface to create powerful Java Servlets.

JSP pages provide tags that allow developers to perform most dynamic content operations without writing complex Java code. Advanced developers can add the full power of the Java programming language to perform advanced operations in JSP pages.

Template Pages

Clearly, the most effective way to make a page respond dynamically would be to simply modify the static page. Ideally, special sections to the page could be added that would be changed dynamically by the server. In this case pages become more like a page template for the server to process before sending. These are no longer normal Web pages—they are now server pages.

On a server page, the client requests a Web page, the server replaces some sections of a template with new data, and sends this newly modified page to the client (See Figure 1–3).

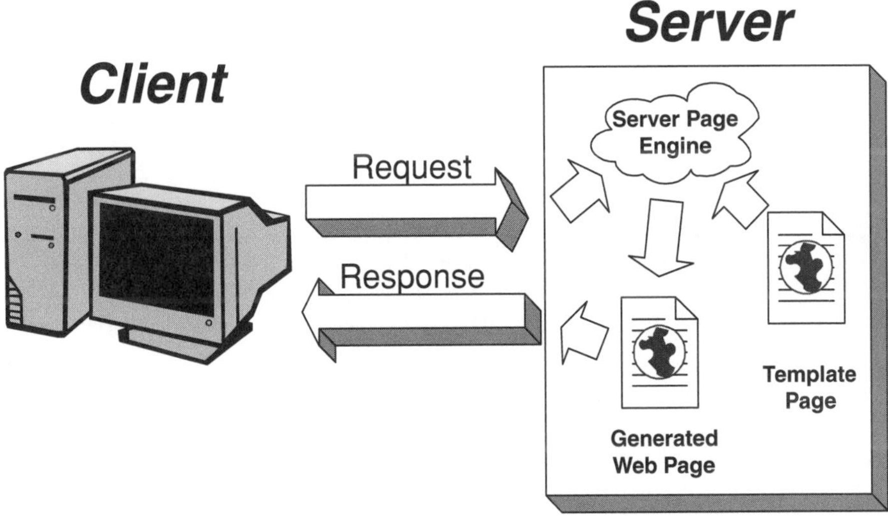

Figure 1–3 Server Page

Since the processing occurs on the server, the client receives what appears to be static data. As far as the client is concerned there is no difference between a server page and a standard Web page. This creates a solution for dynamic pages that does not consume client resources and is completely browser neutral.

Static Data vs. Dynamic Elements

Since JSP pages are designed around static pages, they can be composed of the same kind of static data as a standard Web page. JSP pages use HTML or XML to build the format and layout of the page. As long as a normal Web page could contain the data, so can the JSP page.

In order to replace sections of a page, the server needs to be able to recognize the sections it needs to change. A JSP page usually has a special set of "tags" to identify a portion of the page that should be modified by the server. JSP uses the `<%` tag to note the start of a JSP section, and the `%>` tag to note the end of a JSP section. JSP will interpret anything within these tags as a special section.

JSP pages usually contain a mixture of both static data and dynamic elements. It is important to understand the distinction between the two forms. Static data is never changed in the server page, and dynamic elements will always be interpreted and replaced before reaching the client.

A Simple JSP Page

Often the easiest way to understand something is to see it. Listing 1.1 shows a very simple JSP page.

Listing 1.1 simpleDate.jsp

```
<!DOCTYPE HTML PUBLIC "-//W3C//DTD HTML 4.0 Final//EN">
<HTML>
<HEAD>
<TITLE>A simple date example</TITLE>
</HEAD>

<BODY COLOR=#ffffff>
```

Listing 1.1 simpleDate.jsp (continued)

```
The time on the server is
<%= new java.util.Date() %>
</BODY>
</HTML>
```

Don't worry too much about what the JSP page is doing; that will be covered in later chapters. It is important to notice the two types of data in the page: static data and dynamic data. Understanding the difference between these builds an essential foundation for creating JSP pages.

When the client requests this JSP page, the client will receive a document as HTML. The translation is displayed in Figure 1–4.

When compiled and sent to the browser, the page should look like Figure 1–5.

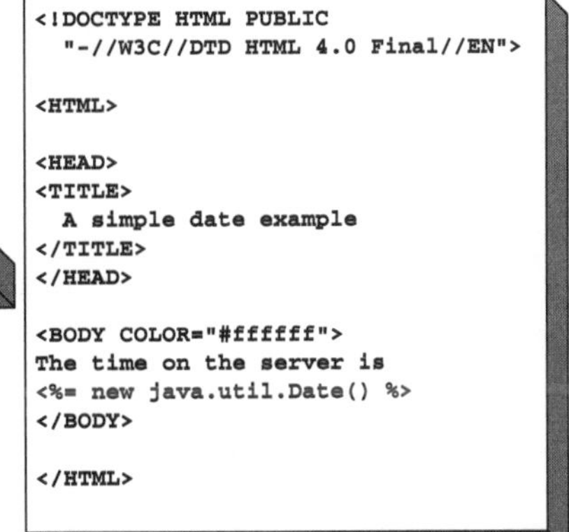
Resulting HTML
<!DOCTYPE HTML PUBLIC
"-//W3C//DTD HTML 4.0 Final//EN">
<HTML>
<HEAD>
<TITLE>
A simple date example
</TITLE>
</HEAD>
<BODY COLOR="#ffffff">
The time on the server is
Wed Dec 08 16:11:09 PST 1999
</BODY>
</HTML>
Server Page Template
<!DOCTYPE HTML PUBLIC
"-//W3C//DTD HTML 4.0 Final//EN">
<HTML>
<HEAD>
<TITLE>
A simple date example
</TITLE>
</HEAD>
<BODY COLOR="#ffffff">
The time on the server is
<%= new java.util.Date() %>
</BODY>
</HTML>

Figure 1–4 A Server Page into HTML Data

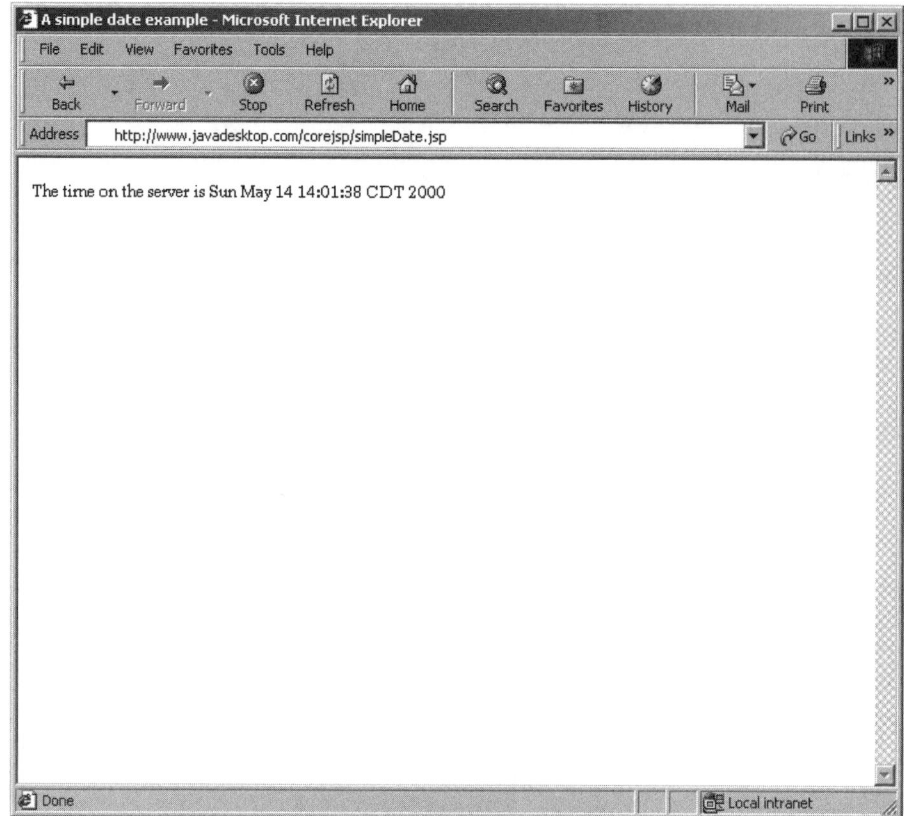

Figure 1–5 A Simple JSP Page.

JavaServer Pages

Most Web servers that understand JSP will look for a specific filename extension. Typically, any filename that ends in .jsp will interpreted and processed by the JSP engine. Often the actual extension is configurable, but for the sake of clarity this book will use .jsp throughout.

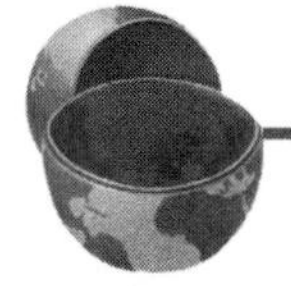

CORE Note: JSP pages without JSP tags.

Since a JSP can handle the same static data as an HTML file, any HTML file can be changed to the extension .jsp. If the JSP server is running, these files will now run through the JSP engine. Without specific tags to identify dynamic sections, this document will come out exactly the same as the original HTML file, but it will take more resources because the JSP engine will be attempting to parse and execute the file

1.3 The Power of Java

JSP pages inherit many of their advantages from the underlying Java programming language and Java Servlet technology. They also gain advantages over alternate methods of development by integrating into the component model. Beyond these advantages the JSP specification is extremely well designed, enabling extensibility and integration with other languages and specifications.

Write Once, Run Anywhere

Because JSP pages utilize the Java programming language, they automatically gain many advantages. First and foremost is the high level of portability offered by Java's well-defined and accepted API. A JSP page developed on one platform can be deployed on a large number of systems. For example, a JSP page developed on a Windows NT system tested on the JSP Reference Implementation can be easily deployed on a Linux box running Allaire Software's JRun Application Server.

Further, JSP pages avoid the few troublesome areas of cross-platform Java development. Since JSP pages run on the server, applications do not need to be tested with several different client platforms, as is often necessary with Java applets. The sometimes troublesome GUI systems developed in Java, such as AWT and Swing, are also avoided in JSP pages.

The Java API

Probably one of the first things noticed when writing JSP pages is that the JSP author has the full power of the Java API. The core Java APIs offer the power of networking, multithreading, database connectivity, internationalization, image manipulation, object serialization, remote method invocation, CORBA access, and more. Standard extensions to Java—such as the Java Naming and Directory Interface (JNDI) and the Java Mail API—offer powerful extensions to Web applications.

With Java classes, JavaBeans, and Enterprise JavaBeans components offered by numerous software vendors it is easy to add powerful code to Web applications. Using the JavaBeans component framework, JSP pages can form the presentation layer of multi-tier applications.

JSP pages can be written that communicate directly to applets, allowing the same code to be leveraged on both the server and the client. This opens a whole new world of client/server application development.

Security and Safety

Another advantage inherited from the Java programming language is strong type safety. Unlike common scripting languages, JSP pages and the underlying Java Servlet API manipulate data in their native types instead of strings. Java also avoids many memory issues with automatic garbage collection and the absence of pointers.

Java is also known for its excellent exception handling. When an error occurs JSP pages can safely catch the exception and notify the user, instead of potentially crashing the server. This built-in feature is considered far superior to the add-on extensions and modules often implemented in other Web application environments.

Finally, a Java application server can utilize the Java security manager, protecting itself from poorly written JSP pages that could potentially affect server performance or damage the host file system. The Java security manager controls rights to resources that could be used to damage the system, only allowing processes with the proper rights to gain access to protected resources. This is a fundamental part of the Java programming language.

Scalability

The Java programming language, as well as the Java Servlet API, adds several scalability components to JSP pages. After a JSP page is loaded, it generally is maintained in memory. When a new request comes in for the JSP page the server makes a simple method invocation. This is very different from traditional CGI applications, which often spawn a process and an interpreter for every request. The underlying server handles multiple requests concurrently by utilizing separate threads, making JSP pages highly scaleable.

When integrated into the JavaBean component framework, JSP pages become even more scaleable. For example, a JDBC JavaBean can handle multiple requests from JSP pages and maintain a single, efficient connection to the back-end database. This is especially efficient when integrated with Enterprise JavaBeans, which add transaction and security services to Web applications, as well as middleware support for Java components.

Extensibility

Another area where JSP pages often outshine their competitors is in their extensibility. The JSP specification itself is an extension of the Java Servlet extension. Within JSP pages, the JSP specification can be extended to create custom tags. These tags allow the JSP "language" to be extended in a portable fashion. One good idea, for example, would be to create a custom tag library filled with embedded database queries. By making these tag libraries portable, and by giving them a common interface, JSP pages can express the component model internally.

The JSP specification authors also left room for further extensibility by making the elements utilized by JSP independent of any certain scripting language. Currently the JSP specification only supports the Java programming language for scripting, but JSP engines can choose to support other languages.

JSP's close relationship to the Extensible Markup Language (XML) is also very important, due to the extensibility and highly organized structure of XML. A properly formed JSP page can actually be written as a valid XML document. Simple XML generation can be done in JSP pages utilizing static templates. Dynamic XML generation can be done with custom tag components, JavaBeans, or Enterprise JavaBean components. XML can also be received as request data and sent directly to custom tag components, JavaBeans, or Enterprise JavaBean components.

Components

An extremely powerful feature of JSP pages is its ability to integrate into the JavaBean component framework. This opens the door for large-scale, enterprise applications created by development teams. As Web applications become more complex, utilizing the component nature of JSP helps break down the complex tasks into simpler, manageable modules. JSP helps separate presentation logic from business logic, and allows the separation of static and dynamic data.

Because of this component-centric nature, both Java programmers and non-Java programmers alike can utilize JSP. It allows Java programmers to make and use JavaBeans, and to create dynamic Web pages utilizing fine control over those beans. Non-Java programmers can use JSP tags to connect to JavaBeans created by experienced Java developers.

1.4 Understanding HTTP

The JSP specification does not define any limitations on the protocol used by JSP. It does require that JSP support HTTP (Hypertext Transfer Protocol). Virtually all current uses of JSP utilize HTTP to deliver content.

The JSP author does not need to understand the intricacies of HTTP, but HTTP does create some restrictions and limitations for JSP. A basic outline of HTTP is included here, and more specific details will be included in following chapters.

The Basics of HTTP

HTTP is a generic, lightweight protocol that is used for the delivery of HTML and XML. HTTP is the primary protocol used to deliver information across the World Wide Web.

HTTP is also a stateless protocol that keeps no association between requests. This means that when the client makes a request to a server, the server sends a response, and the transaction is closed. A second request from the same client is a whole new transaction, unrelated to the first request.

The HTTP Request

The client requests information by sending a special "request message" to the server. This request contains a single line that represents the request itself, and may also contain additional information that describes the client.

The first line of the HTTP request is called the *request header* and contains all of the information required to complete the request. The request header is composed of three parts; the request method, part of a URL for the specific data to be retrieved, and the version of the protocol that should be used. The request header is the only portion that is required to create a valid request.

Additional information is often provided about the client, such as the type of browser or the preferred language of the user. This allows the server to process the request in a way that may have specific responses directed toward a specific client.

Finally, the request can contain parameter information that may be specific to the request. For example, when an HTML form is completed and returned via the `POST` request method, that information is sent through the HTTP request.

The example below shows a typical request:

```
GET /simpleDate.jsp HTTP/1.1
accept: image/gif, image/jpeg, image/png, */*
accept-charset: iso-8859-1,*,utf-8
host: www.javadesktop.com
accept-language: en
user-agent: Mozilla/5.0 [en] (Win98; U)
```

The first line defines the request. The request method is `GET`, the URL is `/simpleDate.jsp`, and uses `HTTP` version `1.1` to respond. The following lines describe the client, the types of files that will be accepted, the character set used, the language used, etc.

CORE Note: Request Method

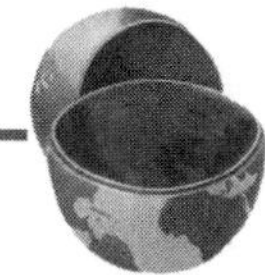

The most common request method used for reading data into the browser is GET. Every page requested by the browser that does not have a request method defined will default to the GET method. The GET request method was intended for reading data only, however practical usage shows that it can provide parameter data by appending information to the URL (i.e., -`/index.html?name=Zella`). The GET passes data in a form that is visible to the user, is cacheable and bookmarkable, and the maximum length of the URL limits the amount of parameter data.

The other common request method is POST. The POST method was designed for sending data and does so by appending name-value pairs in the HTTP request. Since the POST data is in the request, it is not viewable by the user, cannot be cached or bookmarked, and allows for unlimited parameter data.

When using JSP, the parameter information is accessed in the same manner whether sent via GET or POST. The JSP author will need to determine the request method based on the requirements of the parameter data being sent.

The HTTP Response

When the server responds to a request it sends the data in a special "response" format. This response contains a status line, response headers, and a body containing the actual data.

The status line consists of the protocol used, and status integer, and often includes a human-readable value of the status. The status line can indicate fairly specific success or failure results. A more detailed explanation of the status codes gets fairly complex, and is not within the scope of this book.

Immediately following the status line are a series of name/value pairs that represent the response headers. These can be used to describe the server, send additional information, or ask the client to take specific actions.

Finally, the requested document is attached as the response body. This can be a single HTML document or contain several multipart MIME sections. It is not important to know what each line represents, but it is useful to see the kind of information that may be available. In particular, the JSP author can set certain values in the HTTP response header that will change the behavior of the page.

The following is an example of a typical HTTP response:

```
HTTP/1.1 200 OK
Date: Sun, 08 Dec 1999 18:16:31 GMT
Server: Apache/1.3.9 (Unix) ApacheJServ/1.0
Last-Modified: Tue, 22 Jun 1999 05:12:38 GMT
ETag: "d828b-371-376f1b46"
Accept-Ranges: bytes
Connection: close
Content-Type: text/html

<!DOCTYPE HTML PUBLIC "-//W3C//DTD HTML 4.0 Final//EN">
<HTML>
<HEAD>
<TITLE>
  A simple date example
</TITLE>
</HEAD>
<BODY COLOR="#ffffff">
The time on the server is
Wed Dec 08 16:17:57 PST 1999
</BODY>
</HTML>
```

In closing, JSP offers significant benefits over legacy Web-development technologies. Its use of the Java programming language gives it security, reliability, and access to a powerful API. Its memory and threading models offer significant speed enhancements. Additionally JSP is built around a component model that helps separate business logic from presentation logic.

The next chapter, "The Scripting Elements," takes an in-depth look at the JSP language itself.

THE SCRIPTING ELEMENTS

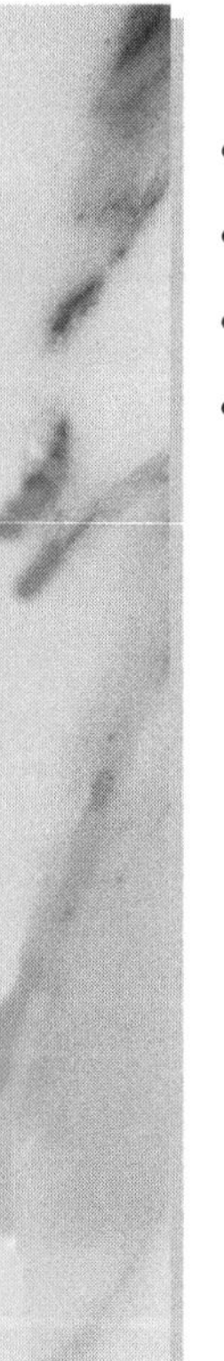

Topics in this Chapter:

- The Three Scripting Elements
- Embedded Control Flow Statements
- Using Comments
- Scripting Elements Applied

Chapter 2

Having seen the syntax of a simple JSP page, the next step is to get a better understanding of the different types of tags or scripting elements used in JSP. There are five basic types of elements, as well as a special format for comments.

The first three elements—Scriptlets, Expressions, and Declarations—are collectively called *scripting elements*. The Scriptlet element allows Java code to be embedded directly into a JSP page. An Expression element is a Java language expression whose value is evaluated and returned as a string to the page. A Declaration element is used to declare methods and variables that are initialized with the page.

CORE Note: Scripting Language

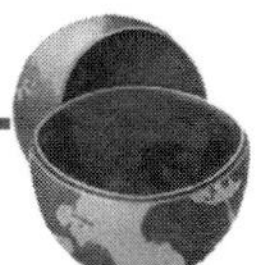

The writers of the JavaServer Pages specification did not define a requirement that Java be the scripting language for a JSP page. Currently the majority of JSP engines only support the use of Java, but in the future other languages such as JavaScript, VBScript, or others could be used as the scripting language.

The two other elements are Actions and Directives. Action elements provide information for the translation phase of the JSP page, and consist of a set of standard, built-in methods. Custom actions can also be created in the form of custom tags. This is a new feature of the JSP 1.1 specification. Directive elements contain global information that is applicable to the whole page. A detailed description of Actions and Directives is given in Chapter 3.

It is also important to note that there are two different formats for most elements. The first type is called the JSP syntax. It is based on the syntax of other Server Pages, so it might seem very familiar. It is symbolized by: `<% script %>`. The JSP specification refers to this format as the "friendly" syntax, as it is meant for hand-authoring. The second format is an XML standard format for creating JSP pages. This format is symbolized by: `<jsp:element />`. While some find it more time consuming to author with the XML syntax, it would produce the same results. While XML syntax is included here, JSP syntax is recommended for authoring. Most of the examples in this book will be in the JSP format. For more information about how JSP and XML interrelate see Chapter 10.

2.1 The Scriptlet Element

JSP Syntax: `<% code %>`
XML Syntax: `<jsp:scriptlet > code </jsp:scriptlet>`

The simplest type of JSP element is the Scriptlet element. A Scriptlet element is simply a section of Java code encapsulated within the opening and closing JSP tags. It is important to note that individual Scriptlets cannot span multiple pages, and that all of the Scriptlets on a single page put together must form a valid block of Java code. Scriptlets can produce output to the page, but don't necessarily have to produce any output. If a Scriptlet needs to produce output it is generally done through the implicit `out` object.

Listing 2.1 shows a very simple implementation of a dynamic JSP page utilizing a Scriptlet. The JSP open tag (`<%`) begins the Java fragment. The `println()` method of the implicit out object is called. Within the `println()` a new `Date` object is created. The `println()` method returns a `String` comprised of the current date in the format of the current locale and time zone.

CORE Note: The Implicit *`out`* Object

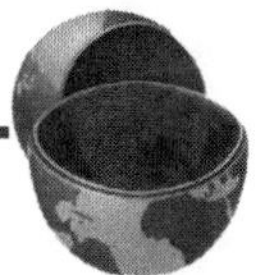

In the JSP 1.x specifications `out` is an instance of the `javax.servlet.jsp.JspWriter` class. `JspWriter` object is created in order to buffer output. If a page needs to be buffered all output goes to the `JspWriter` object, and when the buffer is full or the page is completed a `PrintWriter` object is created to output the data. If the page is not buffered the `JspWriter` simply funnels the output directly to a `PrintWriter` object. Buffering pages is further described in Chapter 4. Both the `print()` and `println()` methods perform the same function on `JspWriter` as they do with a `PrintWriter` object. They take an object as an argument and send it to the output stream. If necessary the object is converted to a `String`.

Listing 2.1 date.jsp

```
<!DOCTYPE HTML PUBLIC "-//W3C//DTD HTML 4.0 Final//EN">
<HTML>
<HEAD>
<TITLE>Current Date</TITLE>
</HEAD>
<BODY>

The current date is:
<% out.println(new java.util.Date()); %>

</BODY>
</HTML>
```

The output of this example should look similar to Figure 2–1. It is important to note that the output of this Scriptlet shows the date of the server, which may be very different from the date where the client resides. A client-side technology such as JavaScript would have to be used to print out the local date.

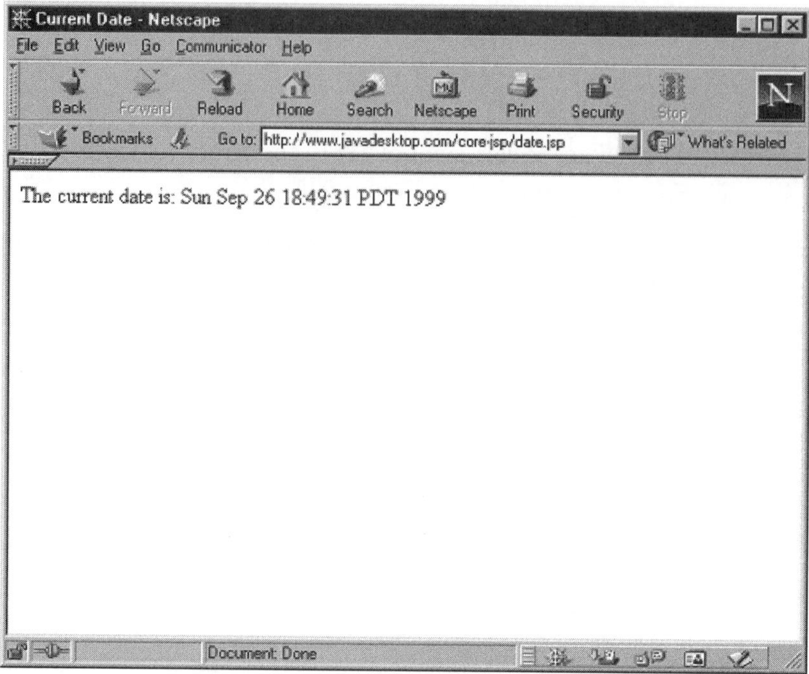

Figure 2–1 date.jsp output.

2.2 Expression Element Syntax

JSP Syntax: `<%= code %>`

XML Syntax: `<jsp:expression > code </jsp:expression>`

It turns out that printing the output of a Java fragment is one of the most common tasks utilized in JSP pages. Having several `out.println()` method tends to be cumbersome. Realizing this, the authors of the JSP specification created the Expression element.

The Expression element begins with the standard JSP start tag followed by an equals sign (`<%=`). Take a look at Listing 2.2 to see the previous example of printing the current date, only this time as an Expression element.

Notice that the Java fragment does not end in a semicolon, as do standard Java statements. The JSP engine takes the Java fragment and evaluates it. It then returns the output of the statement to the implicit *out* object. Notice that the `out.println()` method is removed, and immediately after the opening JSP tag there is an equals symbol. This code returns exactly the same result as our previous example (see Figure 2–1).

Listing 2.2 date2.jsp

```
<!DOCTYPE HTML PUBLIC "-//W3C//DTD HTML 4.0 Final//EN">

<HTML>
<HEAD>
<TITLE>Current Date</TITLE>
</HEAD>
<BODY>

The current date is:
<%= new java.util.Date() %>

</BODY>
</HTML>
```

At first glance the functionality of the Expression element seems simple. It appears to just wrap an `out.print()` method around the Java fragment. This is in fact true. However, the rich set of data types in Java sets it apart from other scripting languages such as JavaScript or VBScript. While other languages deal mostly with strings, Java can deal with numerous data types, as well as user-creatable data types. So how can it print the value of an expression that does not return a `String`?

The `println()` (as well as `print()`) methods of the `JspWriter` class are overloaded to accept most common data types as input. Overloading is the process of giving functions the same name. This is possible as long as the functions differ in number, type, or order of their parameters. The data type is then converted to a `String`, most often using the `String.valueOf()` method. The result `String` is translated into bytes and written in exactly the manner of the `write(int)` method of the `java.io.Writer` object.

2.3 Declaration Element Syntax

JSP Syntax: *<%! code %>*

XML Syntax: *<jsp:declaration> code </jsp:declaration>*

The third type of Scripting element is the Declaration element. The purpose of a Declaration element is to initialize variables and methods and make them available to other Declarations, Scriptlets, and Expressions. Variables and methods created within Declaration elements are effectively nonlocalized, or "global." The syntax of the Declaration element begins with the standard JSP open tag followed by an exclamation point (`<%!`).

The Declaration element must be a complete Java statement. It ends with a semicolon, just as the Scriptlet element does. It is also important to note that Declaration elements are not able to produce any output, as Expression and Scriptlet elements can.

Listing 2.3 rewrites our previous two examples utilizing a Declaration element. The standard JSP open tag followed by the exclamation point symbolize the beginning of the Declaration element. Here the new method, called `PrintDate()`, is declared as a public method that returns a `Date` object. The body of the method simply returns the `Date` object.

Since a Declaration element cannot send output to the `out` object, an Expression element is called to return the output of the `PrintDate()` method. Again the resulting page sent to the client is the same (see Figure 2–1).

Listing 2.3 date3.jsp

```
<!DOCTYPE HTML PUBLIC "-//W3C//DTD HTML 4.0 Final//EN">

<%! public java.util.Date PrintDate()
     {
       return(new java.util.Date());
     }
%>

<HTML>
<HEAD>
<TITLE>Current Date</TITLE>
</HEAD>
```

Listing 2.3 date3.jsp (continued)

```
<BODY>

The current date is:
<%= PrintDate() %>

</BODY>
</HTML>
```

2.4 Embedded Control-Flow Statements

These three Scripting elements themselves are an extremely powerful set of tools to work with. One of their most powerful features comes from one simple fact: together, Scripting elements must form a complete Java statement. The key word is *together*. Blocks of Java code do not have to be kept within one Scriptlet or Expression. This adds the ability to use Java control–flow statements directly within HTML. While other tools, such as JavaScript, can add data to a Web page, they cannot directly control the static HTML content.

This means that decision-making, looping, and exception blocks can be added directly into HTML. The blocks do not have to be in a single Scriptlet or Expression, but can be broken up into several elements distributed throughout the HTML code.

Listing 2.4 ControlFlow.jsp

```
<!DOCTYPE HTML PUBLIC "-//W3C//DTD HTML 4.0 Final//EN">
<%
   // A calendar object is created to get an integer value
   // of the current day of the week
      java.util.Calendar thisCal = Calendar.getInstance();
      int day   = thisCal.get(thisCal.DAY_OF_WEEK);

   // Two arrays are created for demonstrating examples
      String[] wordArray = {"The", "quick", "brown",
                            "fox", ". . ."};
      String[] colorArray = {"red", "green", "blue",
                             "orange",  "black"};
```

Listing 2.4 ControlFlow.jsp (continued)

```
   // Here a random number between 0 and 1 is selected
      java.util.Random rand = new java.util.Random();
      int randomNumber = rand.nextInt(2);
%>
<HTML>
<HEAD>
<TITLE>Control Flow Statements</TITLE>
</HEAD>
<BODY>

<TABLE BORDER="1" WIDTH="600" CELLPADDING="3"
CELLSPACING="0">
<TR><TD BGCOLOR="#AAAAAA" ALIGN="center">
<FONT SIZE="+3" COLOR="white">
Control Flow Statements</FONT>
</TD></TR>
<TR><TD>

<!-- ************************************************** -->
<H3>Decision Making Statements</H3>
<H4><code>if . . . else</code> Statements</H4>

<BLOCKQUOTE>
<%  if (day == 1 | day == 7) { %>
              <FONT COLOR="red" SIZE="+1">It's the
weekend!</FONT>
<%  } else { %>
        <FONT COLOR="red" SIZE="+1">Still in the work week.
        </FONT>
<%  } %>
</BLOCKQUOTE>

<!-- ************************************************** -->
<H4><code>switch . . . case</code> Statements</H4>

<BLOCKQUOTE>
<FONT COLOR="blue">The current day is:<br></FONT>
<% switch (day) { %>
<% case 1: %>
     <FONT COLOR="blue" SIZE="+1">Sunday</FONT>
     <% break; %>
<% case 2: %>
     <FONT COLOR="blue" SIZE="+1">Monday</FONT>
     <% break; %>
<% case 3: %>
     <FONT COLOR="blue" SIZE="+1">Tuesday</FONT>
```

Listing 2.4 ControlFlow.jsp (continued)

```
     <% break; %>
<% case 4: %>
     <FONT COLOR="blue" SIZE="+1">Wednesday</FONT>
     <% break; %>
<% case 5: %>
     <FONT COLOR="blue" SIZE="+1">Thursday</FONT>
     <% break; %>
<% case 6: %>
     <FONT COLOR="blue" SIZE="+1">Friday</FONT>
     <% break; %>
<% case 7: %>
     <FONT COLOR="blue" SIZE="+1">Saturday</FONT>
     <% break; %>
<% default: %>
     <FONT COLOR="blue" SIZE="+1">Error! Bad day!</FONT>
     <% break; %>
<% } %>
</BLOCKQUOTE>

</TD></TR><TR><TD>

<!-- ************************************************ -->
<H3>Loop Statements</H3>
<H4><code>for</code> Statements</H4>
<BLOCKQUOTE>
<% for (int fontSize=1; fontSize <= 5; fontSize++) { %>
   <FONT COLOR="green" SIZE="<%= fontSize %>">
     The Quick Brown Fox . . .</FONT><br>
<% } %>
</BLOCKQUOTE>

<!-- ************************************************ -->
<H4><code>while</code> Statements</H4>
<BLOCKQUOTE>
<% int counter = 0; %>
<% while( counter <= 4) { %>
   <FONT COLOR="<%=colorArray[counter] %>" SIZE="+1">
   <%= wordArray[counter] %></FONT>
   <% counter++; %>
<% } %>
</BLOCKQUOTE>

</TD></TR><TR><TD>

<!-- ************************************************ -->
```

Listing 2.4 ControlFlow.jsp (continued)

```
<H3>Exception Statements</H3>
<H4><code>try . . . catch</code> Statements</H4>
<BLOCKQUOTE>
<FONT COLOR="orange">Trying to divide by
this random number: <%= randomNumber %></FONT><BR>
<% try { %>
    <% int result = 100 / randomNumber; %>
    <FONT COLOR="orange" SIZE="+1">Success!</FONT>
<% } catch (Exception e) { %>
    <FONT COLOR="orange" SIZE="+1">Failure! </FONT>
    <FONT COLOR="red" SIZE="+1">
    Error Message: <%= e.getMessage() %></FONT>
<% } %>
</BLOCKQUOTE>
</TD></TR>
</TABLE>

</BODY>
</HTML>
```

When run, `ControlFlow.jsp` creates a web page similar to Figure 2–2. `ControlFlow.jsp` starts out with the common HTML `DOCTYPE` statement. It then has a Scriptlet that defines a few variables that will be used to demonstrate the abilities of control-flow statements.

```
<%
   // A calendar object is created to get an integer value
   // of the current day of the week
      java.util.Calendar thisCal = Calendar.getInstance();
      int day   = thisCal.get(thisCal.DAY_OF_WEEK);

   // Two arrays are created for demonstrating examples
      String[] wordArray = {"The", "quick", "brown",
                             "fox", ". . ."};
      String[] colorArray = {"red", "green", "blue",
                        "orange",  "black"};

   // Here a random number between 0 and 1 is selected
      java.util.Random rand = new java.util.Random();
      int randomNumber = rand.nextInt(2);
%>
```

The first variable, `thisCal`, is used to get an integer value of the day of the week and place it into the integer `day`. The next part of the Scriptlet creates two `String` arrays. The final section creates an instance of `java.util.Random` and sets the value of `randomNumber` to a random number between zero and one.

The next section is some standard HTML to format the examples. After this section is three different table cells describing decision-making, looping, and exception statements.

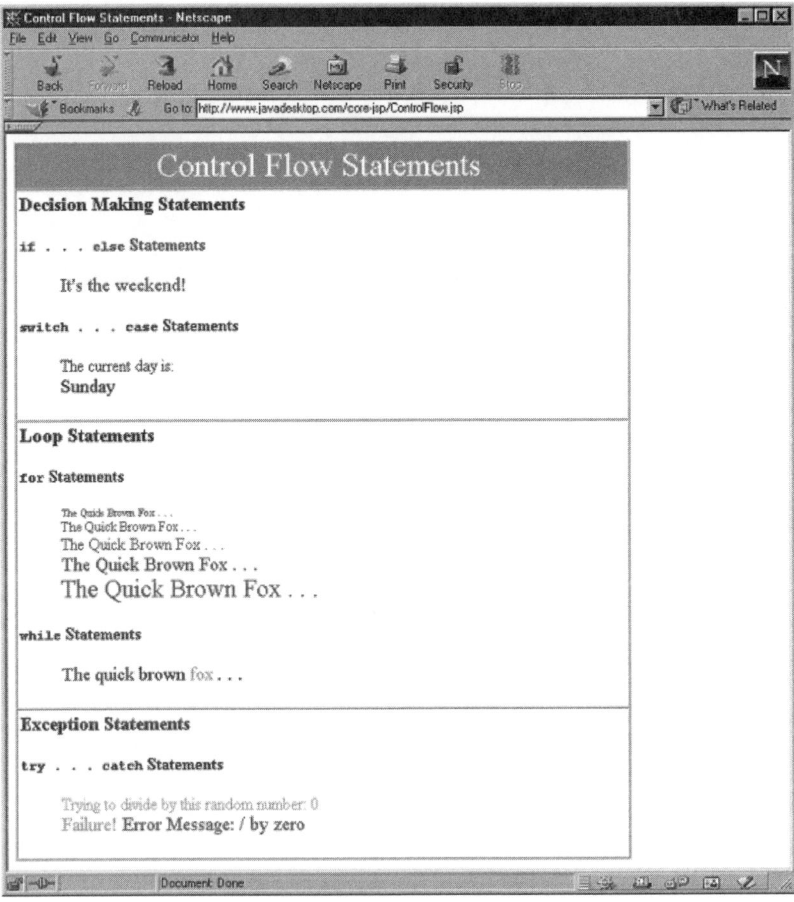

Figure 2–2 The Output of ControlFlow.jsp

Decision-Making Statements

There are two basic types of decision-making blocks in Java: `if…else` blocks and `case` blocks. Another type of block, called a branching statement, is very similar to decision-making statements, but is used less frequently. The branching statements are symbolized by utilizing *`label:`* statements and the `break` and `continue` keywords.

The `if` block starts out like an ordinary Scriptlet, but the Scriptlet is closed at each line with HTML text included between Scriptlet tags.

```
<%  if (day == 1 | day == 7) { %>
<FONT COLOR="red" SIZE="+1">It's the weekend!</FONT>
<%  } else { %>
        <FONT COLOR="red" SIZE="+1">Still in the work week.
         </FONT>
<%  } %>
```

This means that the actual `if` block is spread over three different Scriptlet tags. The three lines of static HTML text are actually the actions to take based on the condition. How does this work? Remembering back to the discussion about the Expression element, the JSP engine simply wraps `out.print()` methods around the internal data in the Expression tag. The Java code is then evaluated and sent to the `out` object. The JSP engine handles template data, or raw HTML data, the same way. It simply wraps them in `out.print()` methods. This is how the resulting Java program will see this block of code:

```
if (day == 1 | day == 7) {
    out.print("<FONT COLOR=\"red\" SIZE=\"+1\">It\'s the
      weekend!</FONT>");
} else {
    out.print("<FONT COLOR=\"red\" SIZE=\"+1\">Still in the
      work week.");
    out.print("</FONT>");
}
```

Could this section of Java code simply be enclosed in a Scriptlet tag to produce the same result? Certainly. There are benefits gained from separating the template data from the application logic. Simply writing the block above in a Scriptlet would mean that either the Java coder would need to know HTML and graphic design, or they would have to convert someone else's HTML to this format every time it changes. JSP can do this, saving time and effort, and defining a division of labor.

Now take a look at the `case` block example:

```
<% switch (day) { %>
<% case 1: %>
      <FONT COLOR="blue" SIZE="+1">Sunday</FONT>
      <% break; %>
<% case 2: %>
      <FONT COLOR="blue" SIZE="+1">Monday</FONT>
      <% break; %>
<% case 3: %>
      <FONT COLOR="blue" SIZE="+1">Tuesday</FONT>
      <% break; %>
<% case 4: %>
      <FONT COLOR="blue" SIZE="+1">Wednesday</FONT>
      <% break; %>
<% case 5: %>
      <FONT COLOR="blue" SIZE="+1">Thursday</FONT>
      <% break; %>
<% case 6: %>
      <FONT COLOR="blue" SIZE="+1">Friday</FONT>
      <% break; %>
<% case 7: %>
      <FONT COLOR="blue" SIZE="+1">Saturday</FONT>
      <% break; %>
<% default: %>
      <FONT COLOR="blue" SIZE="+1">Error! Bad day!</FONT>
      <% break; %>
<% } %>
```

While on the surface the code may seem more complex than the `if` statement, the logic is actually the same. Each line of the `case` statement is enclosed in a Scriptlet tag. Eighteen actual Scriptlet tags and eight HTML strings contribute to this single case block. All of this to produce one line of HTML code.

Loop Statements

There are three basic types of looping blocks in Java: `for`, `while`, and `do...while` blocks. First, take a look at the `for` example in Listing 2.4:

```
<% for (int fontSize=1; fontSize <= 5; fontSize++) { %>
   <FONT COLOR="green" SIZE="<%= fontSize %>">
     The Quick Brown Fox . . .</FONT><br>
<% } %>
```

Once the concept is understood the logic is quite clear. The JSP elements and static HTML data work in unison to form a single `for` block. One difference here is the use of an Expression tag (<%= ... %>). This is mainly for convenience, but again shows the versatility of JSP. Each time through the loop the size of the font is increased by one.

The `for` statement can be seen as a very valuable tool. For example, a table can be created with an unknown number of rows. The number of rows could be determined from a request variable, and each row printed in the `for` loop with the appropriate variables substituted.

Now take a look at the `while` loop:

```
<% int counter = 0; %>
<% while( counter <= 4) { %>
   <FONT COLOR="<%=colorArray[counter] %>" SIZE="+1">
   <%= wordArray[counter] %></FONT>
   <% counter++; %>
<% } %>
```

Once again HTML template data and JSP elements are mixed to create a valid Java statement. Again an Expression is mixed directly in with the HTML data. This example uses Java arrays corresponding to the number of times the HTML data is to be printed. Again this structure could be used to display a variable set of HTML constructs depending on a request variable.

Exception Statements

Exception statements, using the `try...catch...finally` keywords, are one of the more powerful constructs in Java. There is even a built-in method in JSP to handle general exceptions caught by the JSP engine. This will be covered in Chapter 3.

One must be very careful with any situation that involves getting data from a user and then using it in programming logic. Even with data validation it is often necessary to catch any problem thrown from bad input. In this situation the exception block excels. Take a look at the Exception example:

```
<% try { %>
    <% int result = 100 / randomNumber; %>
    <FONT COLOR="orange" SIZE="+1">Success!</FONT>
<% } catch (Exception e) { %>
    <FONT COLOR="orange" SIZE="+1">Failure! </FONT>
    <FONT COLOR="red" SIZE="+1">
    Error Message: <%= e.getMessage() %></FONT>
<% } %>
```

Again, the blending of HTML data and JSP tags works well. The number 100 is divided by a randomly generated number between zero and one. Approximately half of the times this page is loaded zero will be chosen for the random number, and create a divide by zero error. The simple way to handle this exception is to enclose it in a `try` block. This way, if the exception occurs, the page is still rendered and the error message can be displayed.

ControlFlow.jsp is a good example of how the JSP Scripting elements add power to static HTML data. HTML pages can be displayed with decision-making, looping, and exception-handling statements. At the same time they separate the presentation logic from the business logic, allowing for design and programming teams to work separately to produce tightly integrated applications.

2.5 Comment Syntax

Syntax:

```
<%-- comment --%>
<!-- comment -->
```

There are two different types of comments in JSP. The difference between the types of comments lies in whether the comments are viewable after the JSP engine parses the JSP page. The first type of comment is the standard HTML (and XML) comment, which is delineated by: <!-- comment -->. This comment is ignored by both the JSP engine and the browser, and is left intact. In effect all comments in HTML style are considered Template Data. To view a comment like this, simply choose to view source in an HTML browser.

The second type of comment is called a JSP or "hidden" comment. The JSP engine removes JSP comments before the page is built. Thus, it is viewable on the JSP page on the server, but not on the browser. The JSP comment syntax is <%-- comment --%>. JSP comments are treated as Element Data, and are parsed by the server.

CORE Note: JSP Comments

Several implementations of JSP engines—specifically certain versions of JRun and Netscape Web Server 4—do not handle JSP comments correctly. They simply remove the <% and %> tags and leave the comment "as-is". This can cause a compile-time error. A simple work-around is to create the comments as Scriptlet elements. For example

```
<% // This is a comment in a Scriptlet  %>
```

This creates a Java statement that is commented out. It behaves like a JSP comment, and is not sent to the browser. This format should work on any platform.

There are a couple of interesting things that can be done with comments that are extremely useful when developing JSP pages. First, JSP elements can be included within HTML comments. This might be helpful in debugging a script. An Expression statement can be included in a comment to show the current value of a variable. This would not be viewable on the HTML page, but viewable via the browser's "view source" function.

The second helpful task is commenting out JSP code so it doesn't get compiled. Surrounding normal JSP elements with a JSP comment causes the JSP engine to ignore the JSP code. This allows the selective removal of certain parts of the JSP page.

Take a look at Listing 2.5 and Figure 2–3 to see how different comments will be displayed. Listing 2.5 is the source on the server, and Figure 2–3 is the source viewed on the client. In a normal browser window nothing would be displayed. Anything displayed on the server side that is surrounded by the JSP comment syntax is removed completely. Also notice that the JSP element that was included inside the JSP comment was not executed.

Listing 2.5 Comments.jsp on the Server

```
<!DOCTYPE HTML PUBLIC "-//W3C//DTD HTML 4.0 Final//EN">

<HTML>
<HEAD>
<TITLE>Using Comments</TITLE>
</HEAD>
<BODY>

<!-- This is a HTML Style comment -->

<%-- This is a JSP Style comment --%>

<!-- In this HTML comment. I can dynamically retrieve the
URL of the current page:  <%= request.getRequestURI()%> -->

<%--
Here I am commenting out the following JSP code:
<%= request.getServerName()%>
--%>

</BODY>
</HTML>
```

All items that were inside HTML style comments were treated as template data and left alone, with the exception of the JSP element inside the HTML comment, which was parsed and executed.

If the `request.getRequestURI()` and `request.getServerName()` bits of code seem confusing, don't worry. These Expressions are calling methods of the built-in JSP request object. `request.getRequestURI()` returns the relative URL of the current page, and `request.getServerName()` returns the name of the server receiving the web page.

CORE Note: `request` Object

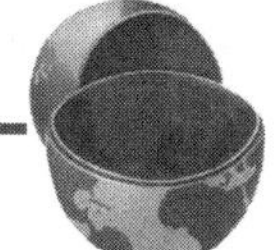

The `request` object, just like the `out` object, is an implicit object to the JSP page. It represents the request parameters associated with the page. This can include query strings (GET requests) and encoded post requests (POST requests), as well as several other pieces of information that are sent with the HTTP request. The `request` object will be examined in detail in Chapter 5.

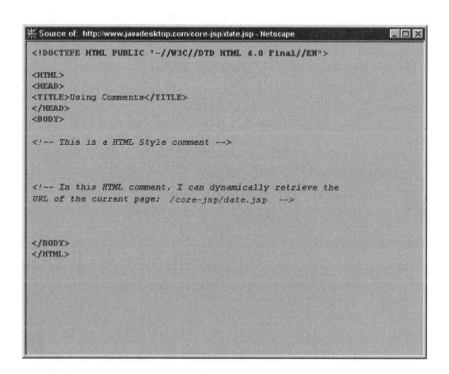

Source of: http://www.javadesktop.com/core-jsp/date.jsp - Netscape

```
<!DOCTYPE HTML PUBLIC "-//W3C//DTD HTML 4.0 Final//EN">

<HTML>
<HEAD>
<TITLE>Using Comments</TITLE>
</HEAD>
<BODY>

<!-- This is a HTML Style comment -->



<!-- In this HTML comment. I can dynamically retrieve the
URL of the current page:  /core-jsp/date.jsp  -->



</BODY>
</HTML>
```

Figure 2–3 comments.jsp on the client (View Source)

2.6 Scripting Elements Applied: Calendar.jsp

After seeing Scriptlets, Declarations, and Expressions, it is obvious that very complex applications can be created with just these three elements. While these three elements are very similar to elements in other server pages technology, JSP has the added benefit of a full-featured programming language: Java.

Listing 2.6 shows a good example of real world JSP use of Expressions, Declarations, and Scriptlets, as well as utilizing a powerful feature of Java not seen in JavaScript, VBScript, and other scripting languages. Listing 2.6 creates an HTML calendar, created from the Java `Calendar` object.

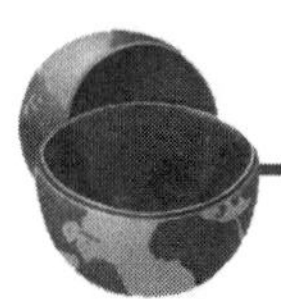

CORE Note: The Java Calendar Object

The `java.util.Calendar` object is new to the Java 1.1 and Java 1.2 API specifications. Previous to the 1.1 spec the features of the `Calendar` object (as well as the features of the `DateFormat` object) were included in the Java `Date` object. The `Date` object represents a single moment in time with millisecond precision. It represents a major leap forward beyond older programming languages where dates are represented as text strings. The absence of Year 2000 bugs with Java is a testament to this fact.

Unfortunately, the `Date` object was not very east to internationalize. Specifically, converting between date objects and integer fields such as YEAR, DAY, and HOUR is not very straightforward, especially when needing to format a single `Date` object to different locales and calendar systems. Thus the `Calendar` object was created. It is an abstract class that can be subclassed with specific calendar systems. The example will use the `GregorianCalendar` subclass, which is built-in to the 1.1 and 1.2 API specs. It also uses the `DateFormat` class to format a representation of the current date to title our HTML calendar.

Listing 2.6 Calendar.jsp on the Server

```
<!DOCTYPE HTML PUBLIC "-//W3C//DTD HTML 4.0 Final//EN">

<%!
  public String FormatTitle(java.util.Calendar thisCal) {
    java.text.SimpleDateFormat formatter =
```

Listing 2.6 Calendar.jsp on the Server (continued)

```
    new java.text.SimpleDateFormat ("MMMMMMMMM d, yyyy");

    return (formatter.format(thisCal.getTime()));
  }
%>

<%
  java.util.Calendar currentCal =
     java.util.Calendar.getInstance();
%>

<HTML>
<HEAD>
<TITLE>Calendar</TITLE>
<STYLE TYPE="text/css">
<!--
TD {
  font-family: Arial, Helvetica, sans-serif;
  font-size: 10pt; text-align: center;
}

.currentDay {
  color: #FF0000; background-color: #EEEEEE;
}

.otherDay {
  color: #666699; background-color: #EEEEEE;
}

.dayHeading {
  font-size: 9pt; color: #666699;
}

.titleStyle {
  font-size: 14pt; color: #FFFFFF;
  background-color: #666699; text-align: center;
  font-weight: bold;
}

-->
</STYLE>
</HEAD>
```

Listing 2.6 Calendar.jsp on the Server (continued)

```
<BODY>

<TABLE BORDER='0' CELLPADDING='1' CELLSPACING='2'>
  <TR><TD CLASS='titleStyle' COLSPAN='7'>
      <%= FormatTitle(currentCal) %>
  </TD></TR>

  <TR>
    <TD WIDTH=14% CLASS='dayHeading'>SUN</TD>
    <TD WIDTH=14% CLASS='dayHeading'>MON</TD>
    <TD WIDTH=14% CLASS='dayHeading'>TUE</TD>
    <TD WIDTH=14% CLASS='dayHeading'>WED</TD>
    <TD WIDTH=14% CLASS='dayHeading'>THU</TD>
    <TD WIDTH=14% CLASS='dayHeading'>FRI</TD>
    <TD WIDTH=14% CLASS='dayHeading'>SAT</TD>
  </TR>


<%  // Set the current day of the month
    int currentDay =
     currentCal.get(currentCal.DAY_OF_MONTH);

    // Calculate the totals days in the month
    int daysInMonth =
    currentCal.getActualMaximum(currentCal.DAY_OF_MONTH);

    // Calculate the day of the week for the first
    currentCal.set(currentCal.DAY_OF_MONTH, 1);
    int dayOfWeek = currentCal.get(currentCal.DAY_OF_WEEK);

    // Prefill the calendar with blank spaces
    if (dayOfWeek != 1) {
      out.println("    <TD COLSPAN=" + (dayOfWeek-1) +
      "> </TD>");
    }

    // Fill in dates
    for (int day=1; day <= daysInMonth; day++) {

      if (day == currentDay) {
        out.println("    <TD CLASS='currentDay'>" + day +
```

Listing 2.6 Calendar.jsp on the Server (continued)

```
          "</TD>");
        } else {
          out.println("    <TD CLASS='otherDay'>" + day +
          "</TD>");
        }

        if (dayOfWeek == 7) {
          out.println("  </TR>\n\n  <TR>");
          dayOfWeek = 1;
        } else {
          dayOfWeek++;
        }
      }

      // Postfill the calendar with blank spaces
      if ((8-dayOfWeek) != 0) {
        out.println("    <TD COLSPAN=" + (8-dayOfWeek) +
        "> </TD>");
      }
%>
</TR>
</TABLE>

</BODY>
</HTML>
```

When run `Calendar.jsp` creates a Web page similar to Figure 2–4.

Calendar.jsp starts out with the standard HTML document identification string, and then defines a method called `FormatTitle()` in a Declaration element. One of the first things noticed here is the explicit naming of the `java.util.Calendar` and `java.text.SimpleDateFormat` objects. Without `import` statements there is no way to use the shorter alias for these objects. `import` statements cannot simply be included in a Scriptlet, as the Java specification states they have to appear at the very beginning of the Java code. JSP pages, being transformed into Java Servlet programs, cannot guarantee where a Scriptlet will actually be placed into the Java program. `import` statements can be used within the `page` directive, which is covered in Chapter 3. Using the full domain name, while less common, is a perfectly legal way of specifying objects.

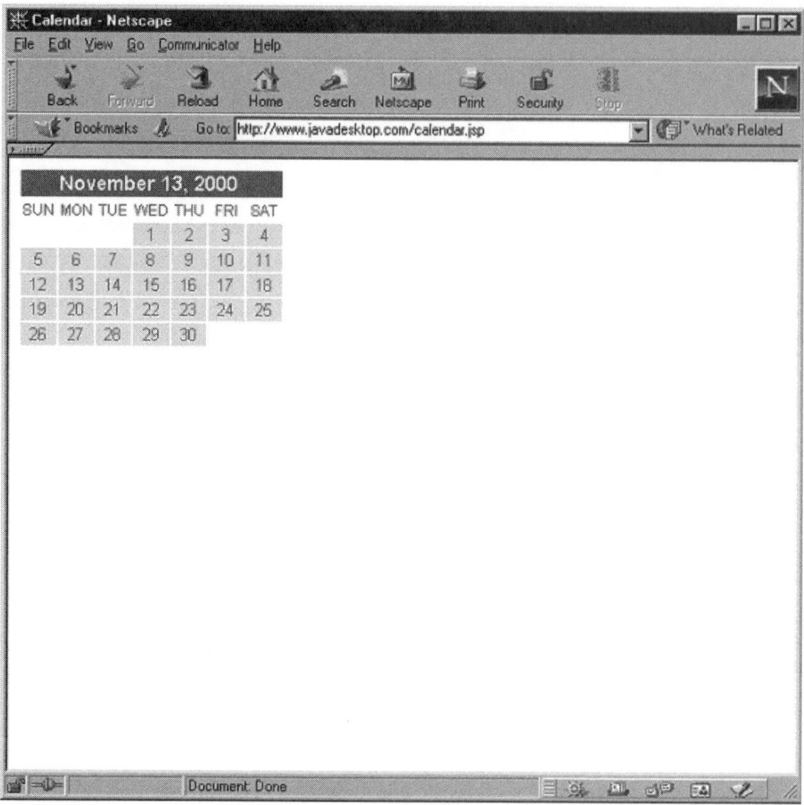

Figure 2–4 calendar.jsp on the server

The `FormatTitle()` method receives a `Calendar` object and returns a `String` with the current date formatted as specified. A `Date` or `Calendar` object must be converted to a string to be displayed in HTML. Earlier the `Date` object was displayed by utilizing the `println()` or `print()` methods of the `JspWriter` object. The `println()` and `print()` methods are very smart. Realizing they are sent a `Date` object, they automatically convert the `Date` object to a `String` using the `String.valueOf(Date)` method. This does the job of converting the `Date` object to a `String`, but only with the default format.

```
<!DOCTYPE HTML PUBLIC "-//W3C//DTD HTML 4.0 Final//EN">

<%!
  Public String FormatTitle(java.util.Calendar thisCal) {
    java.text.SimpleDateFormat formatter =
```

```
      new java.text.SimpleDateFormat ("MMMMMMMMM d, yyyy");

    return (formatter.format(thisCal.getTime()));
  }
%>
```

For the title of the HTML calendar a shortened date is desired, only displaying the month, day, and year. To do this the `SimpleDateFormat` class is used. Similar to the `Calendar` class, `SimpleDateFormat`'s features were originally part of the `Date` object before Java 1.1. `SimpleDateFormat` takes a text string that specifies the `String` format desired for the date. First the `SimpleDateFormat` object is created and is labeled `formatter`. Then the `format()` method of the `SimpleDateFormat` object is called and applied it to the Calendar object received. This object is called `thisCal`. As the `format()` method returns a string it is simply inserted into the return method of the `FormatTitle()` method to return the current date in the specified format.

The format of this text string is based on the ISO 8601 date and time standard. It is also very similar to the string used by the ANSI C function `strftime()` or the UNIX date command. The format string here is: `"MMMMMMMMM d, yyyy"`. The capital *M* stands for the month, both numeric and alphabetic representations. If there are more than three capital *M*s the method decides the alphabetic version is desired and fills in as many characters as there are *M*s, ignoring any extra *M*s for short month names. There are nine *M*s listed to make sure every letter of the month is used, as the longest month (September) has 9 characters.

Next there is a lowercase *D*, representing the numeric version of the day of the month, whether one or two digits. Finally there are four lowercase *Y*s. This represents the year. If three or less lowercase *Y*s are specified, the date is returned in a two-digit format (not Year 2000 compliant). Four are specified here to specify the four-digit version.

It is important to note that while this method was listed at the top of the JSP page for convenience, it could have been placed anywhere on the page and supplied the same desired results. While it will be included as a part of the JSP page's class file, it is a separate and standalone method.

Next comes the creation of the Calendar object within a Scriptlet:

```
<%
  java.util.Calendar currentCal = Calendar.getInstance();
%>
```

Again note the explicit naming of the `Calendar` object, as there is no import statement specified. Also note that here the order is very important. The Calendar object cannot be referenced anywhere in the page until it is initialized. The `getInstance()` method of the `Calendar` object creates a new `Calendar` object, assigning it the current date and time. The new `Calendar` object is named `currentCal`.

Now comes the standard HTML, HEAD, and TITLE tags. This is followed by some style definitions. These definitions are part of Cascading Style Sheets (CSS), which are a part of the HTML 4.0 specification.

```
<STYLE TYPE="text/css">
<!--
TD {
  font-family: Arial, Helvetica, sans-serif;
  font-size: 10pt; text-align: center;
}

.currentDay {
  color: #FF0000; background-color: #EEEEEE;
}

.otherDay {
  color: #666699; background-color: #EEEEEE;
}

.dayHeading {
  font-size: 9pt; color: #666699;
}

.titleStyle {
  font-size: 14pt; color: #FFFFFF;
  background-color: #666699; text-align: center;
  font-weight: bold;
}

-->
</STYLE>
```

There are five different styles listed. The first one, named `TD`, will match the specified style to any TD tag occurring in the HTML page. The HTML table construct is used to create the calendar. `currentDay` specifies the style used by the table element that contains the current day. The current day is differentiated here with a red font. `otherDay` specifies any other day in the table. `dayHeading` designates a style for the column labels of the days of the week, and `titleStyle` designates the style used for the calendar title.

After the style definitions is the beginning of the table construct that will create the HTML calendar. Included in the first table row definition, which spans all seven rows, is the following JSP Expression:

```
<%= FormatTitle(currentCal) %>
```

This calls the method defined earlier in the page. It sends the `currentCal` `Calendar` object and returns a `String` formatted to be the calendar title.

The next row simply prints the static three-letter representations of each day of the week. After this row comes the meat of this JSP page, the Scriptlet that actually creates the HTML calendar. To create a calendar, two pieces of information are needed: the number of days in the current month, and what day of the week the first day falls on. Additionally, the current day must be recorded if it is to be highlighted with a red font. To obtain these values the `get()` and `set()` methods of the Calendar object are called. The `Calendar` object has several fields that define information that can be retrieved via the `get()` method.

The first line of the Scriptlet creates a new integer called `currentDay`:

```
<%  // Set the current day of the month
    int currentDay = currentCal.get(currentCal.DAY_OF_MONTH);
```

Here the `Calendar` object named `currentCal` calls its `get()` method and sends the field `DAY_OF_MONTH`. This field stands for the current day of the month, and the `get()` method returns this value and it is assigned to `currentDay`.

Next comes the number of days in the month. The new integer is aptly named `daysInMonth`. Similar to the `get()` method called to retrieve the current day, the field name `DAY_OF_MONTH` is called, only this time it is sent in a special method of the `Calendar` object called `getActualMaximum()`.

```
        // Calculate the totals days in the month
    int daysInMonth =
        currenCal.getActualMaximum(currentCal.DAY_OF_MONTH);
```

This method returns the maximum value for the given field, and since the maximum days in the month is requested it returns the total number of days in the month.

The third piece of information needed is the day of the week for the first day of the month. The simplest way to do this is to change the current day of the month in the `Calendar` object created to the first day of the month. This is done through the `Calendar set()` method. The two values sent of the `set()` method are the field value to be changed, and the new value. Then the `get()` method of the `Calendar` class can be called with the field specific to the day of the week:

```
    // Calculate the day of the week for the first
    currentCal.set(currentCal.DAY_OF_MONTH, 1);
    int dayOfWeek = currentCal.get(currentCal.DAY_OF_WEEK);
```

It is important to note that the day of the week starts with one instead of zero, as do many `date` methods in Java. Most likely this is to match the lack of zero in the Gregorian calendar.

Now that the needed information is obtained, the calendar can be generated. The first step is to generate blank spaces for the days preceding the first day of the month. The `colspan` HTML tag makes this easy. A table definition is created and assigned the value of `dayOfWeek` minus one. To be safe, this is wrapped in an `if` statement that makes sure a `colspan` of zero is not specified:

```
 // Prefill the calendar with blank spaces
if (dayOfWeek != 1) {
  out.println("    <TD COLSPAN=" + (dayOfWeek-1) +
  "> </TD>");
}
```

Now the table elements that contain dates can be printed. This is done by using a `for` statement that starts at one and ends when the value of `daysInMonth` is reached.

```
// Fill in dates
    for (int day=1; day <= daysInMonth; day++) {

      if (day == currentDay) {
        out.println("    <TD CLASS='currentDay'>" + day +
      "</TD>");
      } else {
        out.println("    <TD CLASS='otherDay'>" + day +
      "</TD>");
      }

      if (dayOfWeek == 7) {
        out.println("  </TR>\n\n  <TR>");
        dayOfWeek = 1;
      } else {
        dayOfWeek++;
      }
    }
```

Two `if` statements are in the `for` loop. The first prints the current day. If it is equal to the `currentDay` it specifies the CSS style that contains the red font. Otherwise it specifies the `otherDay` style. The second `if` statement checks to see if the current `dayOfWeek` integer is equal to seven, and if so it closes the current table row and creates a new one. It also resets the `dayOfWeek` integer to one. If `dayOfWeek` is not equal to seven, it increments `dayOfWeek` by one.

To finish up this Scriptlet, the closing empty table elements need to be filled in. This is accomplished by specifying another table element with a COLSPAN attribute to fill the remaining cells. Again, an `if` statement is used to make sure that a value of zero is not used:

```
    // Postfill the calendar with blank spaces
    if ((8-dayOfWeek) != 0) {
      out.println("    <TD COLSPAN=" + (8-dayOfWeek) +
       "> </TD>");
    }
%>
```

With close TABLE, BODY, and HTML tags the JSP page is complete.

One issue not covered in Listing 2.6 is localization. As with the previous `Date` examples, our HTML calendar will show the calendar for the time and date of the server. This might be very different from the time and date of the browser viewing the JSP page. One way to solve this issue is to make the calendar object configurable by the viewer, such as creating a form where the local date could be set. This information could be then stored in a cookie or user database. This is a common issue with personalization and portal sites.

Another issue not covered is specific ways of viewing the `GregorianCalendar`. For example, in France the first day of the week is traditionally Monday, while Listing 2.6 follows the American tradition of listing Sunday as the first day of the week.

`Calendar.jsp` is a good example of using Scripting elements. It uses a method that is enclosed in a Declaration. It utilizes an Expression to call the method and insert information into the `out` object. The bulk of the processing itself is done in Scriptlets. The page is integrated into an HTML table that utilizes Cascading Style Sheets. It uses a Java date object, showing the power added to JSP pages by the Java programming language.

`Calendar.jsp` also gives clues to the other powerful features in JSP pages. For example, how can Java domains be imported? While `Calendar.jsp` creates a nice HTML calendar, the code itself is not very reusable or modular. What if several calendars are needed—should the code be copied several times? Chapter 3 answers these questions by revealing further features of JSP pages. It reveals JSP Resource Actions, where the output of `Calendar.jsp` can be included in other JSP pages. It introduces the JSP Bean Actions, where code from JavaBeans can be used and reused in a component model. It further describes the `page` and `include` directives, where changes to the underlying Java program that is created from the JSP page can be specified.

ACTIONS AND DIRECTIVES

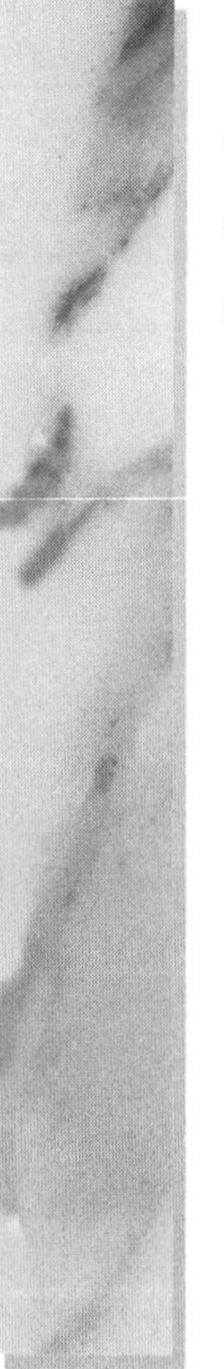

Topics in this Chapter:

- Resource and JavaBean Actions
- JSP Directives
- Handling Errors

Chapter 3

3.1 Action Element Syntax

The Action element is very different from the Scripting elements. There is only one syntax for the Action element, as it conforms to the XML standard.

Syntax: `<jsp:action_name />`

Action elements are basically predefined functions. The JSP specification comes with several built-in actions, and with JSP specification 1.1 custom tags can be created through the `jsp:taglib` directive. An Action element can modify the `out` stream, as well as create and use objects. Another interesting feature of the Action element is that the `request` object of the JSP page can directly influence its actions.

Following the XML standard, Action elements can also have attributes—another difference from the other standard elements. Attributes are a part of the Action element tag and follow the `jsp:action_name` text. For example:

```
<jsp:action_name attribute="value" />.
```

Id attribute

There are two attributes that are common to all Action elements: the id attribute and the `scope` attribute. The `id` attribute uniquely identifies the Action element, and allows the action to be referenced inside the JSP page. If the Action creates an instance of an object the `id` value can be used to reference it through the implicit object `PageContext`.

Scope attribute

The second common attribute is the `scope` attribute, which identifies the lifecycle of the Action element. The `id` attribute and the `scope` attribute are directly related, as the `scope` attribute determines the lifespan of the object associated with the `id`. The `scope` attribute has four possible values: page, request, session, and application. Each of these values refers to an implicit object in the JSP page, similar to the `out` object referenced above.

When the `scope` attribute is set to `page` it ties the object instantiated by the Action tag to the `page` implicit object. The `page` object can be thought of as a synonym for "`this`" in the body of the page. An Action with a scope of page can be thought of as a "one time" object to be used and destroyed separately by each request to a JSP page.

With a `scope` attribute of `request` the named object is made available from the `ServletRequest` object. This is accessed via the `getAttribute()` method.

With the value of `session` the `scope` attribute stays alive while the session remains valid. The named object is also available from the `ServletRequest` object and is retrieved using the `getValue()` method.

A `scope` value of `application` associates the named object with the `ServletContext` object. This means that the object remains alive for the life of the current application or Servlet. The application is normally kept alive unless the `jspDestroy()` method is called, the JSP page or associated class files change, or the JSP engine is restarted.

Table 3.1 describes the four different scopes in greater detail.

Table 3.1 JSP Scope

Scope	*Summary*
page	Objects with page scope are accessible only as a part of the page that they are created in. References to objects with a scope of page are released after the response is sent back to the client from the JSP page or the request is forwarded somewhere else. References to objects with page scope are stored in the `pageContext` object.

Table 3.1 JSP Scope (continued)

request	Objects with *request* scope are accessible from pages processing the same request where they were created. When the request is processed any object with a scope of request will be released. This is similar to the page scope, except that the object will still be accessible if the request object is passed to another JSP page. References to objects with `request` scope are stored in the `request` object.
session	Objects with `session` scope are accessible from pages processing requests that are in the same session as the one in which they were created. Before an object can be created with a session of scope the JSP page must be declared session-aware (in the `page` directive). All references to an object with a scope of session are released after the associated session ends. References to objects with *session* scope are stored in the `session` object.
application	Objects with *application* scope are accessible from pages processing requests that are in the same application as they one in which they were created. All objects of application scope will be released when the JSP page is ended by the `ServletContext`, usually through the server shutdown, the page timeout, or a call to the `jspDestroy()` method. References to objects with *application* scope are stored in the `application` object.

Standard Actions

The JSP 1.0 and 1.1 specifications define six standard actions, which can be grouped into two distinct categories. Each of these actions should be available regardless of the JSP engine or Web server environment.

The first set of standard actions all tie together to utilize JavaBeans. `useBean`, `setProperty`, and `getProperty` are called the JavaBean Actions.

The second set of standard actions is called the Resource Actions. They allow the use of outside resources to be used within JSP pages.

The JavaBean Actions

The JavaBean actions differ from the Resource actions because they all relate to using server side JavaBeans within a JSP page. The `useBean` action is used to instantiate a new JavaBean for use later on the JSP page. The `getProperty` and `setProperty` actions are used to get and set properties that have been defined within a JavaBean.

The JavaBean actions fulfill a crucial role in the component model of JSP pages. By placing all business logic within JavaBeans, and placing all presentation logic into the JSP page, Web applications can be written as separate, reusable, and scaleable components. The JavaBean actions are the key to tying together the JavaBean business logic and JSP page presentation logic.

While the semantics of using JavaBean actions will be covered here, a detailed explanation of JavaBeans and Enterprise JavaBeans, as well as real examples, will be covered in Chapter 8.

<jsp:useBean>

The `useBean` action finds or creates an instance of an object. It also associates this object with an implicit object specified by the scope attribute (page, request, session, and application). It identifies this new object with the value of the `id` attribute. It also creates a new scripting variable under the name of the `id` attribute that references the object.

The `useBean` action is quite versatile. It first searches for an existing object utilizing the `id` and `scope` variables. If an object is not found, it then tries to create the specified object. It can even be used to simply give a local name to an object defined somewhere else. This can be done by specifying the `type` attribute, but not using `class` or `beanName`.

Either the `class` attribute or the `type` attribute must be specified. The `class` attribute specifies the code from which the new object is to be created. The `type` attribute specifies the type of object, so that an existing object might be found. It is not legal to specify both `class` and `beanName` attributes. The `beanName` attribute identifies the new object with a Java Bean. If both `class` and `type` are specified, `class` must be assignable to the specified type.

The following chart describes the valid and invalid ways to use or combine the `class`, `type`, and `beanName` parameters of a `useBean` tag:

Table 3.2 The useBean Tag

`class`	***VALID***
type	VALID—Does not create a new object, but finds an object in the given `scope` and gives it a local name.
beanName	INVALID
beanName type	VALID

Table 3.2 The useBean Tag (continued)

type class	VALID—The class must be assignable to type.
`class` `beanName`	INVALID

The `useBean` tag may or may not have a body. The following example illustrates a `useBean` action without a body:

```
<jsp:useBean id="newBean" class="com.javadesktop.MyBean" />
```

Note the slash before the closing bracket, symbolizing the end of the tag. Now take a look at a similar `useBean` action that sets a property of the Bean:

```
<jsp:useBean id="newBean" class="com.javadesktop.TableBean">

<jsp:setProperty name="newBean" property="border" value="0">

</jsp:useBean>
```

Table 3.3 <jsp:useBean> Attributes

`id`	The id attribute identifies the object within the specified scope's implicit object. It also creates a new scripting variable that is used to reference the object. Like any other scripting variable it is case sensitive and must conform to Java naming conventions. The id attribute is required.
`scope`	The scope attribute defines the implicit object within which the object's reference will be available. Legal values are page, session, request, and application. The default value is page.
`class`	The class that defines the implementation of the object. Without specifying the class name or beanName the object must be available within the given scope.
`type`	The type attribute defines the type of scripting variable that is created. This allows the type of the scripting variable to be different, although related, to the type of the object it references. The type is required to be the class itself, a superclass, or an interface of the class specified. If unspecified, the default is the type of the class attribute.
`beanName`	The name of the bean, as specified by the `instantiate()` method of the `java.beans.Beans` class. This can be specified at request time by an expression.

<jsp:setProperty>

The setProperty action sets the properties of a Bean. The Bean must have been previously defined before this action.

There are two basic ways to use the setProperty action: to set the value of a property to a request parameter, or to set the value with a string. When setting the value of a property to a string, either a string constant (a string literal enclosed by double quotes) or the value of another JSP expression can be used. For example:

```
<jsp:setProperty id="TableBean" property="border" value="i+1"
      />
```

```
<jsp:setProperty id="TableBean" property="label"
      value=<%= TableName + "Label" %> />
```

The param attribute is used to set a property to the value of a request parameter. The value of the request parameter matching the param attribute value becomes the value of the property specified:

```
<jsp:setProperty id="TableBean" property="border"
      param="borderWidth" />
```

If the request parameter name and the property name match, the property attribute can be omitted:

```
<jsp:setProperty id="TableBean" param="border" />
```

One of the most powerful features of the setProperty action is the ability to set the property attribute to asterisk:

```
<jsp:setProperty id="beanName" property="*" />
```

This causes the JSP engine to cycle through the request parameters sent to the JSP page. These parameters are part of the ServletRequest object. Using introspection the JSP engine tries to match each parameter to a settable property of the Bean. It finds a match when the request name matches the name of a Bean property, and the type of the request value matches the type of the property value.

Table 3.4 <jsp:setProperty> Attributes

`name`	The name of the Bean that has a property to be set. The Bean must have been previously defined. With both the JSP 1.1 and 1.0 specifications the Bean must have been defined by using the useBean action. The property to be set must exist in the Bean.
`property`	The property attribute is the name of the Bean property to be set. If the property attribute is specified, but the param and value attributes are omitted, the property name is matched to a request parameter of the corresponding name.
`param`	The param attribute is the name of the request parameter whose value the property is to receive. The the parameter's value is null, or the parameter does not exist, the `setProperty` action is ignored. A param attribute and a value attribute are not legal in the same `setProperty` action.
`value`	The value that is to be assigned to the given property. A value attribute and a param attribute are not legal in the same `setProperty` action.

<jsp:getProperty>

The `getProperty` action is used to retrieve the value of a given property and print it. This simply means inserting it into the implicit `out` object. The Bean specified by the required name attribute must have been defined previously. In the JSP 1.1 and 1.0 specifications this means that the Bean must have been defined with the `useBean` action.

The Bean property value is converted to a String using the `toString()` method of the specified object. The getProperty action has only two attributes, both of which are required. For example:

```
<jsp:getProperty name="TableBean" property="borderWidth" />
```

Table 3.5 <jsp:getProperty> Attributes

`name`	The name of the Bean that has a property to be retrieved. The Bean must have been previously defined. The property to be retrieved must exist in the Bean. This is a required attribute.
`property`	The property attribute is the name of the Bean property to be retrieved. This is a required attribute.

The Resource Actions

Resource actions specify external resources that should be used with the JSP page. The `include` and `forward` actions allow interactions with other resources such as JSP pages, HTML pages, and XML pages. The `plugin` action allows automatically generated HTML to be written for specific browser constructs. This means that the appropriate construct (`<EMBED>` or `<OBJECT>`) will be created that will result in the appropriate plugin being downloaded (if needed) and execution of the Applet or JavaBean code.

There are two elements specifically associated with Resource actions. The `param` element is used with the `plugin` action to specify the parameters to the JavaBean or Applet. With the `include` and `forward` actions the `param` element allows GET operands to be specified for the associated resource (The `param` element is available for the `include` and `forward` actions beginning with the JSP 1.1 specification.) The `fallback` element is used with the `plugin` action if there is no appropriate construct for the particular browser, or if the Applet or JavaBean fails to load for some other reason.

<jsp:include>

The `include` action can be used to insert the output of both static and dynamic pages into the current page. When the include action is encountered the current processing is halted. The `JspWriter out` object is then released to receive the output of the resource identified with the "`page`" attribute. The output of the resource is completely received and any existing buffers flushed before the data is inserted into the `out` object. The output of the resource is not parsed by the JSP engine, but included "as is."

This is very different from the include directive: `<%@ include file="filename" %>`. The `include` directive retrieves the resource specified by the file attribute and inserts it into the current JSP page before the page is parsed. The `include` directive is covered extensively later in this chapter.

To use the include directive simply specify a resource. This is done by setting the value of the `page` attribute. The value must be on the local Web server and the `flush` attribute must be specified:

```
<jsp:include page="/data/footer.html" flush="true" />
```

Table 3.6 <jsp:include> Attributes

`page`	The relative URL of the page to be included. It must be an existing resource on the local Web server.
`flush`	The flush attribute determines whether the included resource has its buffer flushed before it is included. This attribute is required to have a Boolean value. With the JSP 1.0 and 1.1 specifications, "true" is the only legal attribute. This is due to the structure of the underlying Servlet specification. This is a required attribute.

With the JSP 1.1 specification an optional `param` attribute can specify request parameters to be sent to the resource:

```
<jsp:include page="/data/login.jsp" flush="yes">

<jsp:param name="user" value="Joe Blow" />
</jsp:include>
```

The following example demonstrates including the previous date example in a new JSP page:

Listing 3.1 include.jsp

```
<!DOCTYPE HTML PUBLIC "-//W3C//DTD HTML 4.0 Final//EN">

<HTML>
<HEAD>
<TITLE>Using Comments</TITLE>
</HEAD>
<BODY>

<P>Here I am including the page /core-jsp/date.jsp:

<P><jsp:include page="date.jsp" flush="true" />

</BODY>
</HTML>
```

The output of this page is fairly simple (see Figure 3–1):

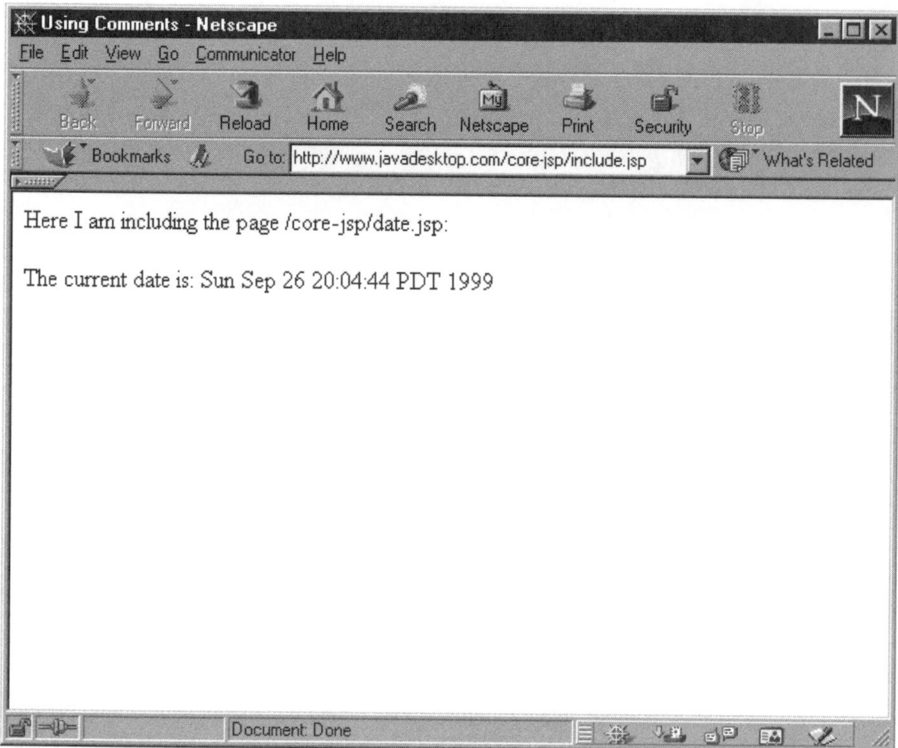

Figure 3–1 Output of include.jsp

What is interesting is the source of the page (see Figure 3–2). Notice that everything on the page was included, even the HTML open and close tags. It is also important to note that it was the output of the date.jsp page that was inserted into the page, not the source of the date.jsp page. The include action is "dumb" in the sense that is does not parse the contents of the page, but inserts them "as is." This means that the page was retrieved just as a normal client would. The JSP elements on date.jsp were processed before it was inserted into include.jsp.

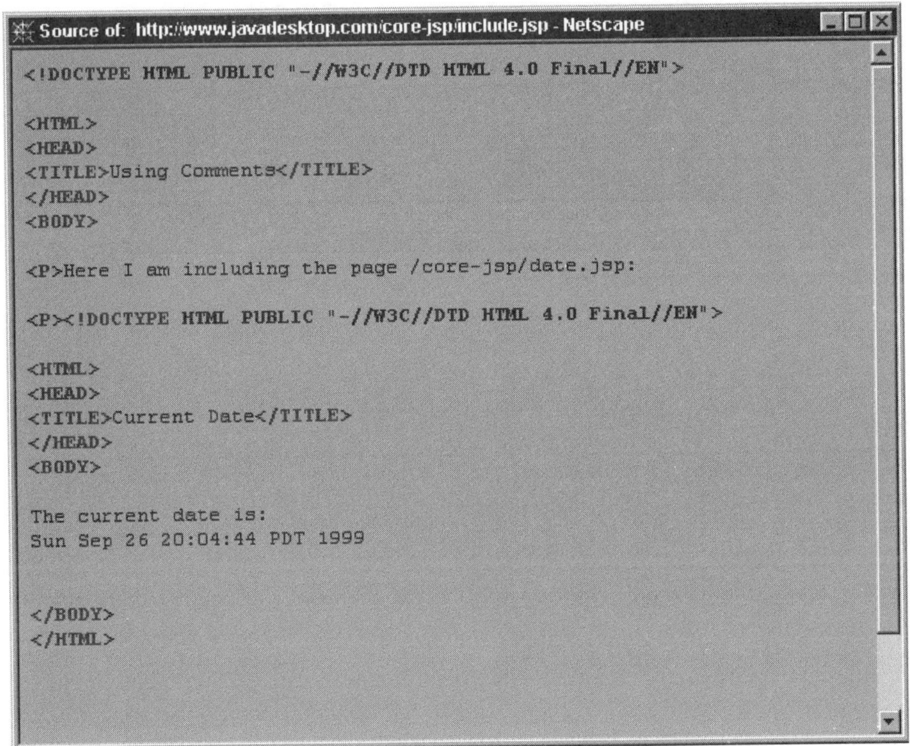
Source of: http://www.javadesktop.com/core-jsp/include.jsp - Netscape
<!DOCTYPE HTML PUBLIC "-//W3C//DTD HTML 4.0 Final//EN">
<HTML>
<HEAD>
<TITLE>Using Comments</TITLE>
</HEAD>
<BODY>
<P>Here I am including the page /core-jsp/date.jsp:
<P><!DOCTYPE HTML PUBLIC "-//W3C//DTD HTML 4.0 Final//EN">
<HTML>
<HEAD>
<TITLE>Current Date</TITLE>
</HEAD>
<BODY>
The current date is:
Sun Sep 26 20:04:44 PDT 1999
</BODY>
</HTML>

Figure 3–2 View source of include.jsp

<jsp:forward>

The `forward` action terminates the action of the current page and forwards the request to another resource, such as a static page, another JSP page, or a Java Servlet. A JSP page or a Servlet must be in the same context. Exactly what is forwarded is determined by the value of the `page` implicit object.

The `forward` action is similar to the HTTP status code 302, where a server tells the browser to forward to a new URL. It is different in the fact that the URL specified must reside on the same server. It is also different in that the browser typically displays the same URL as the original request. In essence, a `forward` action receives a request, forwards it to the new URL, receives the response, and then returns it to the client. The client itself never has an indication that there was a `forward` action, or that the page requested received it's content from another resource.

The `forward` action has only one parameter: page. Similar to the include action the value of the page attribute must be a relative URL on the same Web server.

Listing 3.2 forward.jsp on the Server

```
<!DOCTYPE HTML PUBLIC "-//W3C//DTD HTML 4.0 Final//EN">

<HTML>
<HEAD>
<TITLE>Using Comments</TITLE>
</HEAD>
<BODY>

<jsp:forward page="date.jsp" />

</BODY>
</HTML>
```

Again the same `date.jsp` is being used, although this time it is forwarded to by `forward.jsp`. The output of the page (Figure 3–3) looks almost exactly the same as Figure 3–1, noting that the URL listed is `forward.jsp`. The user has no idea that the page that was really retrieved was `date.jsp`.

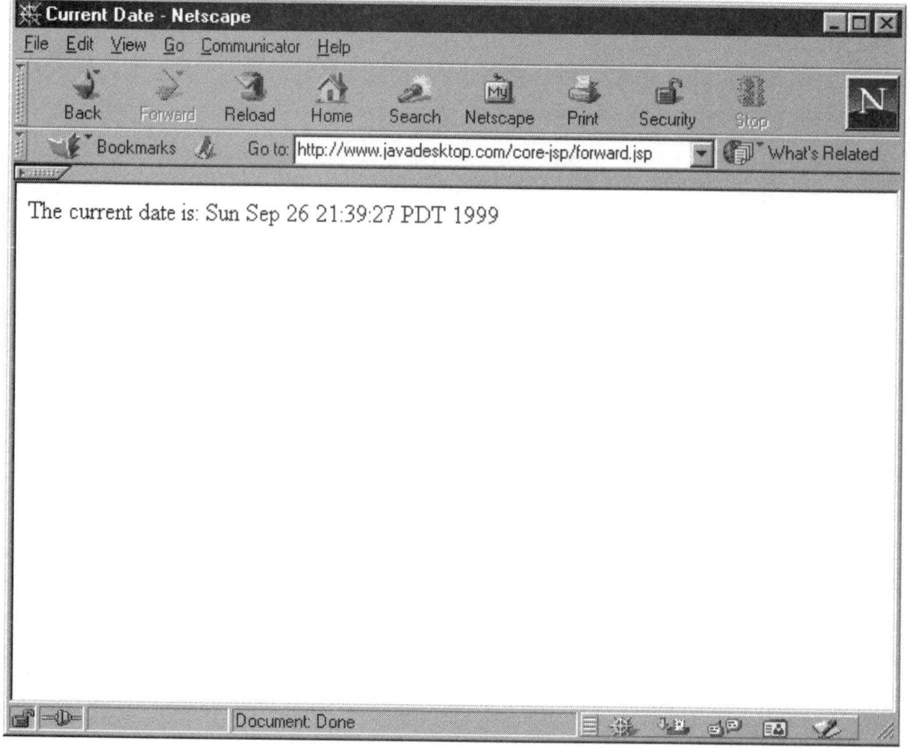

Figure 3–3 Output of forward.jsp

Now take a look at the source of this page (see Figure 3–4).

The important thing to notice is that all of the data before and after the forward action was discarded. This means that the buffer for the actual forward.jsp was discarded. In the event that an original page is not buffered, and there was data sent to the browser, an exception would be raised.

With the JSP 1.1 specification an optional param attribute can specify request parameters to be sent to the resource:

```
<jsp:forward page="/authenticate/verify.jsp">

<jsp:param name="pass" value="dhThs&7" />
  </jsp:forward>
```

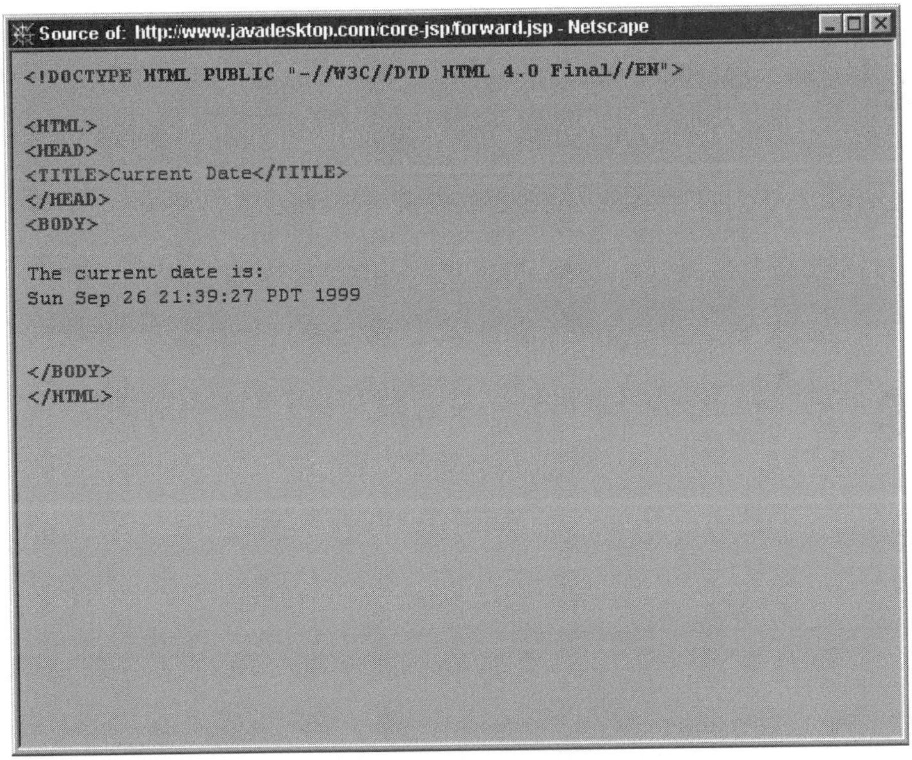

Source of: http://www.javadesktop.com/core-jsp/forward.jsp - Netscape

```
<!DOCTYPE HTML PUBLIC "-//W3C//DTD HTML 4.0 Final//EN">

<HTML>
<HEAD>
<TITLE>Current Date</TITLE>
</HEAD>
<BODY>

The current date is:
Sun Sep 26 21:39:27 PDT 1999


</BODY>
</HTML>
```

Figure 3–4 View source of forward.jsp

<jsp:plugin>

The `plugin` action is used to insert Java components into a JSP page. It determines the type of browser and inserts the `<object>` or `<embed>` tags as needed. If the needed plugin is not present, it downloads the plugin and then executes the Java component. The Java component can be either an Applet or a JavaBean.

It is important to note that any component specified by the plugin URL must be downloaded to the browser and executed on the client. Thus, JavaBeans used with the `plugin` action are run on the client's Java Runtime Environment (JRE), while JavaBeans used with the `useBean` action are executed on the server.

The `plugin` action has several attributes that correspond to common HTML tags used to format Java components. The `param` element can also be used to send parameters to the Applet or Bean. A new element, the `fallback` element, can be used to specify an error string to be sent to the user in case the component fails. How this message is sent to the client is left up to the specific JSP engine implementation. Possibly an error dialog is raised. The component fails if either the browser is not compatible with the `<object>` or `<embed>` tags or if the component could not be successfully started.

The `jrevision` attribute allows a minimum level of Java specification necessary to run the component. With the `iepluginurl` and `nspluginurl` attributes a URL pointing to the appropriate plugin can be specified.

Here is an example plugin action, using several different features:

```
<jsp:plugin type="applet"  code="JavaCharter.class"
      codebase="/java" vspace="0" hspace="0" width="60"
      height="80" jrevision="1.2" >

<jsp:param name="ChartType" value="Bar" />
<jsp:fallback> Unable to initialize Java Plugin
      </jsp:fallback>
</jsp:plugin>
```

Table 3.7 <jsp:plugin> Attributes

`type`	The type of component specified; either JavaBean or Applet.
`jrevision`	Identifies the version of Java Runtime Environment necessary for the component. The default value is 1.1.

Table 3.7 <jsp:plugin> Attributes (continued)	
`iepluginurl`	The URL where the appropriate Java plugin can be found for Microsoft Internet Explorer. The default value is dependent on the JSP engine implementation.
`nspluginurl`	The URL where the appropriate Java plugin can be found for Netscape Navigator. The default value is dependent on the JSP engine implementation.
`code, align, archive, height, hspace, name, vspace, title, and width`	These attributes are defined by the HTML specification, and apply to the `codebase` corresponding HTML tags for the appropriate browser.

3.2 Directives

JSP directives have a very simple purpose: to send messages to the JSP engine. They do not contain business logic. They do not modify the out stream. They simply tell the JSP engine how the JSP page should be compiled. While this purpose is straightforward, understanding directives is somewhat complex. As directives modify how the JSP page is compiled, understanding how they work needs an understanding of the JSP engine. This includes understanding the implicit JSP objects, page scope, error handling, and page buffering.

Directive Syntax

JSP Syntax: `<%@ directive_name %>`

XML Syntax: `<jsp:directive.directive_name />`

The syntax for Directive elements—both JSP and XML versions—is very different from both Action and Scripting element tags. The JSP syntax for the directive elements begins with a standard JSP open tag and an @ symbol (`<%@`). Similar to Action tags it takes attribute value pairs. For example:

```
<%@ include file="mypage.html" %>
```

The XML syntax is specific to the Directive that is being used. In JSP Specification 1.0 there are two Directives, page and include. The JSP 1.1 Specification adds the taglib Directive. The XML versions of the page and include directives are as follows:

```
<jsp:directive.page attribute="value" … />

<jsp:directive.include file="value"/>
```

The `taglib` directive XML syntax is different because its purpose is to define new elements. Instead of being a part of the JSP XML syntax, it extends the JSP XML syntax.

The Page Directive

The page directive allows several different page-specific attributes to be set. It directly influences how the Java program created from the JSP page is formed. The JSP page, including any JSP pages included with the `include` directive, can have any number of page directives. There must not be more than one instance of each attribute/value pair with the single exception of the `import` attribute. Multiple `import` attributes pairs are cumulative.

Page directives always begin with the standard JSP open tag followed by an @ symbol and the keyword page (`<%@ page`). Here are a couple of example page directives:

```
<%@ page import="java.util.Calendar" %>
```

The above page directive imports the `java.utilCalendar` class. This next example sets the scripting language to Java and the page buffer to 32k:

```
<%@ page language="java" buffer="32k" %>
```

It is important to note that the `page` directive is able to affect the overall construction of the Java program that results from the JSP page. For example, the `import` attribute adds to the `import` statements in the Java program, which are location dependent. This means that within the JSP page they are location independent. Wherever the `page` directive is located, it affects the page as a whole.

The `buffer` *and* `autoFlush` *Attributes*

The `buffer` attribute determines whether the JSP page will be buffered, and the buffer size if it is to be buffered. By default the page buffer is at least 8 kb, but the actual value is dependent of the specific JSP engine used. If "none" is specified, the page is not buffered at all, and all output is written directly to a PrintWriter of the ServletResponse object. If a size is specified, such as 16kb, then the output is buffered to a JspWriter object with a buffer no less than the size specified.

The buffer attribute is closely tied to the autoFlush attribute. The autoFlush attribute determines the page's behavior when the page buffer is full or exceeded. By default autoFlush is set to "true". This means that the buffered output is automatically flushed when the buffer is full. By setting the autoFlush attribute to "false" the JSP engine is instructed to raise an exception if the buffer is exceeded.

The forward action can be influenced by the buffer attribute. With a buffer attribute set to "none" a JSP page can have no output before the forward action is encountered or an exception will be raised. Similarly, if the buffer is filled before a forward action is reached, whether or not autoFlush is set, an exception will occur.

The **contentType** *Attribute*

The contentType attribute is used to define the encoding for the JSP page in the response, as well as the MIME type of the response. The contentType attribute can take two different types of values. One form simply specifies the MIME type, and is in the form of "TYPE". Additionally a character set can be set, changing the form of the value to "TYPE; charset=CHARSET". By default the MIME type or "TYPE" value is "text/html" and the character set is ISO-8859-1 (also known as latin-1).

The contentType attribute can be useful in debugging. By setting the value to "text/plain" the output of the JSP file can be seen as source, instead of HTML.

The **errorPage** *and* **isErrorPage** *Attributes*

The errorPage attribute specifies a URL for forwarding exceptions. In the event an exception is thrown in the current JSP page, but not caught, the thrown exception is forwarded to the specified URL. Currently the URL specified must be a JSP page, although this may change in later specifications.

The exception is forwarded by saving the object reference on the common ServletRequest object by using its setAttribute() method. The name used is javax.Servlet.jsp.jspException.

If the current JSP page has buffer="none"—or the buffer has been flushed before the exception is caught, the attempt to forward the exception to the `errorPage` URL might fail. This is similar to the problem discussed above of using a `forward` action after the buffer has been flushed.

The JSP page sent an exception by means of an `errorPage` attribute must have the page attribute of `isErrorPage` set to "`true`". By default this attribute is set to "`false`". If "`true`" an explicit scripting variable called `exception` is created and referenced to the `Throwable` error object from the source JSP page.

CORE Note: Errors and Exceptions

There are two different types of errors that can occur for any given JSP page. The difference between the two types of errors is when they occur in the phase or lifecycle of the JSP page.

The first type of error is referred to a translation-time or compilation-time error. This type of error occurs the first time the JSP page receives a client request, but before a response is sent. The first time a JSP page is requested, the JSP engine must parse the JSP page and create a Java Servlet source file for the JSP page. It then must successfully compile the Java Servlet into a Java class file. Any error occurring during this phase is referred to as a translation-time error, as the error is raised as the JSP source is translated into a Java class file. These errors are not caught by the `errorPage` *attribute of the* `page` *directive, as the Java program itself is not operational. Most occurrences of translation-time errors return an HTTP status code of 500 to the client, signifying an unspecified server problem. Translation-time errors are analogous to fatal errors received when compiling a Java source file.*

The second type of error is referred to as a client-request or request-time error. This is an error that occurs as a client sends a request to the Java class file and a response is sent back to the client. A common cause of a request-time error is receiving incorrect request (GET or POST) data. Request-time errors can be caught by the `errorPage` *attribute of the* `page` *directive, as well as by* `catch` *statements within valid JSP tags. Request-time errors are analogous to exceptions raised when executing a Java class file.*

The `extends` *Attribute*

The `extends` attribute allows the JSP author to specify the superclass from which the current JSP page is transformed. In general, it is recommended that the `extends` attribute be used as little as possible. If no extends attribute is specified the JSP container can utilize special superclasses to improve JSP speed.

In the JSP 1.1 spec, JSP authors have the ability to create new objects with the `taglib` directive. This gives access to new objects and classes, while allowing the JSP container to utilize its own specialized superclasses.

The `import` *Attribute*

The import attribute allows types to be made available to the Java environment. Multiple values can be specified, separated by commas. The `import` attribute is also allowed to be specified more than once in a JSP page or in pages included in an `include` directive.

By default the `java.lang.*`, `javax.Servlet.*`, `javax.Servlet.jsp.*`, and `javax.Servlet.http.*` packages are imported. It is important to note that the `import` attribute is only available when the `language` attribute is set to "java".

The `info` *Attribute*

The `info` attribute simply defines a `String` that is incorporated into the JSP page. This `String` can then be obtained by using the pages' `Servlet.getServletInfo()` method.

The `isThreadSafe` *Attribute*

The `isThreadSafe` attribute specifies the thread safety of the JSP page. By default this attribute is "`true`". A `true` value tells the JSP engine that it is safe to dispatch multiple client requests to this page at the same time. With a value of "`false`" the JSP engine is required to process each page request one at a time, in the order they were received.

It is important to note that even with a value of "`false`" the JSP page must still deal with synchronization issues, especially when concerning the `HttpSession` and `ServletContect` objects. Synchronization is covered in detail in Chapter 4.

The `language` *Attribute*

The `language` attribute of the `page` directive specifies the scripting language utilized within the JSP page. This includes all Scriptlet, Declarations, and Expressions, as well as any pages included with the `include` directive. The default value is "java", and most JSP engines currently only support Java as the scripting language.

Any scripting language utilized in a JSP page has to meet certain conditions. First of all, it must conform to the Java Runtime Environment (JRE). Next, it must expose certain parts of Java to the JSP page. These include the Java object model, as well as the implicit variables, JavaBean properties, and public methods used in the JSP specification.

The `session` *Attribute*

The `session` attribute indicates whether or not the current JSP page should participate in an HTTP session. The default value is "`true`". When true a variable named "`session`" is created with a type of `javax.Servlet.HttpSession`. With a value of "`false`" there is no "`session`" variable created.

HTTP sessions allow information about a particular client to be tracked between requests. Sessions will be discussed thoroughly in Chapter 7.

The Include Directive

The `include` directive allows data from an external URL to be inserted into the current JSP page. Unlike the `page` directive, the `include` directive is position-dependent. Wherever the `include` directive is placed on the page is where the data will be inserted.

The `include` directive inserts the data from the external URL at translation-time. This means that the data is included in the current JSP page before it is compiled. Any JSP tags within the external URL will be processed as a part of the current page. This means that the external resource can affect the current pages' HTTP headers. A drawback is that if the external resource changes, then the current page has no way of being notified. To see any changes in the external URL, the current page would have to be recompiled. Another drawback is that the external resource cannot be specified at request-time, as it is already compiled into the code.

The `include` directive takes only one attribute, `file`, which is required. The following are two examples of the include directive:

```
<%@ include file="footer.jsp" %>

<%@ include file="/products/examples/listing.html" %>
```

The include action vs. the include directive

The `include` directive is very similar to the `include` action. Both take data from an external URL and insert it into the current page. When and how they insert the data create very important differences between the tags.

The `include` action inserts the data from the external URL at request-time. What actually happens is the current JSP page halts and flushes any buffers. It then calls the external URL and inserts the output of the URL into the output stream. After the external page is complete, it resumes processing the original JSP page.

In contrast, the `include` directive inserts the raw data from a URL into the page before it has been compiled. When this happens, a preprocessing step occurs that gathers the appropriate data and inserts the information into a temporary version of the page, then the temporary page is compiled. Since the inserted code is really part of the same JSP page, it can take advantage of other parts of the page or change how the page behaves (such as changing the HTTP headers).

Each approach has powerful and distinct advantages and disadvantages, outlined in Table 3.8.

Table 3.8 `include` action verses `include` directive

	Directive	***Action***
Syntax	`<%@ include ... %>`	`<jsp:include ... >`
Attribute	`file='...'`	`page='...'`
Dynamic include	not allowed	allowed (e.g. page="<%=foo%>")
Processed at	Translation-time	Request-time
Scope	Can effect the rest of the page	Cannot effect other parts of the page
HTTP Headers?	Yes	No

CORE Note: Includes as components

Using either the include action or the include directive provides a simple and effective way of creating modular components.

By creating a wrapper page that includes the components it needs, a large and complex page can be broken into logical blocks. Other pages can then reuse the same blocks—by including the same files—and have the same results. In addition, changing the source of a single block will change each page equally.

This is covered in greater detail in Chapter 12.

The Taglib Directive

The `taglib` directive is new to the JSP 1.1 Specification. It specifies a tag library by which the standard set of JSP tags can be extended. The `taglib` directive accomplishes three tasks: first it tells the JSP engine that this JSP page uses a tag library. This significantly affects the structure of the underlying Java program. Second, it specifies the location of a special jar file containing a Tag Library Descriptor. The Tag Library Descriptor describes the semantics of the new tag library. Finally, the `taglib` directive specifies a tag prefix that will be used to uniquely distinguish the new tags.

There are only two `taglib` attributes and they are both required: `uri` is set to the path of the tag library for the selected set of tags, while `prefix` represents the handle that will represent the library within the page. For example:

```
<%@ taglib uri="http://www.javadesktop.com/sampletags.jar"
                prefix="sample" %>

<sample:tagAction> This is an example </sample:tagAction>
```

In the above example the taglib directive points to a jar file called `sampletags.jar`. It gives the new set of tags the prefix `sample`. Once the new tag library is referenced, an action from the tag library can be used. The example calls the action `tagAction` from the tag library. Further information on extending JSP tags, as well as how to create your own Tag Libraries, is covered in Chapter 11.

It should be obvious that the JSP actions and directives go a step beyond the Scripting Elements to give the JSP author tools to make dynamic Web pages into Web applications. The ability to use standard actions, connect to JavaBeans, and implement custom tags give JSP pages the ability to interact with other systems and become enterprise applications. Now that the external systems JSP interacts with have been discussed, Chapter 4 will take a look under the hood of JSP pages to explore their relationship with Java Servlets.

THE JSP ENGINE: UNDER THE HOOD

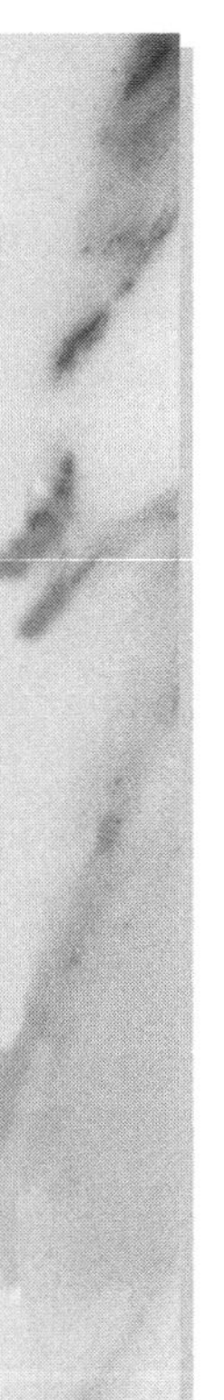

Topics in this Chapter:

- Behind the Scenes
- Multithreading and Persistence
- The Implicit Objects
- The JSP Lifecycle
- A JSP Compiled
- Performance Tuning the JSP

Chapter 4

The previous chapters addressed the background, syntax, and elements of JSP. Until this point many of the technical details of how the JSP engine works have been glossed over or avoided entirely. Developing good JSP applications involves at least a basic understanding of how the JSP engine works.

4.1 Behind the Scenes

When the JSP engine receives a request for a page it converts both static data and dynamic elements of a JSP page into Java code fragments. This translation is actually fairly straightforward.

The dynamic data contained within the JSP elements are already Java code, so these fragments can be used without modification. The static data gets wrapped up into `println()` methods. These Java code fragments are then sequentially put into a special wrapper class.

The JSP wrapper is created automatically by the JSP engine and handles most of the work involved in supporting JSP without the author's involvement. The wrapper usually extends the `javax.servlet.Servlet` class, which means that JSP actually get converted into a special form of Java Servlet code. In many ways JSP could be considered a macro language for creating Java Servlets; JSP pages essentially provide a page-centric interface into the Java Servlet API.

The source code is then compiled into a fully functioning Java Servlet. This new Servlet created by the JSP engine deals with basic exception handling, I/O, threading, and a number of other network and protocol related tasks. It is actually this newly generated Servlet that handles requests and generates the output to clients requesting the JSP page.

Recompiling

The JSP engine could have been designed to recompile each page when a new request is received. Each request would generate its own Servlet to process the response. Fortunately JSP takes a more efficient approach.

JSP pages and Java Servlets create an instance once per page, rather than once per request. When a new request is received it simply creates a thread within the already generated Servlet. This means that the first request to a JSP page will generate a new Servlet, but subsequent requests will simply reuse the Servlet from the initial request.

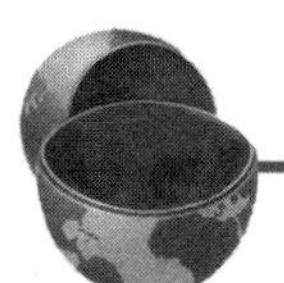

CORE Note: Delay on first request

When a JSP page is first run through the JSP engine there may be a noticeable delay in receiving a response. These delays occur because the JSP engine needs to convert the JSP into Java code, compile it, and initialize it before responding to the first request.

Subsequent requests gain the advantage of using the already compiled Servlet. Requests after the initial request should be significantly faster in processing.

There are specific occurrences that can instruct the JSP engine when to recompile the JSP page. To manage this the JSP engine keeps a record of the JSP page source code and recompiles the page when the source code has been modified. Different implementations of JSP have different rules for when to compile, but all engines are required to recompile when the JSP source code changes.

Keep in mind that external resources to a JSP page, such as a JavaBean or an included JSP page, may not cause the page to recompile. Again, different JSP engines will have different rules on how and when to recompile the page.

CORE Note: The Precompile Protocol

As of JSP1.1, a means of precompiling JSP pages is defined in the specification. To precompile a specific JSP an HTTP request to the JSP must be made with the `jsp_precomile` *parameter set.*

For example, entering the URL `http://www.javadesktop.com/core-jsp/catalog.jsp?jsp_precompile="true"` *should compile this JSP, if it has not already been compiled or the JSP source code had changed.*

The Servlet-JSP Relationship

Because JSP pages are transformed into Java Servlets, JSP displays many of the same behaviors as Java Servlets. JSP inherits powerful advantages and several disadvantages from Java Servlets.

Java Servlets work by creating a single persistent application running in the JVM. New requests are actually handled by running a new thread through this persistent application. Each request to a JSP page is really a new thread in the corresponding Java Servlet.

The Java Servlet also provides the JSP developer with several built-in methods and objects. These provide a direct interface into the behavior of the Servlet and the JSP engine.

4.2 Multithreading and Persistence

JSP inherits multithreading and persistence from Java Servlets. Being persistent allows objects to be instantiated when the Servlet is first created, so the physical memory footprint of the JSP Servlet remains fairly constant between requests. Variables can be created in persistent space to allow the Servlet to perform caching, session tracking, and other functions not normally available in a stateless environment.

The JSP author is insulated from many of the issues involved with threaded programming. The JSP engine handles most of the work involved in creating, destroying, and managing threads. This frees the JSP author from many of the burdens of multithreaded programming. However, the JSP author needs to be aware of several aspects of multithreaded programming that affect JSP pages.

Threads can inadvertently cause harm to other threads. In these situations the JSP programmer needs to understand when and how to protect their pages from threading.

Persistence

Because the Servlet is created once and remains running as a constant instance, it allows persistent variables and objects to be created. Persistent variables and objects are shared between all threads of a single Servlet. Changes to these persistent objects are reflected in all threads.

From the perspective of the JSP author, all objects and variables created within declaration tags (`<%!...%>`) are persistent. Variables and objects created within a thread will not be persistent. Code inside of a scriptlet, expression, and action tags will be run within the new request thread and therefore will not create persistent variables or objects.

Having persistent objects allows the author to keep track of data between page requests. This allows in-memory objects to be used for caching, counters, session data, database connection pooling, and many other useful tasks.

Listing 4.1 shows a counter that uses persistent variables. When the page is first loaded the variable `counter` is created. Since the servlet remains running in memory the variable will remain until the servlet is restarted. Each time the page is requested the variable `counter` is incremented and displayed to the requestor. Each user should see a page count that is one higher than the last time the page was accessed.

Listing 4.1 counter.jsp

```
<!DOCTYPE HTML PUBLIC "-//W3C//DTD HTML 4.0 Final//EN">

<%!
  int counter;
%>

<HTML>

<STYLE>
.pageFooter {
  position: absolute; top: 590px;
  font-family: Arial, Helvetica, sans-serif;
```

Listing 4.1 counter.jsp (continued)

```
  font-size: 8pt; text-align: right;
}
</STYLE>

<BODY>
<DIV CLASS="pageFooter">
This page has been accessed
<% counter++;
   out.print(counter);
 %>
times since last restarted.
</DIV>
</BODY>

</HTML>
```

The Dangers of Threads

Unfortunately, object persistence also presents some potentially significant problems. To avoid these problems the JSP author needs to understand and steer away from these dangers.

The same factors that make persistence useful can also create a significant problem called a "Race Condition." A Race Condition occurs when one thread is preparing to use data and a second thread modifies the data before the first thread has finished using the data.

Consider the above example (Listing 4.1) with two threads running. Take careful note of the value of the counter variable.

Thread 1 – UserA requests the page
Thread 2 – UserB requests the page
Thread 1 – `counter` increases by one
Thread 2 – `counter` increases by one
Thread 1 – `counter` is displayed for UserA
Thread 2 – `counter` is displayed for UserB

In this situation, UserA is actually viewing information that was intended for UserB. This is obviously not the expected result.

The problems caused by the above example are fairly trivial, UserA simply sees an incorrect page count. However, Race Conditions can just as easily result in very significant problems. Imagine if Race Condition occurred while billing a user for an online order.

It is good programming practice to resolve all Race Conditions, whether they appear trivial or not. Threads do not flow in a predictable order, so the results of a Race Condition may appear erratic. Race Conditions can be particularly difficult to spot and can turn from trivial to significant with very minor changes to the processing algorithms.

Thread Safety

In considering thread safety, it is important to first acknowledge that threading is a significant benefit to performance. Thread safety is almost always achieved by "disabling" threading for some portion of the code.

It is also important to understand that Race Conditions occur only with persistent variables. If all the variables and objects used by an application are created by threads, then there will be no Race Conditions. In these cases threading problems are not going to occur.

SingleThreadModel

The simplest method for gaining thread safety is also the least efficient. This is achieved by simply turning off threading for the entire page. Turning off threading is a poor option and should be avoided in most situations, because it avoids the potential problems by sacrificing many advantages.

JSP provides a means to turn off threading through the page directive attribute `isThreadSafe='false'`. This forces the page to be created under the `SingleThreadModel`, which allows only one request to be handled by the page at any time.

This option is still not 100% effective. Variables created in the `session` or `application` scope may still be affected by multiple instances.

synchronized()

A more practical and efficient manner of protecting variables from Race Conditions is to use Java's synchronized interface. This interface imposes a locking mechanism that allows only one thread at a time to process a particular block of code.

Entire methods can be synchronized and protected from Race Conditions, by using the `synchronized` keyword in the methods signature. This will protect all persistent variables accessed within the method. In this case only one thread can access the method at a time.

Blocks of code can also be synchronized by wrapping the code in a `synchronized()` block. In this case an argument is expected, which should represent the object to be locked.

CORE Note: Synchronized flag

Any object derived from `java.lang.Object` *can be used as the argument to the synchronized block. Every object has a special 'lock flag' that is used by* `synchronized()` *to manage threading (synchronized replaces both mutex and semaphore use in C programming). Primitive types in Java do not have this flag and therefore cannot be used as a lock for a synchronized block.*

In creating a synchronized block it is usually most efficient to use the object that most closely represents the data to be synchronized. For example, if a syncronized block is being written that modifies and writes to disk the `foo` *object it is best to use* `synchronized(foo)`*. Of course the* `this` *or* `page` *object can always be used, but that can create bottlenecks by locking the entire page each time the synchronized block is run.*

Listing 4.2 shows a new example of the counter page that uses a synchronized block. In this new example the two lines of code are grouped together within synchronized block. Only one thread is able to process the block at any given time. Each thread will lock the page object, increment the variable, display the variable, and then unlock the page object.

Listing 4.2 counter2.jsp

```
<!DOCTYPE HTML PUBLIC "-//W3C//DTD HTML 4.0 Final//EN">

<%!
  int counter;
%>

<HTML>

<STYLE>
.pageFooter {
  position: absolute; top: 590px;
  font-family: Arial, Helvetica, sans-serif;
  font-size: 8pt; text-align: right;
}
```

Listing 4.2 counter2.jsp (continued)

```
</STYLE>

<BODY>
<DIV CLASS="pageFooter">
This page has been accessed
<% synchronized (page) {
     counter++;
     out.print(counter);
   }
%>
times since last restarted.
</DIV>
</BODY>

</HTML>
```

4.3 The Implicit Objects

The Servlet also creates several objects to be used by the JSP engine. Many of these objects are exposed to the JSP developer and can be called directly without being explicitly declared.

The out Object

The major function of JSP is to describe data being sent to an output stream in response to a client request. This is output stream is exposed to the JSP author through the implicit `out` object.

The `out` object is an instantiation of a `javax.servlet.jsp.JspWriter` object. This object may represent a direct reference to the output stream, a filtered stream, or a nested `JspWriter` from another JSP. Output should never be sent directly to the output stream, because there may be several output streams during the lifecycle of the JSP.

The initial `JspWriter` object is instantiated differently depending on whether the page is buffered or not. By default, every JSP page has buffering turned on, which almost always improves performance. Buffering be easily turned off by using the `buffered='false'` attribute of the page directive.

A buffered `out` object collects and sends data in blocks, typically providing the best total throughput. With buffering the `PrintWriter` is created when the first block is sent, actually the first time that `flush()` is called.

With unbuffered output the `PrintWriter` object will be immediately created and referenced to the `out` object. In this situation, data sent to the `out` object is immediately sent to the output stream. The `PrintWriter` will be created using the default settings and header information determined by the server.

CORE Note: HTTP Headers and Buffering

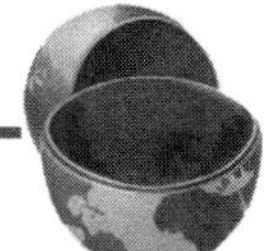

HTTP uses response headers to both describe the server and define certain aspects of the data begin sent to the client. This might include the MIME content type of the page, new cookies, a forwarding URL, or other HTTP "actions."

JSP allows an author to change aspects of the response headers right up until the `OutputStream` *is created. Once the* `OutputStream` *is established the header information cannot be modified, as it is already sent to the client.*

In the case of a buffered `out` *object the* `OutputStream` *is not established until the first time that the buffer is flushed. When the buffer gets flushed depends largely on the* `autoFlush` *and* `bufferSize` *attributes of the page directive. It is usually best to set the header information before anything is sent to the* `out` *object.*

It is very difficult to set page headers with an unbuffered `out` *object. When an unbuffered page is created the* `OutputStream` *is established almost immediately.*

The sending headers after the `OutputStream` *has been established can result in a number of unexpected behaviors. Some headers will simply be ignored, others may generate exceptions such as* `IllegalStateException`.

The `JspWriter` object contains most of the same methods as the `java.io.PrintWriter` class. However, `JspWriter` has some additional methods designed to deal with buffering. Unlike the `PrintWriter` object, `JspWriter` throws `IOExceptions`. In JSP these exceptions need to be explicitly caught and dealt with. More about the `out` object is covered in Chapter 6.

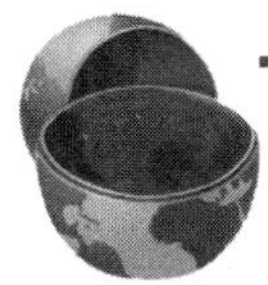

CORE Note: autoFlush()

The default behavior of buffering in JSP is to automatically flush the buffer when it becomes full. However, there are cases where a JSP is actually talking directly to another application. In these cases the desired behavior might be to throw an exception if the buffer size is exceeded.

Setting the `autoFlush='false'` *attribute of the page directives will cause a buffer overflow to throw an exception.*

The request Object

Each time a client requests a page the JSP engine creates a new object to represent that request. This new object is an instance of `javax.servlet.http.HttpServletRequest` and is given parameters describing the request. This object is exposed to the JSP author through the `request` object.

Through the `request` object the JSP page is able to react to input received from the client. Request parameters are stored in special name/value pairs that can be retrieved using the `request.getParameter(name)` method.

The request object also provides methods to retrieve header information and cookie data. It provides means to identify both the client and the server—as previously seen in Chapter 2 (Listing 2.5 uses `request.getRequestURI()` and `request.getServerName()` to identify the server).

The `request` object is inherently limited to the request scope. Regardless of how the page directives have set the scope of the page, this object will always be recreated with each request. For each separate request from a client there will be a corresponding `request` object.

Additional information on using the request object and it methods will be discussed in Chapter 5.

The response Object

Just as the server creates the `request` object, it also creates an object to represent the response to the client. The object is an instance of `javax.servlet.http.HttpServletResponse` and is exposed to the JSP author as the `response` object.

The `response` object deals with the stream of data back to the client. The `out` object is very closely is related to the `response` object. The `response` object also defines the interfaces that deal with creating new HTTP headers. Through this object the JSP author can add new cookies or date stamps, change the MIME content type of the page, or start "server-push" methods.

The `response` object also contains enough information on the HTTP to be able to return HTTP status codes, such as forcing page redirects.

Additional information on using the `response` object and its methods will be discussed in Chapter 6.

The pageContext Object

The `pageContext` object is used to represent the entire JSP page. It is intended as a means to access information about the page while avoiding most of the implementation details.

This object stores references to the `request` and `response` objects for each request. The `application`, `config`, `session`, and `out` objects are derived by accessing attributes of this object. The `pageContext` object also contains information about the directives issued to the JSP page, including the buffering information, the `errorPageURL`, and page scope.

The `pageContext` object does more than just act as a data repository. It is this object that manages nested JSP pages, performing most of the work involved with the `forward` and `include` actions. The `pageContext` object also handles uncaught exceptions.

From the perspective of the JSP author this object is useful in deriving information about the current JSP page's environment. This can be particularly useful in creating components where behavior may be different based on the JSP `page` directives.

The session object

The `session` object is used to track information about a particular client while using stateless connection protocols, such as HTTP. Sessions can be used to store arbitrary information between client requests.

Each session should correspond to only one client and can exist throughout multiple requests. Sessions are often tracked by URL rewriting or cookies, but the method for tracking of the requesting client is not important to the `session` object.

The `session` object is an instance of `javax.servlet.http.HttpSession` and behaves exactly the same way that session objects behave under Java Servlets.

Additional information on the session object and its methods will be discussed in Chapter 7.

The application Object

The `application` object is direct wrapper around the `ServletContext` object for the generated Servlet. It has the same methods and interfaces that the `ServletContext` object does in programming Java Servlets.

This object is a representation of the JSP page through its entire lifecycle. This object is created when the JSP page is initialized and will be removed when the JSP page is removed by the `jspDestroy()` method, the JSP page is recompiled, or the JVM crashes. Information stored in this object remains available to any object used within the JSP page.

The `application` object also provides a means for a JSP to communicate back to the server in a way that does not involve "requests." This can be useful for finding out information about the MIME type of a file, sending log information directly out to the servers log, or communicating with other servers.

The config Object

The `config` object is an instantiation of `javax.servlet.ServletConfig`. This object is a direct wrapper around the `ServletConfig` object for the generated servlet. It has the same methods and interfaces that the `ServletConfig` object does in programming Java Servlets.

This object allows the JSP author access to the initialization parameters for the Servlet or JSP engine. This can be useful in deriving standard global information, such as the paths or file locations.

The page Object

This object is an actual reference to the instance of the page. It can be thought of as an object that represents the entire JSP page.

When the JSP page is first instantiated the `page` object is created by obtaining a reference to the `this` object. So, the `page` object is really a direct synonym for the `this` object.

However, during the JSP lifecycle, the `this` object may not refer to the page itself. Within the context of the JSP page, The `page` object will remain constant and will always represent the entire JSP page.

The exception Object

The error handling methods described in Chapter 3 utilizes this object. It is available only when the previous JSP page throws an uncaught exception and the `<%@ page errorPage="..." %>` tag was used.

The `exception` object is a wrapper containing the exception thrown from the previous page. It is typically used to generate an appropriate response to the error condition.

4.4 The JSP lifecycle

The JSP engine uses three methods to manage the lifecycle of a JSP page and its generated servlet.

The heart of the JSP page is processed using a generated method called _jspService. This is created and managed by the JSP engine itself. _jspService should never be managed by the JSP author; doing so could cause disastrous results. The _jspService method represents the bulk of the JSP page, handling all requests and responses. In fact, new threads are effectively calling the _jspService method.

CORE Note: Reserved names

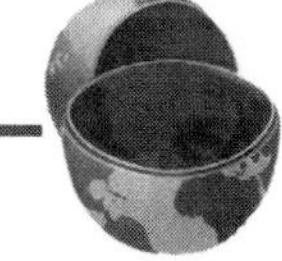

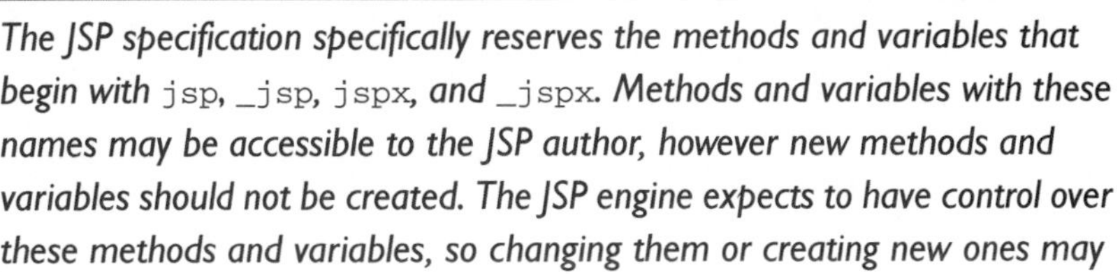

The JSP specification specifically reserves the methods and variables that begin with `jsp`, `_jsp`, `jspx`, *and* `_jspx`. *Methods and variables with these names may be accessible to the JSP author, however new methods and variables should not be created. The JSP engine expects to have control over these methods and variables, so changing them or creating new ones may result in erratic behavior.*

Two other methods, `jspInit()` and `jspDestroy()`, are designed to be overridden by the JSP author. In fact these methods do not exist unless specifically created by the JSP author. They play a special role in managing the lifecycle of a JSP page.

jspInit()

method signature: void jspInit()

`jspInit()` is a method that is run only once when the JSP page is first requested. `jspInit()`is guaranteed to be completely processed before any single request is handled. It is effectively the same as the `init()` method in Java Servlets and Java Applets.

`jspInit()` allows the JSP author a means to create or load objects that may be needed for every request. This can be useful for loading state information, creating database connection pools, and any task that only needs to happen once when the JSP page is first started.

jspDestroy()

method signature: void jspDestroy()

The server calls the `jspDestroy()` method when the Servlet is unloaded from the JVM. It is effectively the same as the `destroy()` method in Java Servlets and Java Applets.

Unlike `jspInit()` this method is not guaranteed to execute. The server will make its best effort attempt to run the method after each thread. Since this method occurs at the end of processing, there are situations—such as the server crashing—where `jspDestroy()` may not be executed.

`jspDestroy()` allows the JSP author a means to execute code just before the Servlet has finished. This is commonly used to free up resources or close connections that are still open. It can also be useful to store state information or other information that should be stored between instances.

JSP Lifecycle Overview

On first request or precompile `jspInit()` will be called, at which point the page is "running" waiting for requests. Now `_jspService` handles most transactions, picking up requests, running threads through, and generating responses. Finally, when a signal is received to shutdown the `jspDestroy()` method is called. The overall lifecycle of a JSP page is shown in Figure 4–1:

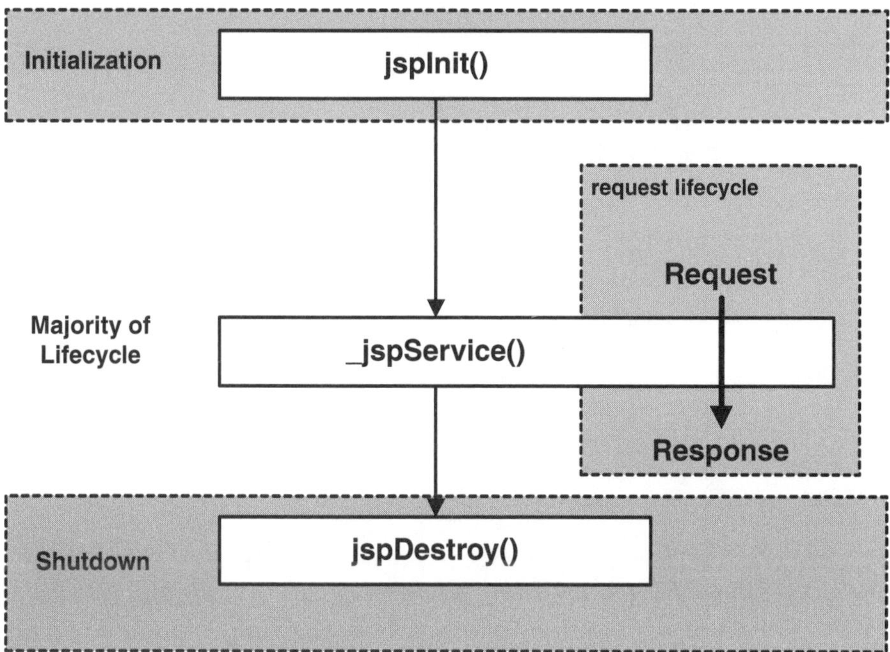

Figure 4–1 The JSP Lifecycle

The counter using jspInit() and jspDestroy()

The previous example of a page counter used a variable stored only in the memory of the running Servlet. It was never written to disk, so if the JSP page is restarted the variable would be reset.

The example shown in Listing 4.3 recovers the variable by using the `jspInit()` method to load the value of the variable when the page is first started. The example also uses the `jspDestroy()` method to write the value of variable to be recovered next time the JSP page is restarted.

Listing 4.3 counter3.jsp

```
<!DOCTYPE HTML PUBLIC "-//W3C//DTD HTML 4.0 Final//EN">

<%@ page import="java.io.*" %>

<%!
  int counter = 0;

  public void jspInit() {
    try {
      FileInputStream countFile =
                        new FileInputStream ("counter.dat");
      DataInputStream countData =
                          new DataInputStream (countFile);
      counter = countData.readInt();
    }
    catch (FileNotFoundException ignore) {
 // No file indicates a new counter.
    }
    catch (IOException e) {
      e.printStackTrace();
    }
  }

  public void jspDestroy() {
    try {
      FileOutputStream countFile =
                       new FileOutputStream ("counter.dat");
      DataOutputStream countData =
                           new DataOutputStream (countFile);
      countData.writeInt(counter);
    }
    catch (IOException e) {
      e.printStackTrace();
    }
  }
     %>

<HTML>

<STYLE>
```

Listing 4.3 counter3.jsp (continued)

```
.pageFooter {
  position: absolute; top: 590px;
  font-family: Arial, Helvetica, sans-serif;
  font-size: 8pt; text-align: right;
}
</STYLE>

<BODY>
<DIV CLASS="pageFooter">
This page has been accessed
<%

  synchronized(page) {
    counter++;
    out.print(counter);
  }
%>
times.
</DIV>
</BODY>

</HTML>
```

4.5 A JSP Compiled

Many implementations of JSP engines leave the Servlet source code that they create in a working directory. Under many engines this is an option that must be explicitly turned on, but it is usually a trivial task to enable.

Reading through the generated source code can be extremely useful in debugging problems that are not readily apparent in the JSP page. In addition, this source code can provide experienced Java developers with additional insight about the inner workings of the JSP implementation.

Listing 4.4 shows the compiled source code from the most recent counter. The source code in this listing is generated from Apache Jakarta Project's Tomcat v3.1; other JSP engines will probably produce slightly different results. The source code was also modified slightly to fit better on the page.

Listing 4.4 counter3_jsp.java

```
import javax.servlet.*;
import javax.servlet.http.*;
import javax.servlet.jsp.*;
import javax.servlet.jsp.tagext.*;
import java.io.PrintWriter;
import java.io.IOException;
import java.io.FileInputStream;
import java.io.ObjectInputStream;
import java.util.Vector;
import org.apache.jasper.runtime.*;
import java.beans.*;
import org.apache.jasper.JasperException;
import java.io.*;

public class _0002fcounter3_0002ejspcounter3_jsp_0
                                 extends HttpJspBase {

 // begin [file="/counter3.jsp";from=(4,3);to=(35,0)]

    int counter = 0;

    public void jspInit() {
      try {
        FileInputStream countFile =
                      new FileInputStream ("counter.dat");
        DataInputStream countData =
                        new DataInputStream (countFile);
        counter = countData.readInt();
      } catch (FileNotFoundException ignore) {
        // No file indicates a new counter.
      } catch (IOException e) {
        e.printStackTrace();
      }
    }

    public void jspDestroy() {
      try {
        FileOutputStream countFile =
```

Listing 4.4 counter3_jsp.java (continued)

```
                    new FileOutputStream ("counter.dat");
        DataOutputStream countData =
                        new DataOutputStream (countFile);
        countData.writeInt(counter);
        } catch (IOException e) {
          e.printStackTrace();
        }
      }
    // end

    static { }

    public _0002fcounter3_0002ejspcounter3_jsp_0( ) { }

    private static boolean _jspx_inited = false;

    public final void _jspx_init() throws JasperException {
}

    public void _jspService(HttpServletRequest request,
                            HttpServletResponse  response)
                      throws IOException, ServletException
 {

        JspFactory _jspxFactory = null;
        PageContext pageContext = null;
        HttpSession session = null;
        ServletContext application = null;
        ServletConfig config = null;
        JspWriter out = null;
        Object page = this;
        String  _value = null;
        try {

            if (_jspx_inited == false) {
                _jspx_init();
                _jspx_inited = true;
```

Listing 4.4 counter3_jsp.java (continued)

```
            }
            _jspxFactory = JspFactory.getDefaultFactory();
            response.setContentType("text/html");
           pageContext = _jspxFactory.getPageContext(this,
                                      request, response,
                                     "", true, 8192, true);

            application = pageContext.getServletContext();
            config = pageContext.getServletConfig();
            session = pageContext.getSession();
            out = pageContext.getOut();

      // begin [file="/counter3.jsp";from=(0,0);to=(2,0)]
                out.write("<!DOCTYPE HTML PUBLIC \"-//W3C//
DTD HTML 4.0 Final//EN\">\r\n\r\n");
      // end
      // begin [file="/counter3.jsp";from=(2,30);to=(4,0)]
                out.write("\r\n\r\n");
      // end
      // begin [file="/counter3.jsp";from=(35,2);to=(50,0)]

out.write("\r\n\r\n<HTML>\r\n\r\n<STYLE>\r\n.pageFooter
{\r\n  position: absolute; top: 590px;\r\n  font-family:
Arial, Helvetica, sans-serif; \r\n  font-size: 8pt; text-
align: right; \r\n}\r\n</STYLE>\r\n\r\n<BODY>\r\n<DIV
CLASS=\"pageFooter\">\r\nThis page has been accessed
\r\n");
      // end
      // begin [file="/counter3.jsp";from=(50,2);to=(55,0)]

                 synchronized(page) {
                   counter++;
                   out.print(counter);
                 }
      // end
```

Listing 4.4 counter3_jsp.java (continued)

```
      // begin [file="/counter3.jsp";from=(55,2);to=(62,0)]
               out.write(" \r\ntimes.\r\n</DIV>\r\n</
BODY>\r\n\r\n</HTML>\r\n\r\n");
      // end

        } catch (Exception ex) {

            if (out.getBufferSize() != 0)
                out.clear();
            pageContext.handlePageException(ex);
        } finally {
            out.flush();
            _jspxFactory.releasePageContext(pageContext);
        }
    }
}
```

4.6 Performance Tuning the Servlet

There are several aspects of Java programming that can have heavy impacts on the performance of a JSP page.

Some of these are not JSP specific, but simply good Java programming techniques overall. The ones listed are the most common efficiency mistakes.

Avoid appending with concatenation

In the course of development it is very easy to use the concatenation operator (+) to join `String` objects. For example:

```
String output;
output += "Item:  " + item + "  ";
output += "Price: " + price + "  ";
println (output);
```

Unfortunately, it is easy to forget that the `String` object is immutable and is not designed to contain modifiable data. The `StringBuffer` object is designed to perform manipulation of strings. Any time a `String` object is modified it really just creates a new `StringBuffer` and a series of new `String` objects, then all the `strings` are appended into the `StringBuffer`, and the old `String` is replaced with the results of `StringBuffer.toString()`.

While processing the above code there will be several new `String` and `StringBuffer` objects created. It's usually significantly more efficient to convert the `String` into a `StringBuffer` or even start out with a `StringBuffer` object. For example:

```
StringBuffer output;
output.append(new String("Item:  "));
output.append(item);
output.append(new String(" "));
output.append(new String("Price: "));
output.append(price)
output.append(new String(" "));
println (output.toString());
```

Use syncronize() carefully

While protecting objects from thread Race Conditions is extremely important, it is easy to create performance bottlenecks in the process of synchronizing.

Make sure that synchronized blocks contain the fewest lines of code possible. When many threads are waiting on a block of code, even reducing one line of code within the synchronized block can make a large difference.

Also, it is always good to synchronize on the most appropriate locking object as possible. Usually it is best to synchronize on the object that is threatened by the Race Condition. Avoid using the `this` or `page` object as the locking object as much as possible.

Overall it is obvious that the JSP engine is built to take advantage of the extremely powerful Java Servlet architecture. While threading is a significant enhancement, care needs to be taken to prevent the "Race Condition." Other techniques based on Java Servlet tuning can be used to fine-tune the performance of the JSP page and the underlying Java Servlet. Chapter 5 moves on to further discuss the `request` object and how it can be used to create dynamic Web applications.

RETRIEVING INFORMATION

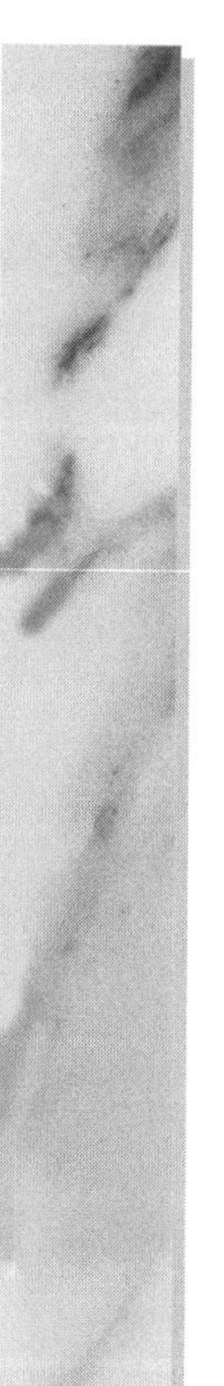

Topics in this Chapter:

- The Request
- Receiving parameter information
- Receiving header information
- Receiving attribute information
- Getting information about the server

Chapter 5

JSP pages, like most Web application platforms, use HTTP as a transport protocol. To understand how a JSP program changes for different requests, one must understand the Web transaction model, which is built on HTTP.

The model itself is very simple, and it applies to many different Web-programming technologies. A good analogy for the Web transaction model is a math function box. Math function boxes are a tool to explain how mathematical functions work. The important thing to understand is that the function box itself never changes. The only reason an output changes is if input changes. It is exactly the same with JSP pages. The JSP page itself does not change, but it generates different output based on different input. (see Figure 5–1).

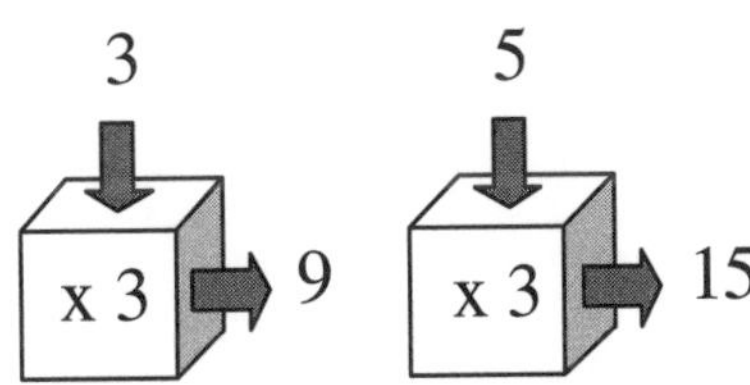

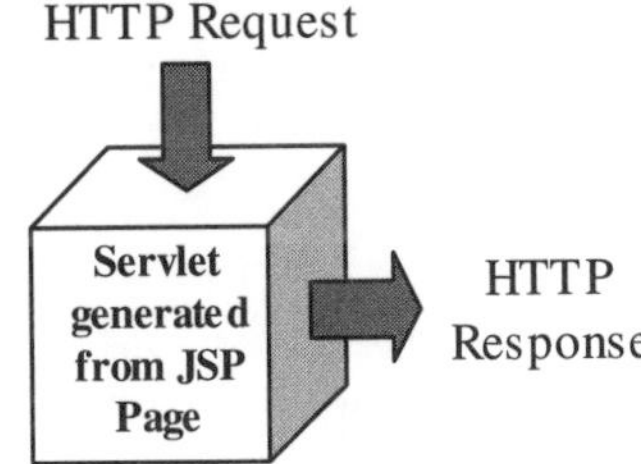

Figure 5–1 Web Transaction Model

This chapter focuses on the input to the JSP page, known as the HTTP request or simply *the request*. The next chapter focuses on the HTTP response, or simply *the response*. By creating a custom response based on the request, the resulting Web page is considered *dynamic*. The next logical step is to group these dynamic Web pages together for a specific Web client. This grouping is known as a *session*. A session is a system by which information about a specific client can be stored between each request/response pair. Sessions are covered in Chapter 7. By maintaining a session, Web pages are considered to be *interactive*. These two characteristics, dynamic content and interactivity, are what distinguish a Web application from a simple Web page.

5.1 The Request

An HTTP request is a simple data structure. It is composed of a block of text that is separated by newline characters. The first line is the request itself. The request line is made up of three sets of data. The first section is the HTTP request type, of which two common types are GET and POST. Next is part of the URL of the document requested, and finally the version of HTTP. An example request line might be:

```
GET /index.html HTTP/1.0
```

The next sets of lines are called headers. Headers consist of name/value pairs separated by a colon. Example headers might be `Server:` followed by the type of server, or `Accept:` followed by the different MIME types the client will accept.

Following the request line and header lines of an HTTP request the client can optionally send a blank line followed by content or "body" data. This is dependent on the type of HTTP request. For example, GET request does not have any body data after the headers section, but can include specific data within the URL. A POST request can include the same data after a blank line in the HTTP request.

It is important to understand that all of the information about a client comes from the HTTP request. This means information about a client—such as browser type or IP address, as well as any data submitted via a form—is included within the HTTP request either in the request line, a header, or content data.

HTTP requests are an intrinsic part of JSP pages. To find out more about HTTP see *Core Web Programming* by Marty Hall (Prentice Hall PTR, 1998).

5.2 The HTTP Request and JSP

As the HTTP request and HTTP response are such a critical part of JSP, they are the two parameters for the Java class generated from any JSP page. The request object is of the type `HttpServletRequest` and is simply named `request`. The authors of the JSP specification provide many different methods for accessing information inside the request, both in raw data format as well as with convenience methods.

Parameters

```
String request.getQueryString()
BufferedReader request.getReader()
ServletInputStream request.getInputStream()
String request.getMethod()
String request.getParameter(String)
Enumeration request.getParameterNames()
String[] request.getParameterValues(String)
```

One of the most common types of data retrieved from a request is referred to as parameters in the JSP specification. Most often this is information sent via a query string in a GET request or form data sent with a POST request. The JSP API specification has two sets of methods for accessing parameter information: getting the information in a "raw" format and allowing the JSP author to process it, and parsing the information for the JSP author in convenience methods.

Raw Parameter Methods

If the author desires, this data is available in its raw format. For GET requests the `request` object has a method called `getQueryString()`, which will return a `String` containing the text after the question mark in the URL string. For POST requests it is more complicated, as the content of the POST is basically seen as a file of the MIME type `text/plain`. The request object contains a method called `getReader()` that will return a `BufferedReader` object containing the POST data.

For other HTTP request types that contain binary content data the `request` object has the `getInputStream()` method that will return a `ServletInputStream` object containing the attached data. To know which of these methods to use, the `getMethod()` method of the `request` object can be called to determine the HTTP request type, whether it is GET, POST, or any other types supported by HTTP.

It is important to note that getting the data in raw format is usually only the first step. For example, a space character sent from a form using GET will be encoded as a "%20" using URL encoding. To use the query string the author would first have to decode the string (i.e., convert the "%20" back into a space). Parsing parameters from a `BufferedReader` object from a POST request is even more difficult, as it involves working directly with Java I/O methods.

CORE Note: UTF-8

UTF-8 stands for Universal Character Set Transformation Format 8. UTF-8 is simply a character set that is agreed on by Web server and browser manufacturers to be the standard for sending and retrieving information in text format. UTF-8 is actually a superset of the Unicode character-encoding standard, with some added benefits. In UTF-8 all ASCII characters are preserved in the standard ASCII format. This means that programs that are not Unicode compatible, but are ASCII aware, can interpret UTF-8 encoded text. This is the case with many operating systems.

Convenience Parameter Methods

Getting parameter data is one of the most common functions in a JSP page, so the JSP specification authors have thoughtfully provided three convenience methods for accessing and utilizing the HTTP request data. Data sent in a GET or POST request is usually in pairs. Thus, the convenience methods work around a name/value paradigm. To this extent the JSP engine automatically parses the query string or POST content data and inserts the name/value pairs in an array stored within the `request` object.

The simplest convenience method is the `getParameter()` method. It takes a `String` as an argument representing the parameter name and returns a `String` containing the value of the specified parameter. For example, given the following URL: `http://www.javadesktop.com/prog.jsp?name=bob`. If `prog.jsp` contained the line:

```
<% String val = request.getParameter("name"); %>
```

then the text contained within the `String val` would be "bob". The same would be true if the request was received via a POST request. If the parameter name "name" did not exist at all, a null would be returned.

This works well if the parameter name is known, but what if the names of the parameters sent is unknown? The JSP specification authors provide the `getParameterNames()` function in this situation. `getParameterNames()` returns an `Enumeration` containing the names of each parameter. An `Enumeration` is an object that is very similar to the `Iterator` object in Java 1.2. It contains a list of objects that can be referenced one at a time with the `nextElement()` method. As the elements within an `Enumeration` are stored as `java.lang.Object` a cast is necessary to assign them to a `String` object. This must be done if they are going to be used to obtain the matching values with the `getParameter()` method. With the `getParameterNames()` and `getParameter()` methods used together all name/value pairs can be displayed:

```
<%
  Enumeration requestNames = request.getParameterNames();
  while (requestNames.hasMoreElements()) {
     String currentName  =
       (String)requestNames.nextElement();
     String currentVal = request.getParameter(currentName);
     out.print(currentName + " = " + currentVal + "<br>");
     }
  }
%>
```

There is still one situation where a problem might occur: in the case that two parameters have the same name but different values. Will the `getParameter()` method work if there is more than one value for a given name? In most cases, yes—but this is JSP-implementation dependent. For example, the JSP engine can choose to either return the first or the last value corresponding to the parameter name. One popular JSP engine returns a single string that is comma delimited and contains all of the values.

In any case the value of the `getParameter()` method is not guaranteed to work the same across all implementations. To solve this problem there is the `getParameterValues()` method. `getParameterValues()` takes a `String` containing the parameter name just as the `getParameter()` method. It returns a `String` array containing all of the values corresponding to the given name.

Combining all three convenience methods, `getParameter()`, `getParameterNames()`, and `getParameterValues()`, allows all data sent from a POST or GET request to be accessed. Listing 5.1 shows a JSP page that uses all three of these methods, as well as the `getMethod()` and `getQueryString()` methods, to retrieve and display all GET and POST data sent.

Listing 5.1 parameters.jsp

```
<!DOCTYPE HTML PUBLIC "-//W3C//DTD HTML 4.0 Final//EN">

<HTML>
<BODY BGCOLOR="white">
<H1> Request Information </H1>
<H2> Request MetaData: </H2>
<BLOCKQUOTE>
<FONT SIZE=4>
Request Method: <CODE><%=  request.getMethod() %></CODE>
<BR>
Query string: <CODE><%= request.getQueryString() %></CODE>
</FONT>
</BLOCKQUOTE>

<H2> Parameter Names and Values: </H2>
<BLOCKQUOTE>
<FONT SIZE=4>
<CODE>
<TABLE BORDER=0>
<%
  Enumeration requestNames = request.getParameterNames();
  StringBuffer outPut = new StringBuffer();

  while (requestNames.hasMoreElements()) {

    String     Name = (String)requestNames.nextElement();
    String[] Values = request.getParameterValues(Name);

    for(int count = 0; count < Values.length; count++){
      outPut.append("<TR>")
             .append("<TD>").append(Name).append("</TD>")
             .append("<TD> = </TD>")
             .append("<TD>")
.append(Values[count]).append("</TD>")
             .append("</TR>\n");
      Name = " ";
    }
  }
  out.print(outPut.toString());
%>
</TABLE>
</CODE></FONT></BLOCKQUOTE>
</BODY>
</HTML>
```

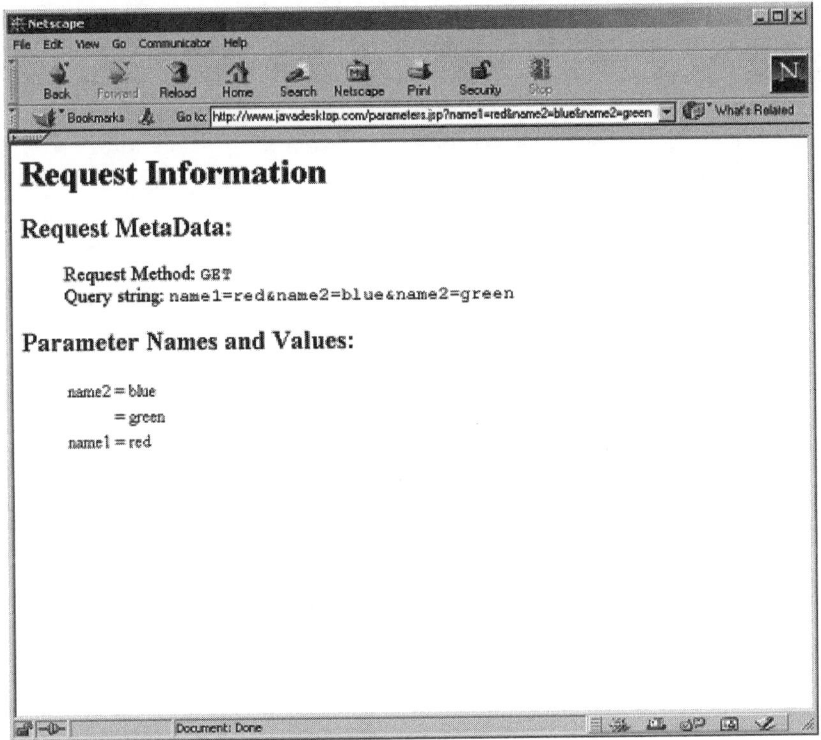

Figure 5–2 Output of parameters.jsp

Notice that the code utilizes a StringBuffer object to store the page output instead of concatenating string objects. This is much more efficient. With a query string of `?name1=red&name2=blue&name2=green` this page will return a page similar to Figure 5–2.

Header Information

```
String request.getHeader(String)
int request.getIntHeader(String)
Date request.getDateHeader(String)
Enumeration request.getHeaderNames()
Enumeration request.getHeaders(String)
String request.getLocale()
Enumeration request.getLocales()
```

Besides parameter information, the HTTP request may include information in request headers. Request headers are information or metadata about the current request. They are most often entered by the Web browser, but can also be added by Web proxy servers. Some examples of information contained in request headers are the name and version of the client, the MIME types the browser supports, and the user's preferred language. See Table 5.1 for a description of some common request headers.

Table 5.1 Common Request Headers

Accept	These are the MIME types accepted by the requesting browser. Optionally they can have a quality factor included.
Accept-Language	Here a browser may indicate which languages it prefers. ISO country codes are used to accomplish this. Some examples are "en" for English or "de" for German. More than one language can be specified, delimited by commas. Optionally they can have a quality factor included
Cookie	If a browser finds a cookie in its cookie file matching the domain of this server it will send it along with every request.
Host	This is the name of the server to which the request was sent. The request line only specifies part of the URL, which does not include the server. The Web server can use this information to see which hostname is explicitly desired and serve the right page. This removes the necessity of having different IP addresses for virtual servers.
Referer	This is the URL of the page on which this server was referred. This is traditionally spelled incorrectly.
User-Agent	This is a browser's ID. It describes the software used, as well as the version. Optionally it includes the default ISO country code.

In the same way parameters can be accessed in "raw" format, the values of HTTP headers can be retrieved "as is." There are also a number of convenience methods for retrieving certain headers and data types.

The basic "raw" method is `getHeader()`. This method takes a `String` argument that describes the header name field. It returns a `String` that contains the value of the requested header, or `null` if the header does not exist. Very similar to `getHeader()` is `getIntHeader()` and `getDateHeader()`. Both `getIntHeader()` and `getDateHeader()` take the same `String` header name argument as does `getHeader()`, but they return an `int` and a `date` object respectively.

Retrieving request header information faces many of the same challenges as getting parameter information, as they both are stored in name/value pairs. For example, what if the names of the headers is unknown? Similar to `getParameterNames()` there is a `getHeaderNames()` that will return an `Enumeration` of the request header field names.

In addition to these four methods, the Java Servlet 2.2 Specification adds three new methods for gathering header information. The Java Servlet 2.2 API is utilized by the JSP 1.1 specification, so any JSP 1.1 compliant engine can recognize these methods. The first method again builds on experience from the parameter methods. While it is rare, multiple headers with the same name bearing different values are possible. In this situation `getHeaders()` can be utilized. `getHeaders()` has a `String` as an argument that describes a header field name. It returns an `Enumeration` of the different values for the specified header.

Additionally, the Servlet 2.2 API Specification adds the `getLocale()` and `getLocales()` methods. These methods are actually inherited from the `ServletRequest` object from which the `HttpServletRequest` object is derived. These methods receive their information from the Accept-Language header. `getLocale()` returns a string that describes the ISO country code of the preferred language. Since more than one value can be specified, the `getLocales()` method is also provided. The `getLocales()` method returns an `Enumeration` of the specified language country codes in order of decreasing preference.

The information stored in headers gives some very specific information about a Web client to the JSP author, and allows for very specific content to be sent to the user. One area where this is especially useful is in internationalization. As the Web grows by leaps and bounds there is a need to expand large sites to multiple languages. Further, if a page can be tailored to the user's language of preference without the user having to specify one, it makes the Web page much more user-friendly. Fortunately, Netscape Communicator 4.0 and above as well as Internet Explorer 4.0 and above do specify which language is preferred in the Accept-Language header.

Take a look at Listing 5.2 to see a page that tailors "Hello World" to the user's preferred language:

Listing 5.2 HelloWorld.jsp

```
<!DOCTYPE HTML PUBLIC "-//W3C//DTD HTML 4.0 Final//EN">

<%@ page contentType="text/html; charset=UTF-8" %>
<%@ page import="java.util.*" %>
<HTML>
<BODY BGCOLOR="white">

<%!
  Hashtable helloHash = new Hashtable();

  public void jspInit() {
    helloHash.put("en",  "Hello World");
    helloHash.put("fr",  "Bonjour Monde");
    helloHash.put("de",  "Hallo Welt");
    helloHash.put("it",  "Ciao Mondo");
    helloHash.put("pt",  "Hello Mundo");
    helloHash.put("es",  "Hola Mundo");
    helloHash.put("ja",  "\u4eca\u65e5\u306f\u4e16\u754c");
    helloHash.put("zh",  "\u4F60\u597D\u4E16\u754C");
    helloHash.put("ko",
      "\uC548\uB155\uD558\uC138\uC694\uC138\uACC4");
    helloHash.put("ru",
      "\u0417\u0434\u0440\u0430\u0432\u0441\u0442"
      + "\u0432\u0443\u0439, \u041C\u0438\u0440");
  }

  public String getGreeting (String Languages) {
    String lang = new String();
    StringTokenizer langPrefs =
new StringTokenizer(Languages, ",");

    while ((!helloHash.containsKey(lang)) &&
           (langPrefs.hasMoreTokens())) {
      lang = langPrefs.nextToken().substring(0,2);
    }

    if ((!helloHash.containsKey(lang)) || (lang == null)) {
      lang = "en";
    }

    return (String)helloHash.get(lang);
  }

%>
```

Listing 5.2 HelloWorld.jsp (continued)

```
<%
  String Languages = request.getHeader("Accept-Language");
%>
<H2>
<%= getGreeting(Languages) %><BR>
</BODY>
</HTML>
```

With Japanese selected as the language of choice, the output of `HelloWorld.jsp` should look something like Figure 5–3.

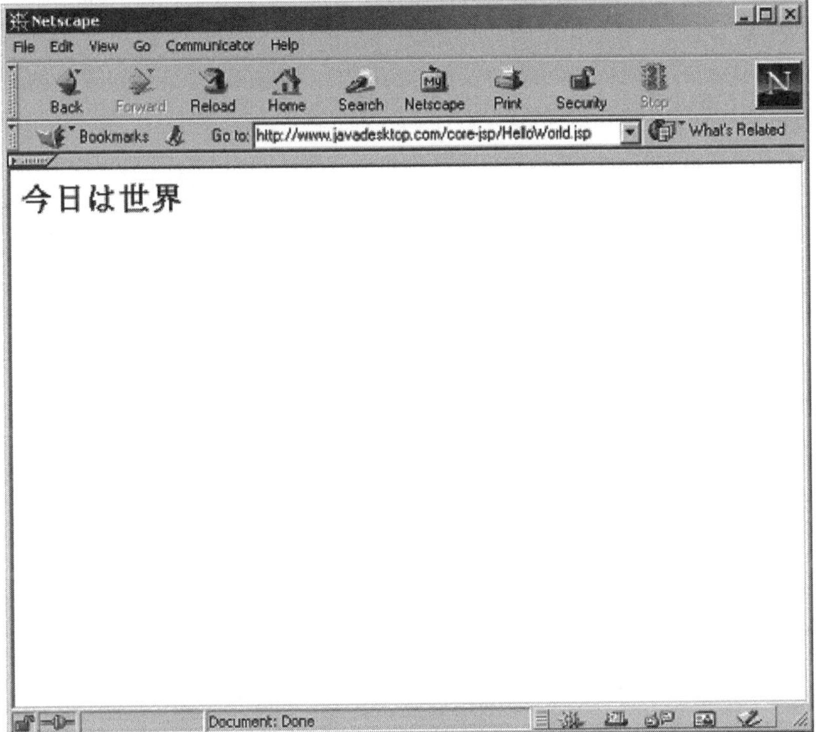

Figure 5–3 Output of HelloWorld.jsp

There is really no magic here. `HelloWorld.jsp` uses Unicode to display its characters, using the UTF-8 characterset. Described simply, Unicode contains all of the characters in the alphabets of several hundred languages. Since the UTF-8 version of Unicode is used here, strings in the standard ASCII range can be added simply by specifying a string. Characters for other languages have to be specified with escape sequences. Unicode character escapes are signified by the string "`\u`" followed by a hexadecimal string of four digits containing the number of the specific character desired. Unicode escapes can be used to display almost every character in the world's common written languages.

Another important thing to point out is that the client must have a font installed that will display the characters needed. There are many font sets available on the Internet that display fonts of a specific language, and even a few which try to cover the range of Unicode. Then the client must have their browser's preferences set to map Unicode or UTF-8 charactersets to the correct font. The client must have also set up their language preferences in their browser.

Take a look at the `jspInit()` function of `HelloWorld.jsp`:

```
helloHash.put("en",  "Hello World");
helloHash.put("fr",  "Bonjour Monde");
helloHash.put("de",  "Hallo Welt");
helloHash.put("it",  "Ciao Mondo");
helloHash.put("pt",  "Hello Mundo");
helloHash.put("es",  "Hola Mundo");
helloHash.put("ja",  "\u4eca\u65e5\u306f\u4e16\u754c");
helloHash.put("zh",  "\u4F60\u597D\u4E16\u754C");
helloHash.put("ko",
  "\uC548\uB155\uD558\uC138\uC694\uC138\uACC4");
helloHash.put("ru",
  "\u0417\u0434\u0440\u0430\u0432\u0441\u0442"
  + "\u0432\u0443\u0439, \u041C\u0438\u0440");
```

Here the ISO country code is entered as a key into a `Hashtable` called `helloHash`. The corresponding string "Hello World" is entered as a value, described in the characters of the specified language. There is no translation done here. The JSP author had to know how to write "Hello World" is the specific characters of each language.

Next, skip down to the bottom of `HelloWorld.jsp` to see the two lines that get the header and call the workhorse function:

```
<%
  String Languages = request.getHeader("Accept-Language");
%>
<H2>
<%= getGreeting(Languages) %><BR>
```

The first line of code simply gets the text value associated with the header Accept-Language. Remember that this is a comma delimited `String` listing the preferred language of the user in order of preference. For example the string might be "`en,ru,ja`" which would mean that the author prefers English, Russian, or Japanese in that order. Note that in a JSP 1.1 compliant engine the `getLocales()` function could be used here to gather the country code information. The JSP Expression then calls the workhorse function `getGreeting()` sending the header value as an argument. This function returns the proper `String` for the specified language to the output stream. Now take a look at `getGreeting()`, which does the real work:

```
public String getGreeting (String Languages) {
  String lang = new String();
  StringTokenizer langPrefs = new StringTokenizer
     (Languages, ",");

  while ((!helloHash.containsKey(lang)) &&
        (langPrefs.hasMoreTokens())) {
    lang = langPrefs.nextToken().substring(0,2);
  }

  if ((!helloHash.containsKey(lang)) || (lang == null)) {
    lang = "en";
  }

  return (String)helloHash.get(lang);
}
```

There are two strings defined—`Language` which is sent from the caller, and `lang` which will serve as a placeholder for the current section of the `Language` string that is being matched. To break `Language` up into the different languages it specifies, a `StringTokenizer` is used, with a comma used to separate each section of data. Using the above example of "`en,ru,ja`" as the `Language` string, `lang` would be set to "`en`", "`ru`", and "`ja`" alternatively each time the through the `while` loop.

The reason why only the first two letters of the country code are taken? Sometimes more information is given for each country. For example, instead of "`zh`" for Chinese, "`zh-TW`" might be specified for the Taiwanese dialect of Chinese. The Web browser might also have appended a numeric weight to each language specified. As the `helloHash Hashtable` is built around only the country code itself, the rest of the information is discarded.

The `while` loop checks to see if the preferred language has a match in the `helloHash Hashtable` by using the method `containsKey()`. If the first language has no match, it goes on to each other language specified. If there is a match the `while` loop is broken with `lang` still set to the language that had a match. In this way each language specified by the user is checked for a match until one is found that is supported by the JSP page. If no match is found, or if there was no language specified (where `lang == null`), the last `if` statement will set `lang` to "en" for English, which was chosen as the default language. The final line returns the `helloHash` value for `lang`.

The `HelloWorld.jsp` example makes it obvious that there is a lot of information that can be derived from headers to create very specific responses for a client.

Cookies

```
Cookie[] request.getCookie()
```

No discussion of request header information could be complete without mentioning cookies. A cookie is a system by which a server can store information on a client's machine. A server sets a cookie by sending it in a response header. Each cookie has a specific time length before it will "expire" and be removed from the client machine. By default this is when the current Web client application is closed.

When a cookie is set, it is matched to a specific URL. When the client requests a URL, the Web browser checks to see if it has a cookie in its cookie file that matches the URL. If there is a match, the cookie is included in the request header. To store cookies the Java Servlet API, on which the Java JSP API is built, creates a `Cookie` object.

While cookie information can be received as a `String` by using the method `getHeader("cookie")`, managing multiple cookies and translating them into `Cookie` objects is a surmountable task. Luckily the `getCookie()` method is provided to do just that. The `getCookie()` method takes no argument, and returns an array of `Cookie` objects. If there were no cookies specified, it returns `null`.

Attributes

```
String request.getAttribute(String)
Enumeration request.getAttributeNames()
```

Besides parameters and headers there is a third type of information that can be derived from the `request` object called attributes. Attributes are JSP engine specific and contain information about the `request` object itself, or `request` metadata. To get attribute information the request object provides the `getAttribute()` method. One common attribute is the SSL certificate used by the client to make an encrypted session. For example:

```
<%= request.getAttribute("javax.servlet.request.X509Certificate") %>
```

This will only work if the JSP engine supports this attribute and the actual connection made by a client was done using SSL. Similar to parameters and headers, attributes have a `getAttributeNames()` function. This function takes no argument and returns an `Enumeration` object listing the attributes for the current request object. The only way to find out all of the request attributes supported a given JSP engine is to read the JSP engine's specific documentation.

Server Information

```
String application.getServerInfo()
String application.getRealPath(String)
```

In addition to the `request` object, information about the specific configuration of the JSP engine can be accessed through the implicit `application` object. Remember that the `application` object is an instance of `javax.servlet.ServletContext`. This means it has specific information about the JSP engine as well as the operating system as it relates to the server.

One piece of information made available to the application object is the JSP engine name and version number. This data also may contain other information, such as Java Runtime Engine (JRE) version or operating system. This string can be obtained by using the `getServerInfo()` method. It takes no arguments and returns a `String`. For example:

```
<%= application.getServerInfo() %>
```

will return a string similar to: `JavaServer Web Dev Kit/1.0 EA (JSP 1.0; Servlet 2.1; Java 1.2.2; Windows NT 5.0 x86; java.vendor=Sun Microsystems Inc.)`. This string was returned by the JSWDK on a Windows 2000 box.

Another method of the `ServletContext` object is `getRealPath()`. The `getRealPath()` method takes a `String` that describes a part of a URL. The method returns a `String` that contains the full path of the file that matches the URL. For example:

```
<%= application.getRealPath(request.getRequestURI()) %>
```

This takes the URL of the current page and returns the path of the file on the local file system. In this case it returns: `D:\jswdk-1.0\javadesktop\test.jsp`.

Overall, the JSP API Specification provides several different methods for accessing information about a client's request and the local server environment. It is important to remember that this is the only information that a JSP program can use to define specific content. The response object will be covered in detail in Chapter 6. In Chapter 7, sessions will be discussed, which help tie specific sets of request/response pairs to an individual client.

SENDING INFORMATION

Topics in this Chapter:

- Using the Response Object
- HTTP Status Codes
- HTTP Headers
- Setting Cookies
- Handling Errors

Chapter 6

JSP can perform a lot of complex tasks on the server, ranging from managing a database to performing complex math. However, it is important to keep in mind that JSP is primarily designed to describe data being sent back to the user.

The examples in previous chapters have shown how easy it is to send simple information from a JSP page. Using the HTML or XML template, the methods of the `out` object, or the expression tags (`<%=...%>`), the JSP author can generate content for the resulting page. The process of sending simple data really does not involve much more than that.

Unfortunately, real-world data is often not quite so simple that it will easily fall into the default categories. In many cases, the JSP author will need to be able to take control of the output and give the server explicit instructions on how the response should be constructed.

6.1 Using the Response Object

A client requests a page by building an HTTP request and the results are sent back in an HTTP response. The HTTP response can contain the data returned from the request or an error indicating that the request was not successful. Typically a successful request will include the data and information describing the data in the HTTP response.

Normally the HTTP response is managed entirely by the server. All information passed through the server gets treated the same; a standard response is built, and then sent back to the client.

In order to send data that is not managed entirely by the server requires manipulating the HTTP response. Carefully controlling the HTTP response is the most important aspect of sending complex information. JSP provides an interface into manipulating the response through the `HttpServletResponse` object, which is exposed to the JSP author through the implicit `response` object.

In Chapter 1 the HTTP response was shown to be composed of three basic parts: the status, headers, and data. To send more complex information a more detailed understanding of these three components is required.

The HTTP Status

The HTTP status is set to indicate the actual status of the request. Typically this will contain "succeed," "failed," or other condition information that directs the client how to respond. In essence, the HTTP status line defines how the rest of the response is received.

A typical HTTP status line is shown here:

```
HTTP/1.1 200 OK
```

The HTTP status begins by stating the protocol it is going to use. Since this is an HTTP status, the protocol information typically reflects the specific version of HTTP to follow—1.0 or 1.1.

Following that is an integer value that represents the actual results of the request. This may also be followed by a human-readable value corresponding to the integer result.

Table 6.1 shows some of the more common HTTP status codes, followed by their Java Servlet constant, and a description of the status. The "404 Not Found" or "500 Internal Server Error" status codes may look very familiar to some people—others are only ever used behind the scenes.

Table 6.1 Common HTTP status codes

Status	Constant
200 OK	Sc_OK
This status is sent when the request was processed completely and without errors	
204 No Content	SC_NO_CONTENT
Indicates that the requested was processed, but there is no data to return	
301 Moved Permanently	SC_MOVED_PERMANENTLY
This indicates that the URI has been changed permanently. Most clients will look in the header information for a new location.	
302 Moved Temporarily	SC_MOVED_TEMPORARILY
The URI is temporarily relocated. Most clients will look in the header information for a new location.	
401 Unauthorized	SC_UNAUTHORIZED
Authentication was not successful and access is being denied.	
403 Forbidden	SC_FORBIDDEN
This indicates that the page is restricted and the client is not allowed access.	
404 Not Found	SC_NOT_FOUND
The requested document does not exist.	
500 Internal Server Error	SC_INTERNAL_SERVER_ERROR
Errors on the server prevent the request from being completed.	
503 Service Unavailable	SC_SERVICE_UNAVAILABLE
The server is temporarily overloaded and unable to complete the request.	

The response object `sendError()` and `setStatus()` methods allow the JSP author to set the HTTP status code that is sent back to the user.

Both of these methods behave in a similar fashion. Some extra logic separates `sendError()` as the method to send status codes that indicate a failed request. The `setStatus()` method should be used to set all other HTTP status codes.

These methods typically accept an integer value or constant as the argument, which will correspond directly to the value sent. Some of these methods also allow an error to include a text message.

```
void response.sendError(int sc)
void response.sendError(int sc, String msg)
void response.setStatus(int sc)
void response.setStatus(int sc, String msg)
```

(Note: Errors are really the only form of HTTP status that may need an expanded message, so `void response.sendStatus(int sc, String msg)` has been deprecated as being "ambiguous".)

The HTTP Headers

Immediately following the HTTP status line are the HTTP headers. These are a series of name/value pairs that contain information about the server and the document being returned. The HTTP header section can be any length, and a single blank line marks its end.

A typical set of HTTP headers is displayed here:

```
Date: Sun, 08 Dec 1999 18:16:31 GMT
Server: Apache/1.3.9 (Unix) ApacheJServ/1.0
Last-Modified: Tue, 22 Jun 1999 05:12:38 GMT
ETag: "d828b-371-376f1b46"
Accept-Ranges: bytes
Connection: close
Content-Type: text/html
```

The most important thing to note about HTTP headers is that this is information the server specifically wants the client to have. They may not trigger a response on the client side, but they are intended to direct the behavior of the client. This may include time stamps for client-side caching, the type of data that will be sent, or information to identify the server.

While there is no complete list of HTTP headers that can be used, there are some very common headers. Table 6.2 shows some of the more common HTTP headers, used by many Web pages:

Table 6.2 Common HTTP Headers

Content-type	This is the MIME-type of the data being sent in the HTTP response body
Connection	This indicates whether the server will maintain a constantly open connection. If the server will support this, the value is set to `keep-alive`. Otherwise, the value is `close`.
Location	This header is only read by the client when the server sets the status to `301 Moved Permanently` or `302 Moved Temporarily`. This specifies a URI that should be used for a new location. Most browsers will automatically follow this link when the status is set appropriately.
Expires	This date field specifies when the document should become invalid for caching purposes.
Cache-Control	(HTTP 1.1 only) This allows control over specific caching issues that relate to this document. Common values are `no-cache`, `no-store` (`no-store` indicates that the client, caching proxies, and squid engines should never cache the document), and *`maxage=n` (to expire the document in `n` seconds).*
Pragma	(HTTP 1.0 - replaced by "Cache-Control" in HTTP 1.1) Pragma allows extremely limited control on the cache. The only valid value is no-cache, which instructs the browser to never cache this document.

The response object provides the JSP author with several methods than can be used to manipulate the response headers:

```
void response.addHeader(String name, String value)
void response.setHeader(String name, String value)

void response.addIntHeader(String name, int value)
void response.setIntHeader(String name, int value)

void response.addDateHeader(String name, long date)
void response.setDateHeader(String name, long date)
```

The primary difference between these methods is the type of data that each sets in the response header. The type of data accepted by each method is fairly self-explanatory by the method signature.

Understanding the difference between `add` and `set` methods is less obvious. The difference really involves the fact that HTTP headers can have more than one entry with the same named key. The `add` methods will create a new name/value pair that may be in addition to an already existing pair with that same name. The set methods will overwrite the previous pairs that have the same named key.

These methods allow the JSP author to modify or create an HTTP header. However, there are a series of convenience methods that modify the most often used headers.

`Content-type` is very important header that defines the MIME type of the document being sent. A method has been made to allow easier access to changing the MIME type of the document:

```
void response.setContentType(String type)
```

CORE Note: Content-Type

`Content-type` is almost always included to define the MIME type of the data carried in the response body. By default the server, based on what the server knows of the data, sets `Content-type`.

Changing the `Content-type` header can dramatically change the response on the client. For example, a `Content-type` of `text/html` will be interpreted as HTML, however setting it to `image/png` will force the browser to interpret the data as a `.png` graphic file. The Unicode example in Chapter 5 used the `Content-type` to define the data, as `UTF-8` data, as opposed to standard `html/text`.

Of course, many of these methods would not be useful unless the JSP author can check the header for a specific named key. This is exactly what the `containsHeader()` method is provided for.

```
boolean response.containsHeader(String name)
```

The `containsHeader` method simple returns `true` if the named key exists, allowing the JSP author a means to check before overwriting.

Other Methods of the Response Object

The response object also has some methods, which do not deal with just the HTTP status or the HTTP headers. Some of these methods involve merging the status and header information, and others are convenience methods that have no direct relation to the HTTP response.

Redirecting a client to an alternate URI is a relatively common occurrence. This could be done by first setting the status to `SC_MOVED_TEMPORARILY`, and then setting the location header to the destination URI. For example:

```
response.setStatus(SC_MOVED_TEMPORARILY);
response.setHeader ("Location", "http://localhost:8080/");
```

These two method calls are so interdependent that they have been converted into a single method:

```
void response.sendRedirect ("http://localhost:8080/");
```

The example shown in Listing 6.1 shows a simple JSP page that does a "round robin" load balancing. "Round robin" is a way to distribute requests across multiple servers—it's not very sophisticated, but it works in many situations.

The "round robin" is accomplished by using the `sendRedirect` method of the `response` object. The actual list of servers is implemented using a circular queue stored in a Vector.

Some people may notice that some HTML information was included in the bottom of the JSP page. This is done because some browsers process the page enough to make the screen "blink" before forwarding. The small amount of HTML sets the background color to the color of the new page, which makes the "blink" significantly less noticeable.

Listing 6.1 roundRobin.jsp

```
<!DOCTYPE HTML PUBLIC "-//W3C//DTD HTML 4.0 Final//EN">

<%@ page import ="java.util.Vector"%>

<%!
  Vector servers = new Vector();

  public void jspInit() {
    servers.addElement("http://server1.javadesktop.com/");
    servers.addElement("http://server2.javadesktop.com/");
    servers.addElement("http://server3.javadesktop.com/");
  }

  synchronized public String nextInQueue (Vector queue) {
    // impliment a cyclic queue
```

Listing 6.1 roundRobin.jsp (continued)

```
    String item = (String)queue.firstElement();
    queue.removeElementAt(0);
    queue.addElement (item);
    return (item);
  }
%>

<%
  response.sendRedirect(nextInQueue(servers));
%>

<HTML>
<BODY BGCOLOR="#ffffff">
</BODY>
</HTML>
```

A visual example of the effect of roundrobin.j-sp can be seen in Figure 6-1.

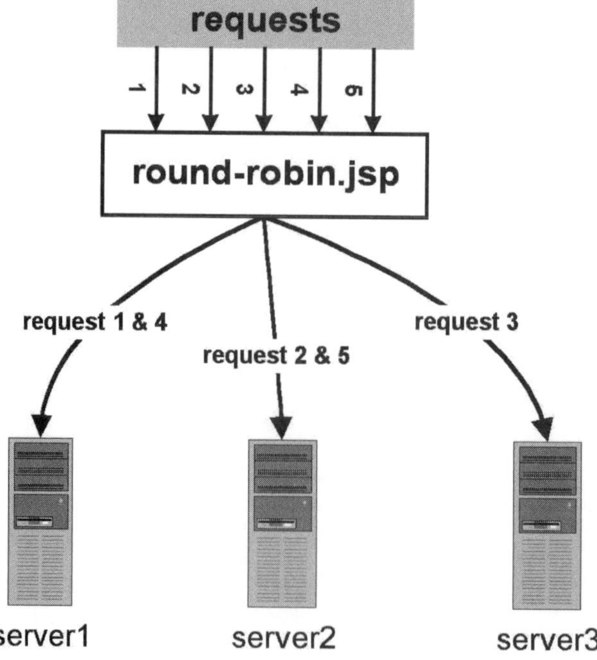

Figure 6–1 The effect of roundrobin.jsp

In this figure, five requests are sent and divided equally between the three servers. If a sixth request comes in, it will wind up at server three, because that server is next in the queue to receive a request.

6.2 Setting Cookies

Quite often a server will send cookies to a client in order to store little bits of information. This information is managed by the client and may be requested by the server at a later time.

Information on retrieving cookies was discussed in Chapter 5. Setting cookies is a little more complicated, because it involves first creating the cookie, then sending to the client.

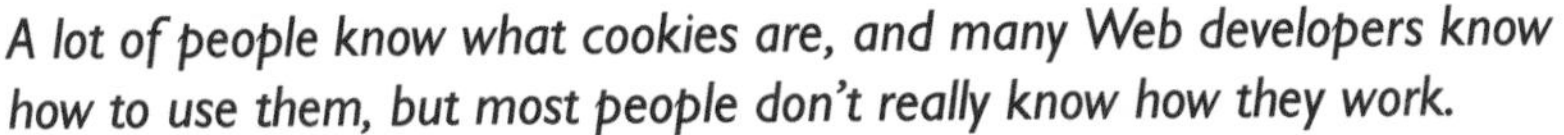

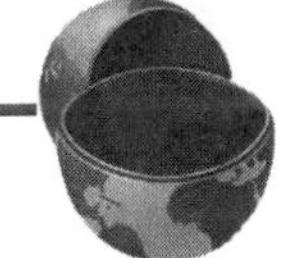

CORE Note: Cookies

A lot of people know what cookies are, and many Web developers know how to use them, but most people don't really know how they work.

In reality, cookies are just a special kind of HTTP header. This special header contains a comma-separated list of values that describes a name/value pair, an expiration date, and some control information.

Unlike a standard HTTP response header, the information sent in a cookie is saved on the client. The client will then send information back to the server if it matches the URI and hostname specified in the cookie.

Since the client manages the cookie, the client can impose additional restrictions about how cookies are accepted. It is also the responsibility of the client to expire old cookies.

Building the Cookie

JSP represents cookies with a `Cookie` object. This object is created with the constructor:

```
public Cookie (String name, String Value)
```

A cookie is normally composed of several attributes. The most important data is the name/value pair, which is the data the server would retrieve from the cookie. But the cookie also contains information on when to expire the cookie and when to give out the cookie.

The name/value pair that is stored in the cookie is established when the cookie is first instantiated using `new Cookie (String name, String`

Value). Other attributes default to standard values determined by the server, but they can be changed using methods of the cookie object.

```
void Cookie.setMaxAge (int expiry)
```

By using the `setMaxAge` method the JSP author can set the lifespan of a cookie. By default, the maximum age is set to a negative value. This makes the cookie "temporary"; the cookie will be destroyed when the browser exits.

Cookies can also be made psuedo-permanent by setting a positive integer value. A cookie has a lifespan that is measured in seconds since it was received. These kind of cookies are discarded by the client when they get too old.

Cookies can also be destroyed by setting the `setMaxAge` method. By setting the value to zero, the browser will destroy the cookie immediately.

```
void Cookie.setDomain (String pattern)
```

This method restricts accessing cookies based on the name of the server. The default is set to match only the server that sent the cookie. This prevents any other server from retrieving a cookie set by that server.

`setDomain` can be set to either match-specific domain names or a pattern. Domain patterns can allow a set of servers under a similar subdomain to have access to the same cookie. Domain name patterns always begin with a dot and will only allow access to hosts (not subdomains) that match this pattern. For example, by setting a domain pattern of `'.javadesktop.com'`, a cookie could be received by `'www.javadesktop.com'` and `'www2.javadesktop.com'`.

```
void Cookie.setPath (String uri)
```

A specific path on the server can also restrict the cookie by using the `setPath` method. Applications at the same directory level or under the specified URI are also able to access the cookie. For example, if setPath was set to `/JSP/catalog`, then `/JSP/catalog/list.jsp` and `/JSP/catalog/admin/addNewItem.jsp` would be able to access the same cookies.

```
void Cookie.setSecure (boolean flag)
```

The `setSecure` method will require a cookie to be sent only via a secure channel, such as an SSL connection. By default, cookies do not have this restriction.

Sending the Cookie

With a cookie created and configured properly, it still needs to be send out to the client. This is done using the `addCookie()` method provided by the `response` object.

```
void response.addCookie(Cookie cookie)
```

This method will add the cookie to the response headers. When the page is sent the cookie will be retrieved and stored by the server. The next request sent by the client should contain the cookie information.

Using Cookies

Listing 6.2 shows an example of getting and setting cookies. This is a fairly complex example that stores the name of the user.

Listing 6.2 userGreeting.jsp

```
<!DOCTYPE HTML PUBLIC "-//W3C//DTD HTML 4.0 Final//EN">

<%@ page import ="java.util.*"%>

<%!
  Hashtable cookieTable (Cookie[] cookies) {
    Hashtable cookieTable = new Hashtable();

    if (cookies != null) {
      for (int i=0; i < cookies.length; i++) {
        cookieTable.put(cookies[i].getName(),
          cookies[i].getValue());
      }
    }

    return cookieTable;
  }
%>

<%
  Cookie myCookie;
  String username = new String();
  Hashtable cookies = cookieTable(request.getCookies());
  String newLogin = request.getParameter("name");

  if (cookies.containsKey("name")) {
```

Listing 6.2 userGreeting.jsp (continued)

```
    username = (String)cookies.get("name");
  }

  if (newLogin != null) {
    if (newLogin.equals("")) {
      myCookie = new Cookie("name", "");
      myCookie.setMaxAge(0);
      username = null;
    } else {
      myCookie = new Cookie("name", newLogin);
      myCookie.setMaxAge(3600);
      username = newLogin;
    }

    /*
       It is important to change the domain to
       your domain name in order for this to work
    */
    myCookie.setDomain(".javadesktop.com");

    response.addCookie(myCookie);
  }
%>

<HTML>

<STYLE>
.login {
  position: relative; border: 1px; margin: 1px;
  background-color:#bbbbbb; text-align: right;
  font-family: Arial,Helvetica,sans-serif;
  font-size: 9pt; color:#000000;
}
</STYLE>

<BODY BGCOLOR="#ffffff">

<DIV CLASS="login">
<% if (username == null || username.equals("")) { %>

You look like a new user!<BR>
<FORM METHOD="get" ACTION="<%= request.getRequestURI() %>">
Create a login by entering your name:<BR>
<INPUT TYPE="text" SIZE="8" NAME="name">
<INPUT TYPE="submit" VALUE="login">
</FORM>
```

Listing 6.2 userGreeting.jsp (continued)

```
<% } else { %>

Welcome back, <%= username %><BR>
<%= new java.util.Date() %>
<FORM METHOD="get" ACTION="<%= request.getRequestURI() %>">
<INPUT TYPE="hidden" NAME="name" VALUE="">
<INPUT TYPE="submit" VALUE="logout">
</FORM>

<% } %>

</DIV>
</BODY>
</HTML>
```

When run for the first time, the page should look similar to Figure 6-2.

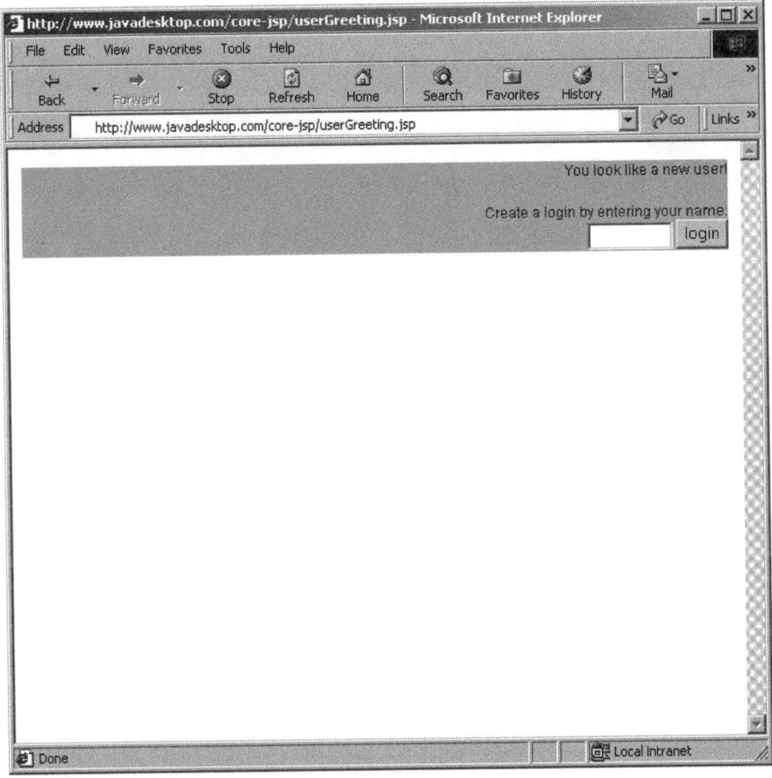

Figure 6-2 userGreeting.jsp

In this example, the cookies are retrieved and read into a `Hashtable` by the `cookieTable` method. Using a `Hashtable` to store the cookies allows for rapid searching to find a particular cookie.

The majority of the work involved in managing the cookies happens here:

```
if (cookies.containsKey("name")) {
  username = (String)cookies.get("name");
}

if (newLogin != null) {
  if (newLogin.equals("")) {
    Cookie newCookie = new Cookie("name", "");
    newCookie.setMaxAge(0);
    username = null;
  } else {
    Cookie newCookie = new Cookie("name", newLogin);
    username = newLogin;
  }
  newCookie.setDomain(".javadesktop.com");
  response.addCookie(newCookie);
}
```

Take particular notice of the functions that were used to manage the cookie. The name/value pair is set at the time of creating the cookie. The cookie is not actually sent to the client until `response.addCookie(newCookie)` is called.

Deleting the cookie is accomplished by changing the value of `setMaxAge` to zero. This instructs the client to expire the cookie immediately.

Also note that `Cookie.setDomain(".javadesktop.com")` sets the domain to match any host on the `javadesktop.com` domain. This prevents multiple webservers from having to manage separate cookies; all hosts on the domain share the same cookie.

6.3 Handling Errors

In a perfect world, things shouldn't ever go wrong. JSP pages released into production should be tested, debugged, and released as enterprise applications.

Of course, in the real world things do go wrong, even with applications that have undergone the most rigorous testing and debugging. Many of these errors can be caught and handled using Java's built-in exception handling. In addition, JSP provides some great resources to help the JSP author manage error conditions.

Sending the fully detailed and ugly error details to the client is not particularly useful. JSP pages should also always specify the `errorPage` page directive attribute. This allows the JSP author to deal with any uncaught exceptions and present a nice looking front-end page to the client.

Using an `errorPage` will also allow the JSP author to build additional functions that should run to help deal with errors appropriately. This might include functions to log the error on the server using the `application.log()` method. It is even possible to forward the resulting problem to another location based on the specific form of problem that occurred.

Below are two examples. Listing 6.3 shows a page that is really not very practical; it is designed to simply throw an error and nothing else. What is interesting is the effect of the `errorPage` shown in Listing 6.4.

Listing 6.3 errorGen.jsp

```
<%@ page errorPage = "errorPage.jsp" %>
<%
  if (true) {
    throw new Exception ("Just testing");
  }
%>
```

Listing 6.4 sets the `isErrorPage` page directive attribute so that it will be recognized as an error page.

Listing 6.4 errorPage.jsp

```
<!DOCTYPE HTML PUBLIC "-//W3C//DTD HTML 4.0 Final//EN">

<%@ page isErrorPage="true" %>
<%@ page import="java.io.*" %>

<%!
  String showError (HttpServletRequest req, Throwable ex)
    Throws IOException {
    StringBuffer err = new StringBuffer();

    err.append("Uncaught runtime error --\n");
    err.append("         URI: ");
    err.append(req.getRequestURI()).append("\n");
    err.append("Extra Path: ");
    err.append(req.getPathInfo()).append("\n");

    ByteArrayOutputStream baos =
new ByteArrayOutputStream();
```

Listing 6.4 errorPage.jsp (continued)

```
    PrintWriter pw = new PrintWriter (baos, true);
    ex.printStackTrace (pw);

    err.append("     Stack: ");
    err.append(baos.toString()).append("\n");

    baos.close();

    return (err.toString());
  }
%>

<%
  response.setStatus (response.SC_INTERNAL_SERVER_ERROR);
%>

<HTML>

<STYLE>
body {
  background-color: #0000ff; color: #ffffff;
}
.error {
  position: absolute; top: 250px;
  font-family: courier, monospaced; font-size: 11pt;
  font-weight: bold;
}
</STYLE>

<BODY>

<%
  String error = showError(request, exception);
  application.log (error);
%>

<DIV CLASS="error">
500 -- Internal Server Error<BR>
Error in: <%= request.getRequestURI() %><BR>
Reason: <%= exception.getMessage() %><BR>
</DIV>

</BODY>

</HTML>
```

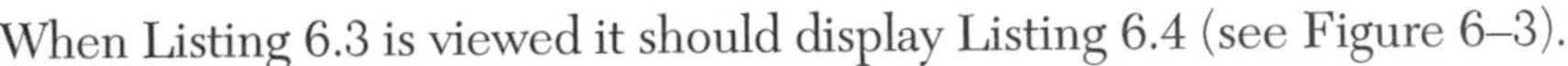

When Listing 6.3 is viewed it should display Listing 6.4 (see Figure 6–3).

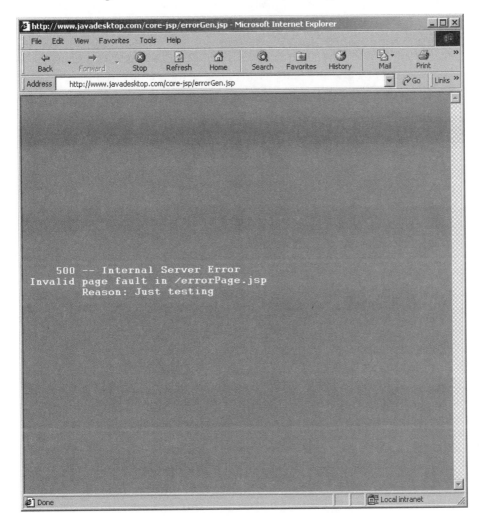

Figure 6–3 errorGen.jsp

Notice that the `request` object used in this example appears the same as the `request` object from the original page. In fact, even the method `getRequestURI()` method returns the URI of the original page and not the error page. The client will also not see a change; the browser will still show the originally requested page in the `Location:` line. Because of this it is possible to direct the error in such a way that the client may never know an error occurred at all.

Also take note of the `exception` object, which contains the exception thrown by the original URI. In this example the information is just logged, but this could also be used to react more appropriately based on the type of error that occurred.

Last, one of the more interesting features of this example is the use of the `application` object. The data is actually being recorded directly to the server's logs by using the `log` method of the `application` object.

```
application.log (error);
```

There are many powerful features in JSP that allow specific client responses. Understanding different HTTP headers and response codes, as well as how to access them with methods of the `response` object, gives the JSP author a low-level ability to manipulate what the user can see. Complex tasks such as manipulating cookies and creating custom error pages are made easy with convenience methods. Chapter 7 will cover how to tie specific request/response pairs to individual clients.

TRACKING SESSIONS

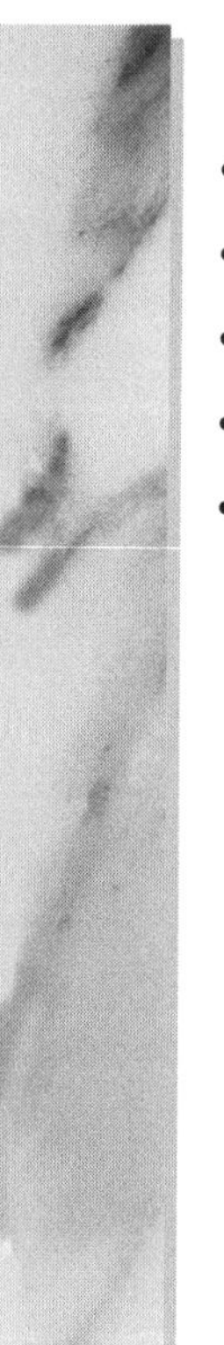

Topics in this Chapter:

- Tracking Data Between Requests
- Hidden Frames and Hidden Form Fields
- Cookies and URL Rewriting
- The `HttpSession` API
- Sessions & Identity

Chapter 7

JSP is typically used to create HTML or XML pages that are delivered using HTTP. Previous chapters have gone through heavy discussions on HTTP requests and responses. One of the limitations of HTTP is that it is a stateless and connectionless protocol. This means that the protocol has no recollection of any transaction that occurred in the past. Each new request from the client creates a whole new transaction that has no relation to any past, concurrent, or future transaction. The client makes a request, the server completes the request to the best of its abilities, and then the transaction is completed and finished.

Without state, each request must contain everything that the server might need to complete the request. In a basic sense this means that even something as simple as displaying the user's name on a page means that the requestor needs to send that information in each request.

Unfortunately, this model does not fulfill the requirements of modern applications. It would be like a dialog between two people where whenever the other person talks, they both forget everything that was said previously.

7.1 Tracking Data between Requests

Needless to say, most applications in use today need to keep at least some constant information about the previous transactions. Knowing whether a user has already logged in, keeping a list of items in a shopping cart, or simply knowing that the user wants to have a blue background would all require some memory of previous requests.

So, of course, many ingenious strategies have been developed to work around these limitations.

Hidden Form Fields

A relatively simple way to track data between user requests is to use an HTML form. Hidden form fields are simple and effective for maintaining small amounts of data between a few forms.

To use hidden form fields the server takes the request data and puts it back into a form on the next page. The server must do this each time or else all the data is lost.

This method puts the majority of the burden back to the client. In essence, the client is told to remember all the previous information and send it next time. To use the previous analogy of a dialog between two people, it would be as if the entire previous conversation had to be repeated before a new idea could be added.

Hidden form fields are one of the oldest methods of preserving state information that is still in use today. The fact that it is still in use seems to indicate that it fills an important need, in particular where the task is not complex but still needs to keep some "state" information. A common case where this might used would be where a user must fill the form that is mailed to the webmaster. If the user forgets an important field it can be specifically requested on the next "page;" all of the previous data is stored on the same page unbeknownst to the user.

It is important to note that this method will only work to and from HTML forms. Changes to state information outside of a form cannot be easily done using hidden form fields.

A Brief Tutorial on JavaMail

The following example sends an e-mail to a user based on the fields put into a form. In this example, e-mail is handled using a Java package called JavaMail. The JavaMail API should already be installed on systems where the Java 2 Enterprise Edition was installed, and can be added to any Java 2 installation. The JavaMail API also requires the JavaBeans Activation Framework (JAF), which is also installed with Java 2 Enterprise Edition, or can be installed separately.

The JavaMail API creates an abstraction from the actual mail system, providing platform-independent and protocol-independent framework to access mail. The system works by providing a basic framework with service providers to implement particular protocols. The JavaMail provides just about every service that an e-mail client or even an e-mail server might need.

In this particular example the requirements are very small. An e-mail needs to get created and sent to a single user. Creating the e-mail in the example is basically separated into three steps; compose the text of the message, setup the server information, and send the e-mail.

The creation of the e-mail message is simple. The actual body of the e-mail just needs to wind up in a `String`. Later when the message is sent it will include this `String`.

Setting up the server information is fairly straightforward. First data from the system is received and anything that might need to change overridden or added. In this case the `mail.smtp.host` is set to the mail delivery host. To set the server properties these two lines are used:

```
Properties props = System.getProperties();
props.put("mail.smtp.host", mailhost);
Session emailsession = Session.getDefaultInstance(props,
null);
```

Finally, the mail is created and sent. This requires filling out the header fields needed to make a valid e-mail, then calling the `Transport.send()` method from JavaMail. The following list of commands is what actually builds and sends the e-mail:

```
Message email = new MimeMessage(emailsession);
email.setFrom(new InternetAddress(req.getServletPath()));
InternetAddress[] address = {
                new InternetAddress(formRecipient) };
email.setRecipients(Message.RecipientType.TO,address);
```

```
email.setSubject(req.getServletPath());
email.setSentDate(new Date());
email.setHeader("X-Mailer","MailFormJava");
email.setText(message);
Transport.send(email);
```

A Mail Form Example

Listing 7.1 shows an example of a very simple form that uses hidden fields to store data between pages. Once all the required fields have been filled, JavaMail is then used to send the e-mail to the user.

The examples in this chapter are setup slightly differently than previous examples, in that they use `<jsp:include>` to add new components to the page. This method is described briefly in Chapter 3. This effectively means that each example will include multiple sets of code, where one of the sets will represent a "wrapper." Listing 7.2 is the wrapper for Listing 7.1, and it generates the proper header and footer to make the page behave properly on a browser.

Listing 7.1 mailForm.jsp

```
<%@ page import =
     "javax.mail.*,javax.mail.internet.*,
      javax.activation.*,java.util.*"
%>

<%!
  private final String formRecipient =
  "webmaster@javadesktop.com";
  private final String mailhost = "mail.javadesktop.com";
  private final String senderAddress =
  "mail-form@javadesktop.com";

  class formField {
    String name;
    boolean required;

    formField (String name, boolean required) {
      this.name = name;
      this.required = required;
    }
  }
```

Listing 7.1 mailForm.jsp (continued)

```
Vector fieldList = new Vector();

public void jspInit() {
  fieldList.add(new formField("Name", true));
  fieldList.add(new formField("Address", false));
  fieldList.add(new formField("City", false));
  fieldList.add(new formField("State", false));
  fieldList.add(new formField("ZIP Code", false));
  fieldList.add(new formField("Day Phone", false));
  fieldList.add(new formField("Evening Phone", false));
  fieldList.add(new formField("Email", true));
  fieldList.add(new formField("Website", false));
}

String displayField (String name) {
  StringBuffer formOut = new StringBuffer();

  formOut.append("<input type=\"text\" name=\"")
           .append(name)
           .append("\">\n");

  return (formOut.toString());
}

String storeField (String name, String value) {
  StringBuffer formOut = new StringBuffer();

  formOut.append("<input type=\"hidden\" name=\"")
           .append(name)
           .append("\" value=\"")
           .append(value)
           .append("\">\n");

  return (formOut.toString());
}

boolean isValidForm (HttpServletRequest req) {
  boolean valid = true;
  Enumeration need = fieldList.elements();

  while (need.hasMoreElements()) {
```

Listing 7.1 mailForm.jsp (continued)

```
    formField field = (formField)need.nextElement();

    if (field.required) {
      String value = req.getParameter(field.name);
      if (value == null || value.equals("")) {
        valid = false;
      }
    }
  }

  return (valid);
}

String mailForm (HttpServletRequest req)
   throws JspException{
  StringBuffer message = new StringBuffer();

Enumeration fields = fieldList.elements();

  while (fields.hasMoreElements()) {
    formField field = (formField)fields.nextElement();

    message.append(field.name)
           .append(" : ")
           .append(req.getParameter(field.name))
           .append("\n");
  }

  // JavaMail here.
  Properties props = System.getProperties();
  props.put("mail.smtp.host", mailhost);
  Session emailsession =
    Session.getDefaultInstance(props, null);

  try {
    Message email = new MimeMessage(emailsession);
    email.setFrom(new InternetAddress(senderAddress));
    InternetAddress[] address = {
                  new InternetAddress(formRecipient) };
   email.setRecipients(Message.RecipientType.TO,address);
    email.setSubject(req.getServletPath());
    email.setSentDate(new Date());
```

Listing 7.1 mailForm.jsp (continued)

```
      email.setHeader("X-Mailer","MailFormJava");
      email.setText(message.toString());
      Transport.send(email);
    } catch (MessagingException e) {
      throw new JspException (e.getMessage());
    }

    return (message.toString());
  }

%>

<%
  if (isValidForm(request)) {
    mailForm(request);
    // need to create a 'thanks for your comments' page
    response.sendRedirect("thanks.jsp");
  }
%>

<STYLE>
<!--
TD {
  font-family: Arial,Helvetica,sans-serif;
  font-size:10pt;
}
TABLE {
  background-color: #ffffcc;
}
-->
</STYLE>

<FORM ACTION="<%=request.getServletPath()%>" METHOD=POST>

<TABLE CELLPADDING=5 CELLSPACING=0 BORDER=0>
<%
  Enumeration fields = fieldList.elements();

  while (fields.hasMoreElements()) {

    formField field = (formField)fields.nextElement();
    String value = request.getParameter(field.name);

    if ( request.getParameter("Init") == null ||
```

Listing 7.1 mailForm.jsp (continued)

```
        ( field.required && value.equals("") )
        ) {
%>
<TR>
<TD ALIGN=RIGHT><%= field.name %> : </TD>
<TD ALIGN=LEFT><%= displayField(field.name) %></TD>
</TR>
<%
    } else {
%>
<%= storeField(field.name, value) %>
<%
    }
  }
%>

<TR>
<TD COLSPAN=2 ALIGN=CENTER>
<INPUT TYPE=HIDDEN NAME="Init" VALUE="No">
<INPUT TYPE=SUBMIT VALUE="Send This">
</TD>
<TR>

</TABLE>

</FORM>
```

Listing 7.2 is a simple form that includes Listing 7.1, `mailForm.jsp`.

Listing 7.2 mailForm-wrapper.jsp

```
<!DOCTYPE HTML PUBLIC "-//W3C//DTD HTML 4.0 Final//EN">
<%@ page errorPage="errorPage.jsp" %>

<HEAD>
<TITLE> Generic Email Form </TITLE>
</HEAD>

<BODY>
A Generic Email Form<BR>
<jsp:include page="mailform.jsp" flush="true" />
</BODY>

</HTML>
```

The output of Listing 7.2 should look similar to Figure 7.1.

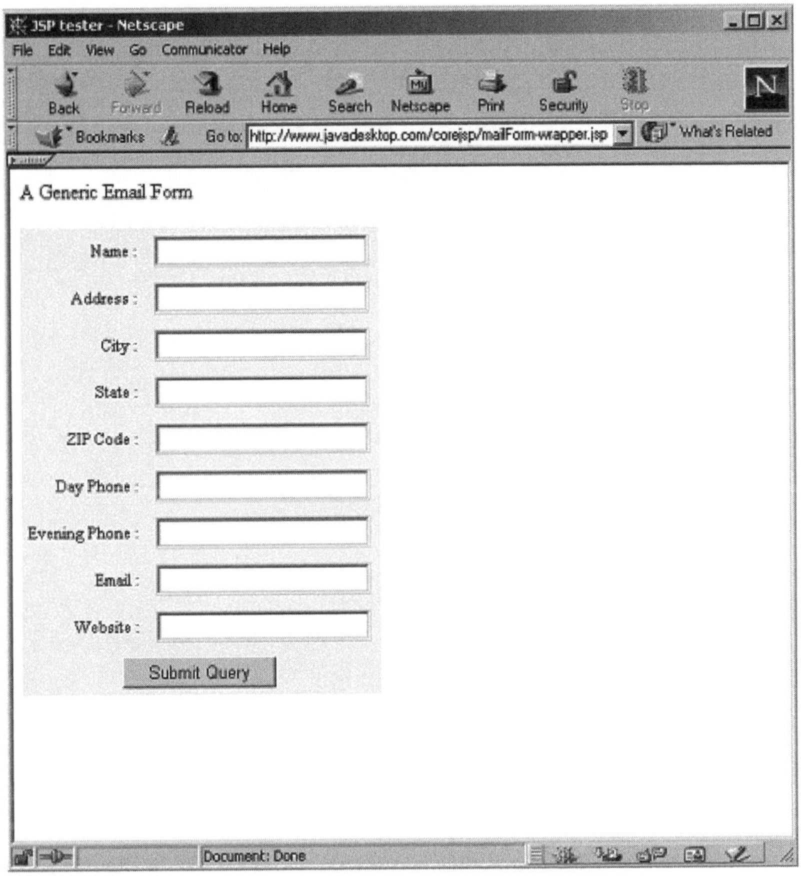

Figure 7–1 Mailform.jsp

Hidden Frames

Another means of getting the client to preserve and send state information is using hidden frames. Implementing hidden frames is outside the scope of this book, but understanding how they work adds perspective to other methods.

By using a client-side scripting language and the browser's Document Object Model it is possible to retrieve and store data from any frame on a browser. It is also possible to create frames that are not seen by the user. Combining these two ideas allows a page author to create a hidden frame that can be used by the developer as a "scratch pad" to add and remove information as needed.

Using hidden frame fields results in an extremely flexible way of preserving state. Unfortunately, not all browsers support hidden frames, and browsers that do support hidden frames often behave differently.

Overall, getting hidden frames to work properly can be a complex combination of client-side and server-side programming that can quickly become daunting and overwhelming.

URL Rewriting

State information can also be preserved by dynamically changing the URL that a user might click on. There are several ways that the URL can be modified and used to include extra information about the transaction.

State information can be put into the URL as standard HTTP GET parameters, for example:

```
http://www.javadesktop.com/catalog?category=books
```

The same general idea can be applied using a custom separator that is recognized by the server but different from the standard HTTP GET separator.

```
http://www.javadesktop.com/catalog;category=books
```

Alternatively, the path information can be parsed by indicating a real page and a separate parameter, for example:

```
http://www.javadesktop.com/catalog/books
```

where `catalog` is the page, and `books` is the parameter.

Ultimately, URL rewriting has similar advantages and disadvantages to using hidden form fields. One advantage is that URL rewriting can change information that does not reside within a form. Additionally, when used with a session ID less data is transferred with each transaction. Unfortunately, URL rewriting is significantly more complex to implement.

URLs are limited in length, so URL rewriting can be limited in the amount of information it can include. This is where session IDs tend to become extremely important. Most URL rewriting in use will add only one parameter, a session ID.

Cookies

Cookies are undoubtedly the most efficient and effective way to store state. In fact, all of the previous listed methods are attempts at using preexisting facilities in new ways to preserve state. Cookies are the only method that is expressly designed from the ground up for preserving information about the state of the client.

Cookies can be set to store name/value pairs that might be needed to store state. Several cookies can be set to create a whole "picture" of the entire session. The actual details of setting, getting, and destroying cookies are discussed in great detail in Chapter 5 and Chapter 6.

In normal usage, it is unusual to store many cookies on a client. More likely, a cookie is sent that contains a session ID or some other piece of information that uniquely identifies the client. Each time the browser sends a request, the cookie gets sent along with that request, allowing the server to maintain the information it needs to preserve state.

7.2 The `HttpSession` API

The actual work of managing sessions using a session ID is a complex task. It involves generating unique keys that must be encoded properly, storing data transactions, and expiring sessions that are too old. Then notable parts from each transaction need to be stored in some internal database and be readily available when given the session ID key.

Fortunately there are methods built into the JSP API that will manage sessions. The API takes almost all the complexities of handling sessions and makes them into a simple and elegant interface that is easy to implement.

CORE Note: Session ID

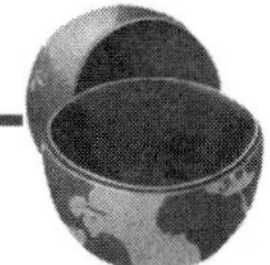

The concept of a key begins to materialize as the amount of information kept about an HTTP connection increases. A session ID is a single value that represents a key to a collection of state information kept on the server.

When the client presents this key the server knows which collection of state data to use. The server is tracking the actual state of the transactions as long as the client preserves the key.

Session IDs have a number of advantages that stem from the fact that most of the data is kept on the server and does not have to be sent to the client. The bandwidth between transactions is reduced, since the state data does not have to be sent back and forth with each transaction. In addition there is increased security, because only the session key is required to be passed between the client and the server.

Basics

Session tracking begins with the server generating a unique ID for the user. The server then either sets a cookie or uses URL rewriting to store the session ID. Most often cookies will be used, but URL rewriting can be utilized (for sites that don't want to use cookies). Many JSP engines are intelligent, in that they will first attempt to set a cookie and revert to URL rewriting if cookies are not enabled on the client browser.

Next, a new instance of `HttpSession` is created. The new `HttpSession` object is accessible by using the session ID as a key value. As long as the client returns the proper key, this same instance of the `HttpSession` object becomes accessible. If there are requests from multiple users, each will have their own `HttpSession` object, which will be accessible from only their own request.

The `HttpSession` object actually serves as a container that can be used to store or retrieve information. This object can store any number of other pieces of information. In fact anything that extends `java.lang.Object` can be placed into the `HttpSession` object. This means that even more abstract data—including I/O streams and database connections—can be placed in the object and associated to a particular user.

Using the Session Object

By default, JSPs have session tracking enabled and a new `HttpSession` object is instantiated for each new client automatically. There is nothing special that the JSP author needs to do to enable session tracking. In fact, actually disabling session tracking requires explicitly turning it off by setting the `page` directive `session` attribute to `false`:

```
<%@ page session="false" %>
```

The JSP engine exposes the `HttpSession` object to the JSP author through the implicit `session` object. Since this object is already provided to the JSP author, the author can immediately begin storing and retrieving data from the object without any initialization or `getSession()`.

CORE Note: New Sessions

Java Servlet programmers will need to take particular note that session tracking is setup by the JSP engine automatically. There is no need to go through the process of creating a new session.

There are a number of methods that can be used from `session` object. The most important and most used methods are the ones directly related to storing and retrieving data.

`void session.putValue(String key, Object value)`

`putValue()` is a fairly simple method that does the actual work of storing the value object within the `session` object. The object specified as the value will get stored under the string `key`.

Only one value may be stored at any particular name. Using `putValue()` on a key name that already contains an object will simply overwrite the old data without any warning.

`Object session.getValue(String name)`

`getValue()` is the compliment to `putValue()`. This method retrieves data from the `session` object. If there is no corresponding value for the key, then a null value is returned.

Since the return value from this method is an `Object`, it will typically need to be cast into the correct object type. For example:

```
String value = (String)session.getvalue(name);
```

`void session.removeValue(String name)`

This method is used to remove a value from the session object. It is important to note that a value cannot be removed by setting the value to null (`session.putValue(name, null)`), in fact this will throw a `nullPointerException`.

`String[] session.getValueNames()`

This method returns a String array that contains the key name of each entry that is stored in the session object. Using method allows for listing or "sniffing" the session data.

CORE Note: Session Object

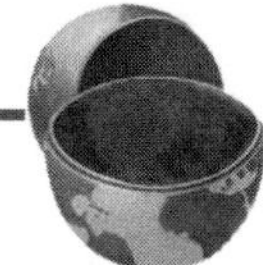

The session object uses method names that resemble the methods used by the collection classes (`HashMap`, etc.), but instead closely resembles the `cookie` object. This being the case there are some things to be particularly wary of.

First off, the `session` object will always require a `String` for the key name. Other classes extended from `java.lang.Object` are not usable as key names.

But most notably, unlike the collection classes, neither the key names nor values of a session object a may contain a `null` value. If a `null` is found then the page will throw a `nullPointerException` at execution time and will not complete properly.

Listing 7.3 show an addition to the previous example from Listing 7.1. The wrapper framework is that contains the included files is shown in Listing 7.4.

The example creates debug page that is included in the framework from the previous `mailForm.jsp` example. This debug mode is transparent until the URL includes a `debug` parameter set to `true` (e.g. `?debug=true`).

Once debug mode is activated that state is stored in the client's session. Thereafter, all the pages that include `debug.jsp` will see the `request` and `session` data until the session expires. Since there are no changes to the standard session, this will typically mean a certain time period of inactivity or closing the browser.

Listing 7.3 debug.jsp

```
<%@ page import ="java.util.*" %>

<%!
  String debugDump (HttpSession session) {
    StringBuffer data = new StringBuffer();

    String names[] = session.getValueNames();

    if (names != null) {

      for (int item=0; item < names.length; item++) {
        data.append("  ").append(names[item])
        data.append(" :  ");
data.append(session.getValue(names[item]));
        data.append("<BR>\n");
      }
    }

    return (data.toString());
  }

  String debugDump (HttpServletRequest request) {
    StringBuffer data = new StringBuffer();

    Enumeration reqdata = request.getParameterNames();
    while(reqdata.hasMoreElements()) {
      String name = (String)reqdata.nextElement();
```

Listing 7.3 debug.jsp (continued)

```
      String values[] = request.getParameterValues(name);

      if (values != null) {

        for (int item=0; item < values.length; item++) {
          data.append("  ").append(name);
          data.append(" [").append(item).append("] ");
          data.append(" : ");
data.append(values[item]).append("<BR>\n");
        }
      }
    }

    return (data.toString());
  }
%>
<%
  String setDebug = request.getParameter("debug");
  if (setDebug != null) {
    session.putValue("debug", setDebug);
  }

  String debug = (String)session.getValue("debug");

  if (debug != null && debug.equals("true")) {
%>
<STYLE>
<!--
.debugtext {
  color: #000000; font-size: 7pt;
  font-family: courier,serif;
  font-weight: 600;
}
-->
</STYLE>


<TABLE BORDER=1 CELLSPACING=0 CELLPADDING=0><TR><TD>
<TABLE BORDER=0 CELLSPACING=0 CELLPADDING=4>

<TR><TD CLASS="debugtext">
```

Listing 7.3 debug.jsp (continued)

```
DEBUG DATA
</TD></TR>

<TR><TD CLASS="debugtext">
SESSION:<BR>
<%= debugDump(session) %><BR>
</TD></TR>

<TR><TD CLASS="debugtext">
REQUEST:<BR>
<%= debugDump(request) %><BR>
</TD></TR>

</TABLE>
</TD></TR></TABLE>

<%
  }
%>
```

Listing 7.4 shows a simple JSP page that includes a form and includes Listing 7.3, `debug.jsp`.

Listing 7.4 mailForm-wrapper2.jsp

```
<!DOCTYPE HTML PUBLIC "-//W3C//DTD HTML 4.0 Final//EN">
<%@ page errorPage="errorPage.jsp" %>

<HEAD>
<TITLE> Generic Email Form </TITLE>
</HEAD>

<BODY>
<jsp:include page="debug.jsp" flush="true" />
A Generic Email Form<BR>
<jsp:include page="mailform.jsp" flush="true" />
</BODY>

</HTML>
```

The new `mailform-wrapper.jsp` with `debug.jsp` included would look like Figure 7-2.

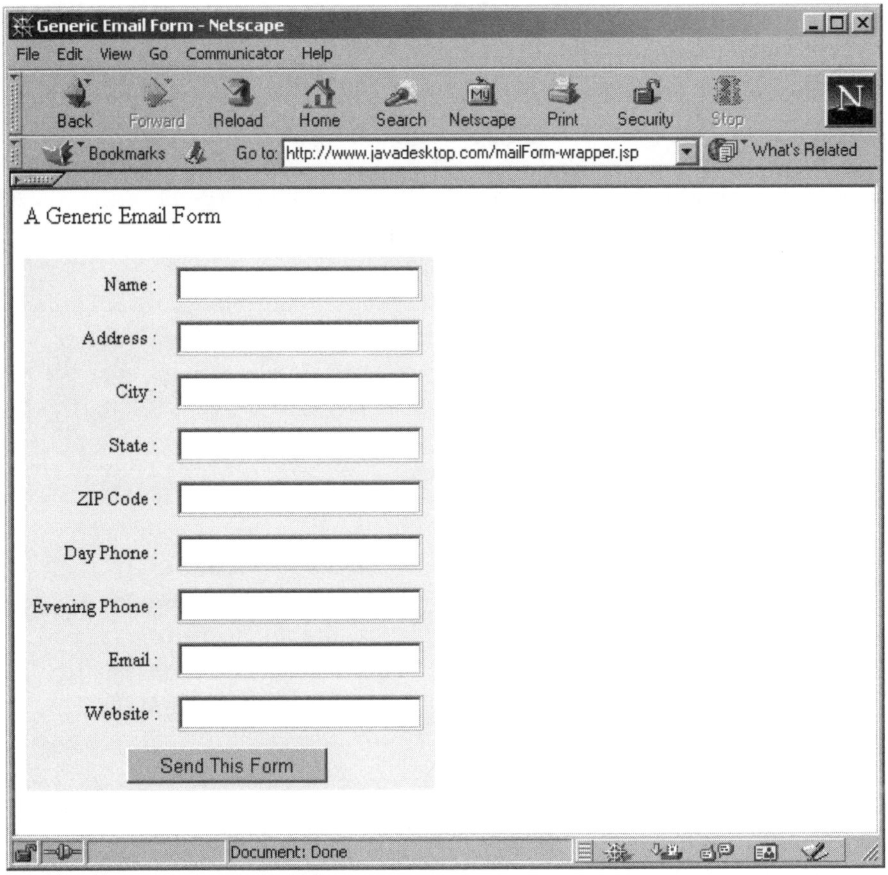

Figure 7-2 Mailform with Debugging information

In theory, the `mailform.jsp` example shown in Listing 7.1 could also be reworked to use session tracking instead of hidden form fields. But this would probably become more complicated because the end results need to be ultimately sent through an HTML form.

The Life of a Session

Sessions are intended to preserve state between transactions; they are not designed to last. If a session is ever lost then its data is irretrievable, whether it was by the intention of the JSP author or by the server crashing.

While sessions are reliable, they are really not intended for the long-term storage of data. Long-term storage of user data should be achieved by using some form of authentication and an external data source, such as a database or file. Sessions still play a very important role in identifying user and associating the user with their data. In fact a common tactic is to use the session as a database cache of sorts.

Sessions keep a series of time stamps to indicate different things. One use of these time stamps is to automatically expire sessions that have been inactive for too long. The default before a session is removed is usually configured in the JSP engine. Of course, the JSP author can remove a particular session at any time.

CORE Note: Session Memory Space

Sessions are an extremely powerful and useful feature, but it's good to bear in mind the memory footprint when putting objects into sessions.

Since session data lasts for a fixed period of time and the session can store large amounts of data, it is relatively easy to saturate memory on a high traffic site. As an example, consider a site that keeps sessions for 1 hour, gets 500 clients per hour, and stores an average of 40k bytes per client. This winds up consuming 20MB of RAM (albeit some of that may get swapped to disk).

Reducing data size per client or reducing the session keep-alive time will reduce the overall memory footprint. But the opposite holds true as well; increasing either of these increases the memory footprint.

There are two simple things that can reduce the memory size. First, be sure to remove specific data from a session when it is no longer useful. Second, don't let sessions hang around when they are known to be closed—explicitly invalidate these sessions.

The session API provides the JSP author with a series of methods that help to check and control the lifecycle of the session.

`int session.getMaxInactiveInterval()`

`void session.setMaxInactiveInterval(int interval)`

`getMaxInactiveInterval()` returns the number of seconds that need to pass before a session will expire. `setMaxInactiveInterval()` allows the JSP author the ability to change the amount of time before the particular session will expire.

long session.getCreationTime()

long session.getLastAccessedTime()

`getCreationTime()` returns the time that the session was created. `getLastAccessedTime()` returns the last time the session was used. Both of these methods return the time as the number of seconds since epoch (12 midnight, Jan. 1, 1970).

void session.invalidate()

`invalidate()` simply destroys the existing session. Once a session has been invalidated there is no way to regain it.

This method is particularly useful in creating "logout" methods. It can also be useful in sweeping out really old sessions that might occur from external applications that might reconnect regularly and never allow the session to expire.

boolean session.isNew()

Allows the JSP author a means to determine if this is a new session. This method returns `true` if this is a newly created session.

String session.getId()

Returns the unique string identifier for the session.

Enumeration session.getIds()

Returns an enumeration of all the currently valid session IDs.

CORE Note: Session ID Security Risk

It's important to point out that giving out the session ID itself presents a security risk. By knowing another user's session ID might allow a mischievous user to piggyback on another user's session and effectively become that user. In most of these cases the safest tactic is simply to never display the session ID back to the user.

7.3 Sessions and Identity

The concept of state implies client identity. As any site becomes more complex and dependent on state, the complexity of the identity of the client grows in scale. Some type of authentication is needed to identify each user, and since state is maintainable it is also possible to manage a login process using the `session` object.

The next example is a session-based login system. This will allow for page-based access by including a small chunk of code at the top of any "secure" page. If the client tries to get to a secure page without having logged in, they are prompted for information.

This example will require several components, Listings 7.5, 7.6, and 7.7. Listing 7.5 shows the JSP file that actually checks that a user has logged in. It would need to be included using a page directive (using `<%@ include file="..." %>`) because it needs to modify the HTTP response headers to redirect requests to a login page. This should be included near the top of any JSP page where the user's identity is important.

Listing 7.5 confirmLogin.jsp

```
<%
  String login = (String)session.getValue("login");

  if ( login == null) {
    StringBuffer loginpoint = new StringBuffer();

    loginpoint.append(request.getScheme())
              .append("://")
              .append(request.getServerName())
              .append(request.getRequestURI());

    session.putValue("loginpoint", loginpoint.toString());

    StringBuffer loginpage = new StringBuffer();

    loginpage.append(request.getScheme())
             .append("://")
             .append(request.getServerName())
             .append("/")
             .append("login.jsp");

    response.sendRedirect(loginpage.toString());
  }
%>
```

Listing 7.6 shows the heart of the login system. This page is presented whenever anyone tries to access a restricted page without having the proper tokens. When they have logged in they are given tokens that identify themselves.

Listing 7.6 login.jsp

```
<%@ page errorPage="errorPage.jsp" %>

<%
  String login = (String)request.getParameter("loginname");

  if (login == null || login.equals("")) {
%>
<!DOCTYPE HTML PUBLIC "-//W3C//DTD HTML 4.0 Final//EN">
<HEAD>
<TITLE>Login Page</TITLE>
<STYLE>
<!--
font.loginhead {
  font-family: Arial,Helvetica,sans-serif;
  font-size:12pt; font-weight: 600; color: #000000;
}
font.loginform {
  font-family: Arial,Helvetica,sans-serif;
  font-size:10pt; font-weight: 600; color: #ffffff;
}
-->
</STYLE>
</HEAD>

<BODY>
<jsp:include page="debug.jsp" flush="true" />

<CENTER>
<FONT CLASS="loginhead">
LOGIN REQUIRED:
</FONT>
<BR>

<FORM NAME="loginform" METHOD=post>
<TABLE BGCOLOR=#990022 BORDER=0 CELLPADDING=5
CELLSPACING=0>

<TR><TD ALIGN=right>
<FONT CLASS="loginform">
Login Name:
</FONT>
</TD><TD ALIGN=left>
<FONT CLASS="loginform">
<INPUT TYPE=text NAME="loginname" SIZE=10>
</FONT>
```

Listing 7.6 login.jsp (continued)

```
</TD></TR>

<TR><TD ALIGN=right>
<FONT CLASS="loginform">
Password:
</FONT>
</TD><TD ALIGN=left>
<FONT CLASS="loginform">
<INPUT TYPE=password NAME="loginpassword" SIZE=10>
</FONT>
</TD></TR>

<TR><TD COLSPAN=2 ALIGN=center>
<FONT CLASS="loginform">
<INPUT TYPE=SUBMIT VALUE="Login">
</FONT>
</TD></TR>
</TABLE>

</FORM>
</CENTER>

</BODY>
</HTML>
<%
  } else {
    /*
      This should check against a database to make sure the
      password is correct, and retrieve user data. Right now
       it doesn't.
    */

    session.putValue("login", login);
    session.setMaxInactiveInterval(600);

    String loginpoint =
(String)session.getValue("loginpoint");
    if (loginpoint == null) {
      StringBuffer defaultpoint = new StringBuffer();
      defaultpoint.append(request.getScheme())
                  .append("://")
                  .append(request.getServerName())
                  .append("/");

      loginpoint = defaultpoint.toString();
```

Listing 7.6 login.jsp (continued)

```
      } else {
        session.removeValue("loginpoint");
      }

      response.sendRedirect(loginpoint);
    }
%>
```

The output of Listing 7.6 should look like Figure 7-3.

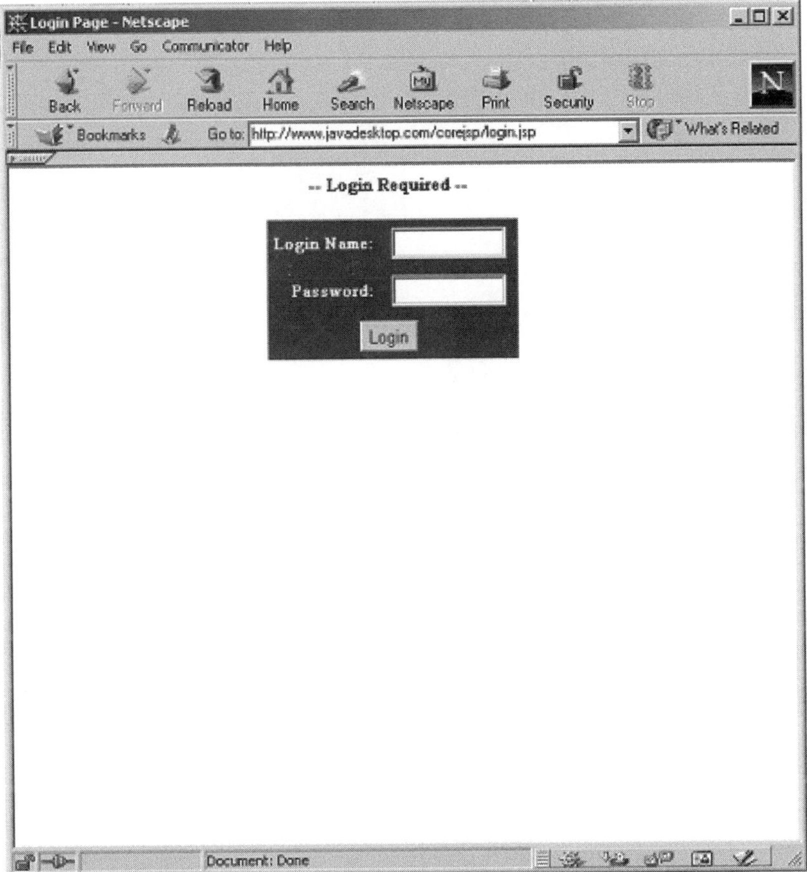

Figure 7-3 Login.jsp

Listing 7.7 shows the logout page. Logging out the user could be accomplished by invalidating the session, which would create a whole new session. Preserving information outside of the login process might also be desired, so the key is simply removed. Finally, the user is redirected to a location that does not require a login.

Listing 7.7 logout.jsp

```
<%
session.removeValue("login");

  /*
    To use logout by destroying the session, uncomment the
    line below.
  */
  //session.invalidate();

  StringBuffer logout = new StringBuffer();

  logout.append(request.getScheme())
        .append("://")
        .append(request.getServerName())
        .append("/");

  response.sendRedirect(logout.toString());
%>
```

Unfortunately, until some form of a database has been introduced this login system only functions as a means of asking for a name. With the addition of a directory service or database this example could be reworked to include true password authentication and preference information.

Another drawback to the above examples is that the login system is fairly passive. It doesn't really have an entry point, only hooks to insert it into other pages. As a mechanism to make this concept work, a navigation bar will also be introduced.

Listing 7.8 is the navigation bar itself. It has been implemented in a way that will leave it open to later expansion. For the time being it works using fairly static options.

Listing 7.8 navbar.jsp

```
<%@ page import ="java.util.*" %>

<%!
  class tab {
    String tabname;
    String location;

    tab (String name, String value) {
      this.tabname = name;
      this.location = value;
    }
  }
%>

<%
  Vector leftnavbar = new Vector();
  Vector rightnavbar = new Vector();

  leftnavbar.add(new tab("Main", "/"));
  leftnavbar.add(new tab("Maillists", "/maillists.jsp"));

  rightnavbar.add(new tab("Logout", "/logout.jsp"));
  rightnavbar.add(new tab("Preferences", "/prefs.jsp"));
%>

<STYLE>
<!--
td.navbar {
  background-color: #990022;
  margin: 1px; padding: 1px; border: 1px;
}
font.navtext {
  font-family: arial,helvetica,sans-serif;
  font-weight: 600; text-decoration: none;
  font-size: 10pt; color: #ffffff;
}
-->
</STYLE>

<TABLE WIDTH=100% BORDER=0 CELLPADDING=0 CELLSPACING=0>
```

Listing 7.8 navbar.jsp (continued)

```
<TR>
<TD ALIGN=LEFT CLASS="navbar">

<TABLE CELLPADDING=3 CELLSPACING=2 BORDER=0>
<TR>
<%

  Enumeration lefttabs = leftnavbar.elements();

  while (lefttabs.hasMoreElements()) {
    tab current = (tab)lefttabs.nextElement();

%>
<TD>
<A HREF="<%=current.location%>">
<FONT CLASS="navtext">
<%=current.tabname%>
</FONT>
</A>
</TD>

<%
  }
%>
</TR>
</TABLE>
</TD>

<TD ALIGN=RIGHT CLASS="navbar">
<TABLE CELLPADDING=5 CELLSPACING=2 BORDER=0>
<TR>
<%

  Enumeration righttabs = rightnavbar.elements();

  while (righttabs.hasMoreElements()) {
    tab current = (tab)righttabs.nextElement();

%>
<TD>
<A HREF="<%=current.location%>">
```

Listing 7.8 navbar.jsp (continued)

```
<FONT CLASS="navtext">
<%=current.tabname%>
</FONT>
</A>
</TD>

<%
  }
%>
</TR>
</TABLE>
</TD>

</TR>
</TABLE>

<BR><BR>
```

Listing 7.9 shows how the framework would change to include the new additions to the site.

Listing 7.9 index-navbar.jsp

```
<%@ page errorPage="errorPage.jsp" %>
<%@ include file="confirmLogin.jsp" %>

<!DOCTYPE HTML PUBLIC "-//W3C//DTD HTML 4.0 Final//EN">

<HEAD>
<TITLE> JSP tester </TITLE>
</HEAD>

<BODY>
<jsp:include page="debug.jsp" flush="true" />
<jsp:include page="navbar.jsp" flush="true" />
</BODY>
</HTML>
```

Security Concerns

As identity becomes more important, the potential for problems from mistaken or stolen identities increases. Some system should be put in place to protect the users access.

Fortunately, because JSP pages are compiled and executed on the server many traditional security concerns are avoided entirely.

Again, keep in mind that the actual data about the session is stored on the server and is not given to the client. This gives sessions a layer of security. Information stored in the session (like a login token) is never passed back to the user and never requested from the user, so there is really nothing that can be spoofed or forged here.

However, it's extremely important to realize that this does not protect JSP pages from evildoers. There are still a number of major considerations in creating secure pages.

Table 7.1 Authentication Security Concerns

- It is usually a bad idea to print the session ID. This is not useful information for most clients. It might be useful in doing debugging work, but it's worth always sending through `application.log()` just in case something doesn't work as planned.
- Never, ever send the entire list of session IDs (using `getIds()`) through `out`. Having another user's session ID will allow a user to piggyback with another user's session.
- Of course, there is not enough that can be said for requiring clients to select decent passwords. Encryption technology today is so powerful that it is most common to have compromises from brute force guessing.
- Always use a secure server (SSL) for any page that the user needs to type in their password. This will help prevent people from getting their passwords "sniffed."

There is no way a full list of all the potential security issues could be printed here. It is beyond the scope of this book. For additional information, there are a number of great resources available on the Web, and there are several very good books on the topic.

The JSP Specification authors understood the value of including a session tracking API in JSP. It effectively adds state information to HTTP. This is a key factor in creating complex Web applications and prepares JSP for bigger and better tasks. The next chapter, JavaBeans, describes how to connect these sessions to enterprise-class Java applications.

JAVABEANS

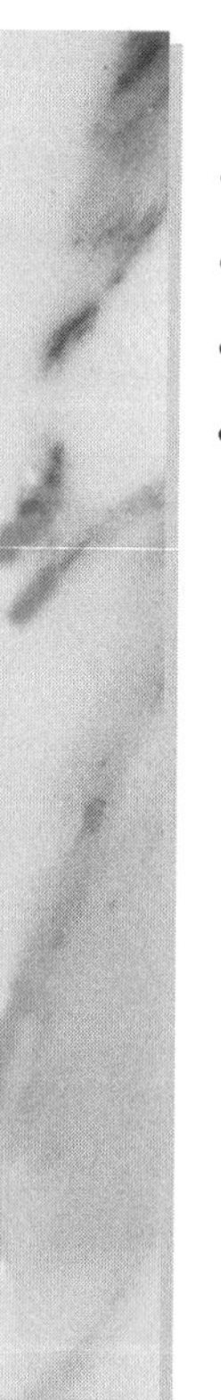

Topics in this Chapter:

- Modularity & Code Reuse
- JavaBeans
- Using JNDI
- An Authentication JavaBean Using LDAP

Chapter 8

Previous examples have made extensive use of embedding JSP using the include action (`<jsp:include />`) and the include directive (`<%@ include %>`). Each of these methods works in slightly different ways, but both present significant scalability problems.

The include directive (`<%@ include %>`) effectively inserts code inline. This can create potential namespace collisions or significant problems with overlapping declarations. The include action (`<jsp:include />`) inserts the output of a second JSP page into the original page. This can create problems in trying to share data or when the secondary JSP does something erratic.

For each of these methods there is also no standardized interface. Each developer creates their own classes and methods each with its own syntax and signature. Finding a second developer that can easily work with another developer's inline code relies heavily on documentation, comments, and the likemindedness of developers that may not exist.

These approaches are also not conducive to separating business logic from presentation. One the most powerful abilities in JSP is its ability to separate the hard code from the presentation of the page into two distinct entities.

8.1 The Component Model

In 1798 the U.S. government decided to end its reliance on foreign countries to supply army muskets. Eli Whitney, made famous for his invention of the cotton gin, secured a contract to produce 10,000 army muskets.

The problem was there were only a handful of skilled machinists in the early American republic. To solve this problem, Whitney invented something far more important than a machine. He invented a system that would permit anyone to create a product that would be just as good as one made by a highly trained machinist.

Whitney based his system on interchangeable parts, and called his solution the "Uniformity System." He later demonstrated that randomly selected individual parts would fit together to create a working musket. Until then, every rifle had been made by hand from stock to barrel. No parts of one gun would fit into another. More important than filling his order, Eli Whitney had created the component model.

Computer programming begins to embrace the component model with the development of an "object model" in object-oriented programming languages such as C++ and Java. While the object model breathed life into the development of complex applications, its distribution was still limited to language libraries and APIs. Joining two complex libraries still takes the skill and finesse of someone well versed in the language and the methods of the APIs.

More recently another model has been applied on top of the object model. This newer model draws on the best advantages of the object model, but it also implements the idea of the interface. Under this new model a packaged set of code is created that communicates with other components through a set of standardized methods called interfaces. In this "component model," plugging together interfaces of different components creates applications.

Using a component architecture grants a powerful level of code reusability and interchangeability. Components should behave the same way everywhere they go and can be "plugged-in" wherever or whenever needed.

The component also provides an extremely powerful ability to abstract the business logic from presentation. Designers continue to work on presentation, yet draw on powerful tools without understanding the programming behind them. A developer that specializes in a very specific technology can develop a component without going over the intricate details of how it works, and still share it with his coworkers and teammates.

The Component Model for JSP

Like many other aspects of JSP, a JSP page uses the component model that is built right into the underlying Java platform. The JavaBean component architecture was introduced in Java 1.1 and further refined in Java 1.2. JSP is designed to take full advantage of this JavaBean component architecture.

JavaBeans were originally designed to be graphical components in a graphical user interface. Fortunately, the architecture and design pattern used by JavaBeans does not really lock them into any specific application model. Even before JSP started to support JavaBeans, they were already beginning to be used to create nongraphical data-centric components.

By using the component architecture that is already built into the language, JSP can leverage a large pool of existing JavaBean components. While many of these data-centric JavaBeans may not have originally been intended for JSP, their component architecture will allow them to plug right in.

Unfortunately, since JavaBeans were used for user interface components for so long the majority of the current documentation on JavaBeans will refer to them as graphical widgets. These JavaBeans really are the same as graphical component JavaBeans and all the concepts remain the same.

8.2 JavaBeans

A JavaBean is basically a standard Java class that adheres to a set of fairly simple design and naming conventions. A JavaBean defines its exported methods and objects in a standardized naming convention that can be easily derived by the calling application. This provides a programmatic entry (interface) into the JavaBean without understanding how the JavaBean works internally.

There are actually no requirements for a JavaBean to extend or super class any other object. Any class that follows the JavaBean conventions is a JavaBean. The true essence of creating new JavaBeans is really a programming paradigm more than calling specific API methods.

The JavaBean API does provide a simple container class that knows how to expose these properties in special ways to create interfaces. This is really not relevant to the JSP author or JavaBean developer. The JavaBean API really applies to applications that "handle" JavaBeans, such as "Bean boxes" or the JSP engine itself.

JavaBean Conventions

By using standard design and naming conventions a JavaBean can be used by applications that do not understand the underlying logic of the JavaBean. Adhering to specific semantics and rules allows applications like JSP pages to analyze the class and methods that are available to derive the method invocation and properties that are available.

These conventions contain specific requirements on how the class must be designed. Fortunately, these design requirements are fairly straightforward and resemble "good" object-oriented programming methodologies.

There are three design requirements for a JavaBean. First, the constructor needs to accept no parameters. Second, all access to the JavaBean is done through specially defined accessor methods. And finally, a JavaBean needs to be distributed in a jar file in a special way.

CORE Note: JavaBean Naming Conventions

The specification for JavaBeans does not require any specific convention for naming classes. They can be named whatever the JavaBean developer believes is most appropriate. However, there is an informal class naming convention that is used to help other developers more easily identify JavaBeans.

Typically a JavaBean will usually follow Java's standard naming convention of beginning each word section with a capital letter. In addition, the JavaBean will usually have a class name that ends in the word "Bean" (for example, "LdapBean," "ClockBean," etc.).

The Constructor

By definition, a JavaBean is required to have a constructor that is instantiated with no parameters. This makes sense considering that the calling application may not know how the JavaBean actually functions. It would be nearly impossible for the calling application to derive an understanding of the specific instantiation parameters that might be required.

While all JavaBeans require a constructor with no parameters, it is certainly possible to overload the constructor with several signatures. This is not uncommon for classes that have been converted from non-JavaBean classes into JavaBeans. But the default `<jsp:useBean>` tag will only actually use the constructor that has no parameters.

Java also supports classes without constructors. When this is the case, the Java compiler creates a constructor that contains no parameters and initializes no values. This means that a JavaBean could even be an empty class file and still remain valid. For example, this is a valid JavaBean:

```
public class EmptyBean {}
```

Properties and Accessor Methods

When working with a JavaBean, every aspect of the JavaBean that is exposed is called a *property*. Properties are really just an external representation of the internal state of the JavaBean.

For each property, there will be accessor methods that define interaction with the property. These accessor methods either set a value or get a value from a specific property. The JavaBean should never have its internal state accessed directly, so every modifiable aspect of the JavaBean should have accessor methods.

Most frequently, a property will have accessor methods that allow setting and getting a value. However, there is no specific requirement that a property must have both of these accessor methods; it could have just one. Some properties may not allow a property to be set, so no accessor method would be available.

Accessor methods are created using a common naming format. Once again this is to allow information about the JavaBean to be derived without explicit knowledge of the JavaBean.

The methods used for retrieving data are called getter methods and follow the format:

```
public {Object-Type} get{Property} ()
```

The compliment to this is the setter methods that allows for placing data into a property. The setter methods follow this format:

```
public void set{Property} ({Object-Type})
```

JavaBeans also provide an additional accessor method that returns a `boolean` value. This accessor method is known as a *Boolean getter* method. It is useful for checking state or other flags in the JavaBean.

```
public boolean is{Property} ()
```

Visibility

Normally the visibility of methods and variables is left open to the developer. However, the JavaBean requires that all accessor methods be declared as `public` methods. The JSP container will only be able to identify properties that are `public` accessor methods, so other non-`public` accessor methods will not be available to JSP pages.

The visibility of internal objects and methods within the JavaBean is still open to the option of the developer. But since the JavaBean is intended as a means of encapsulating logic, it really doesn't make sense to have anything public besides the accessor methods.

Serious consideration should be given to any object within a JavaBean that is declared as `public`. Usually only the constructor and the accessor methods of the JavaBean should be `public`. Most other objects should probably be `protected` or `private` and have their properties exposed through `public` accessor methods. This will keep the users of a JavaBean accessing it through the standard interfaces and prevent potential problems that might occur if the internal implementation of the JavaBean changes.

JavaBean Examples

Listing 8.1 shows a very simple JavaBean that acts as a simple counter. This JavaBean doesn't do anything incredibly interesting, but it does illustrate some of the requirements of a JavaBean.

The constructor takes no parameters and still initializes the variables that will be needed for the JavaBean. In this particular case the bean has only one property, `count`, which is accessed through a getter method for that property.

Listing 8.1 SimpleCountingBean.java

```
public class SimpleCountingBean {
  private int count;

  public SimpleCountingBean() {
    count = 0;
  }

  public int getCount() {
    count++;
    return count;
  }
}
```

CORE Note: Using JavaBeans

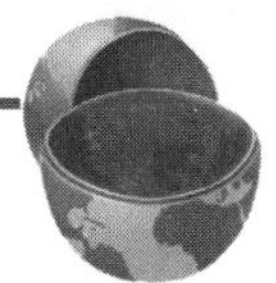

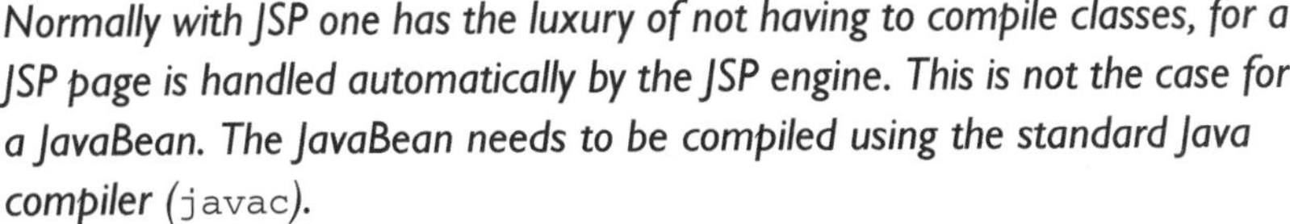

Normally with JSP one has the luxury of not having to compile classes, for a JSP page is handled automatically by the JSP engine. This is not the case for a JavaBean. The JavaBean needs to be compiled using the standard Java compiler (`javac`*).*

The compiled JavaBean is really just a new class, so it needs to be made available the way any other class would be. When the JSP engine goes to compile a JSP page that contains a JavaBean, the JavaBeans class is essentially "`import`*"ed automatically by the JSP engine.*

From the perspective of JSP this means that the first class in the servers `CLASSPATH` *that matches the value defined by the "*`class=`*" attribute in the* `jsp:useBean` *tag. So, any individual* `.class` *file that could be imported and used as a JavaBean will be used as a JavaBean without complaint. Simply being in the* `CLASSPATH` *will allow a JavaBean to behave exactly as anyone would expect.*

Listing 8.2 shows another simple JavaBean, but this one is a bit more complicated. This JavaBean actually represents a user in an address book system. This JavaBean has both getter and setter methods that allow it to actually act as a data repository for information about the user.

Listing 8.2 UserInfoBean.java

```
import java.util.*;

public class Contact {
  private String name=null;
  private String phone=null;
  private String email=null;

  public Contact() { }

  public String getName() {
    return this.name;
  }

  public void setName(String myName) {
    this.name = myName;
```

Listing 8.2 UserInfoBean.java (continued)

```
  }

  public String getPhone() {
    return this.phone;
  }

  public void setPhone(String myPhone) {
    this.phone = myPhone;
  }

  public String getEmail() {
    return this.email;
  }

  public void setEmail(String myEmail) {
    this.email = myEmail;
  }

}
```

Other Requirements

There are some additional requirements in the JavaBean specification that are part of the more traditional form of JavaBeans. However, the JSP engine should not normally require these.

These requirements should be strictly adhered to if the goal is to create fully qualified JavaBeans. If the goal is simply to make a JavaBean that works with JSP, then these are still useful and recommended, but are not required.

Packaging

It looks like a JavaBean, and it behaves like a JavaBean—so is it a JavaBean? Well, it might not be a JavaBean as defined by the JavaBean specification, even though most people wouldn't notice the difference. Technically, it is not a JavaBean until the new class is placed into a jar file that includes a specific manifest option. Each class file that is a JavaBean needs to be marked with the "`Java-Bean: true`" attribute in the manifest file.

Specific examples in how to use these commands will be shown later, as the JavaBean examples are going to be packaged.

Using the `serializable` Interface

Earlier in the chapter it was said that JavaBeans do not need to implement any particular interface, and that is still true for JavaBeans used within JSP. However, the JavaBeans specification actually requires that all JavaBeans implement the `serializable` interface.

Serialization allows JavaBeans to be saved to disk, sent across a network, or written into a database. Later, the same JavaBean can be reread and restored to its state at the time that it was stored.

Serialization turns an object, such as a JavaBean, into a stream of data that resembles a byte array. This data contains representations of the raw data types and all the raw data that is currently contained in the JavaBean. Then this data can be put just about anywhere that a byte array output stream can go. Later when the data needs to be reconstituted, it undergoes a reversing process that deserializes the data back into the same data structures.

Serialized JavaBeans can be extremely powerful in storing data. Rather than storing discrete data segments in a database, the actual JavaBean can be stored and restored using serialization. Consider an e-commerce order from a customer. Traditionally the data would consist of a series of elements from a series of database tables, which can be difficult and expensive to reconstruct. Alternatively, if the order was all done as a JavaBean, it is serialized and stored, reconstructing it is as simple as deserializing the JavaBean.

The `serializable` interface also lets the developer create a JavaBean that is preconfigured. This bypasses the "empty constructor" requirement to some degree by creating the a new JavaBean using a template. When `<jsp:useBean>` tag is given the `beanName` attribute, it will instantiate a new Bean from a serialized file (`*.ser`) that matches the class name of the JavaBean. If there is no serialized file then JSP will create new JavaBean using the empty constructor.

Creating a JavaBean that can be serialized simply involves implementing the `serializable` interface, but making serialization behave properly is a discussion that is beyond the scope of this book.

Beyond the Requirements

So far everything that has been discussed about JavaBeans has been an aspect of the required conventions. JavaBeans also provide a number of other convenience functions that can optionally be used by the JSP developer.

Indexed Properties

Normal properties are restricted to a single value only. There is addition type of a property that supports multiple values, where all the values must be of the same data type. These are called indexed properties and they deal with arrays of data.

Indexed properties have getter and setter methods like normal properties, but there are methods for each that retrieve the entire array or a single value from that array.

The first set handles the entire array, getting or setting the array through a single accessor method:

```
public {Object-Type}[] get{Property} ()
public void set{Property} ({Object-Type}[])
```

The other type of accessor methods for indexed properties refer to a specific index within the array, setting or getting a single value:

```
public {Object-Type} get{Property} (int)
public set{Property} (int, {Object-Type})
```

Introspection

So far, there is no common method or base class for an application to use to derive information about the JavaBean. Somehow an application using a JavaBean knows what accessor methods and properties are available. It is probably time to talk briefly about this process and the underlying technologies.

When a JavaBean is instantiated the JavaBean container starts by going through a process called "introspection." The introspection process will collect data from several sources.

Most of the information obtained comes from another process called "reflection," which simply scans the method signatures of the class. Next, introspection matches the known naming conventions for a JavaBean and builds a list of accessor methods.

Finally, once all the data has come back the process will make some decisions about how accessor methods and properties will actually be exposed. The process of simply looking at method signatures essentially defines the properties and accessor methods.

Overriding Introspection

JavaBeans also provide a mechanism to specifically override introspection. This is actually a combination of a class and an interface that need to be defined. First a class needs to be created that is prefixed by "`BeanInfo`," and the class needs to implement the `java.beans.BeanInfo` interface.

By using `BeanInfo` a developer can explicitly change which internal method is connected to each accessor method or property. A developer can designate any arbitrary method to map across to a specific JavaBean property. This can be particularly useful when an existing non-JavaBean class needs to be converted into a JavaBean but still needs to retain the original method name.

Implementing a `BeanInfo` class can get somewhat complicated and most of the features are designed for use in applications that actually handle JavaBeans, like visual JSP editors. While it is a bit beyond the scope of this book, a simple implementation framework is available with `java.beans.SimpleBeanInfo`.

Using the JavaBean in JSP

Everything up to this point has discussed the process of creating and changing the actual JavaBean itself, but there has been no discussion about actually using them from within JSP.

There is a lengthy discussion on the specific semantic on the tags `<jsp:useBean>`, `<jsp:getProperty>`, and `<jsp:setProperty>`—including the valid signatures for each tag—in Chapter 3.

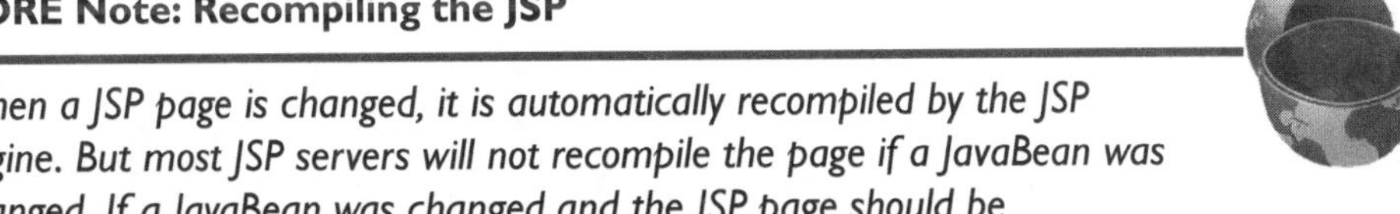

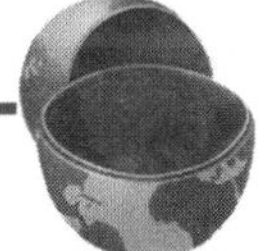

CORE Note: Recompiling the JSP

When a JSP page is changed, it is automatically recompiled by the JSP engine. But most JSP servers will not recompile the page if a JavaBean was changed. If a JavaBean was changed and the JSP page should be recompiled, then the JSP engine will need to be told to recompile the JSP page. This might be as easy as using a "touch" command to update the last-modified date of the file.

JSP Type Conversions

The JSP tags `<jsp:setProperty>` and `<jsp:getProperty>` deal with every value as a scalar; every value they receive is converted into a `String`. This is not a limitation created by the JavaBean; it is simply how the JSP engine handles these tags.

These tags automatically call the `toString()` method associated with the object just before the actual JavaBean is given the value or immediately after the value is received back. For primitive types, the data is converted using the corresponding object in `java.lang.*.toString()` method (for example, a `double` uses `java.lang.Double.toString())`.

Since this occurs in the layer just before the JavaBean, the actual methods that are requested will effectively have these signatures:

```
public String get{Property} ()
public void set{Property} (String n)
```

For example, Listing 8.1 has a method that returns an `int`. In this case when the JSP engine sees the tag `<jsp:getProperty name="counter" property="count">`, it behaves as if an accessor method was called that looks like this:

```
public String getCount()
```

Avoiding JSP Type Conversions

Its possible to avoid the type conversions that occur in JSP by simply not using the standard tags `<jsp:getProperty>` and `<jsp:setProperty>`.

The first and simplest way to avoid these problems is to use the JavaBean the same way a normal class would be used. In this case, the bean is still instantiated as a JavaBean using the `<jsp:useBean>` tag. The properties of the Bean can be accessed by calling the accessor methods directly. For example:

```
<jsp:useBean id="pagecounter" class="SimpleCounterBean">
<%
  int count = pagecounter.getCount();
%>
```

Since this called the accessor method directly (without the JSP interpreting the tag), it will actually return an `int`.

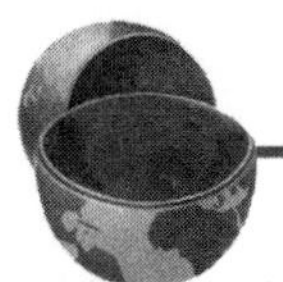

CORE Note: nulls and properties

In addition to converting the resulting values into a string, the `<jsp:setProperty>` *and* `<jsp:getProperty>` *tags don't handle* `nulls` *very well under a large number of JSP engines.*

If either of these tags is given a `null` *as a value, or receives a* `null` *back from an accessor method, then an exception is thrown. This is probably not the behavior that would be expected.*

This can either be avoided by changing the JavaBean or by calling the accessor methods directly.

An alternative method of avoiding JSP type conversions would be to create custom JSP tags that can handle the appropriate data types. A custom tag can be created to accept or return any type of data that might be needed. More information on creating custom tags is available in Chapter 11.

The Scope of a JavaBean

JSP supports using JavaBeans in under the same four different levels of scope that any page can have: request, page, session, and application. Each JavaBean is created with its own scope independent of the page.

This allows the JavaBean to actually have significantly different behaviors under different scopes. JavaBeans can outlive a page, or they can have a shorter lifespan than a page, depending on the context that is needed.

In fact, a JavaBean as simple as the one shown in Listing 8.1 can have significantly different behaviors depending on its scope. While the request and page scope would be pretty useless for this JavaBean (it would count then be discarded), using this JavaBean in the session scope would allow the counter to track how often a particular user has requested a page up until their session expires. Used in the application scope it would track how often a page was accessed by anyone since the server was last restarted.

JavaBeans and Thread Safety

JavaBeans instantiate a lot of objects that are not inherently thread-safe. Since the JSP engine is a threaded environment, JavaBeans may have some problems that come about as a result of threading. In fact, JavaBeans are not thread-safe.

However, a JavaBean can effectively be thread-safe depending on its scope. Since both the request and page scope have an instance based lifespan, it is impossible to have threading problems with a JavaBean within these scopes.

On first glance, session-based JavaBeans seem to be thread-safe. In this case, the JavaBean is only available to one particular session ID so it's not likely that a threading problem will arise, but it is still possible for threading problems to occur. In particular, if a user has two windows open from the same browser or the user clicks on a submit button twice, this will create two separate requests that might wind up causing a race condition. So, in real-world situations it is not useful to view session JavaBeans as thread-safe.

Of course, JavaBeans created in the application scope are simply not thread-safe. If a JavaBean should be used in this scope then the developer will need to make sure that the JavaBean is internally thread-safe.

It's generally a good idea to always try to make JavaBeans that are as thread-safe as possible. This allows the JavaBean developer and JSP authors to work without fear that the Bean might be used in an unexpected scope. Unfortunately, sometimes the nature of a JavaBean can make it difficult or impossible to make the JavaBean completely thread-safe.

8.3 An Authentication JavaBean

Here is where the first really practical JavaBean will come into existence. This new JavaBean is going to authenticate a user against an entry in an LDAP database. (This will dovetail nicely with the login function that was shown in Chapter 7.) The JavaBean will not actually replace existing functionality in those examples; instead it will simply add an extra functionality that those JSP pages will use.

The authentication JavaBean is designed to validate the user by authenticating them against an LDAP database. Java has a package that is designed to access LDAP databases: the Java Naming & Directory Interface (JNDI) package that is included with the Java 2 Enterprise Edition (J2EE). In order to understand how the JavaBean works it's important to understand some of the functions of both JNDI and LDAP.

What is JNDI?

Java's Naming and Directory Interface (JNDI) is an API that allows access into standard naming and directory services. This allows a JSP to find out information about users, hosts, and a large assortment of other useful information. Before going too far into JNDI, the concepts of naming and directory services need to be presented.

Naming

The concept of naming is a fundamental building block to any computer program or operating system. Almost every object that is used by a computer is associated with a name and is retrieved by name. Examples of naming can be seen in a standard file system where files are accessed by name, or out on the Internet where domain names are mapped to IP addresses.

Normally, Naming includes naming conventions to identify logical blocks such as the dot (.) in a domain name. It also does not preclude the concept of references or address-based access.

Naming introduces the concept of binding, which is the relationship of the name to the object (a name is bound to the object). It also introduces the concept of context, a grouping of several bindings with a common root (*www.javadesktop.com* and *mail.javadekstop.com* share the *javadesktop.com* context). These terms later become important in describing the naming relationships.

Directory Services

Many of these naming of services have been extended to associate more to a particular name than just a single object. Names begin to be associated with an object and many attributes. This creates a directory service, where objects become more complex and can be located by searching for particular attributes.

An example of this can be seen in any address book application where an address can be found by entering either the last name or the first name of the person being searched.

How JNDI Works

JNDI is designed as a universal framework that supports the use of plugable modules called an SPI (Service Provider Interface). Generally a single SPI provides an interface into a single naming or directory service.

In fact, without any SPI installed JNDI provides a framework that cannot access anything. If JNDI was installed with the Java 2 Enterprise Edition (J2EE) version 1.3, then several common SPIs should already be installed (including the LDAP SPI for the example). If JNDI was installed separately then one or more SPI will be needed downloaded before JNDI will be useful, in this particular case the LDAP SPI will need to be installed.

JNDI is usually implemented by creating a `Hashtable` that defines the "environment." This contains constants as keys and values that reflect how the internal state of the API and SPI should actually appear. A new directory context is then created and given the "environment" `Hashtable`. As an example, this is how a connection to an LDAP server would be created:

```
Hashtable myEnv = new Hashtable();

myEnv.put(Context.INITIAL_CONTEXT_FACTORY,
                        "com.sun.jndi.ldap.LdapCtxFactory");
```

```
myEnv.put(Context.PROVIDER_URL,
"ldap://ldap.javadesktop.com:389");

DirContext ctx = new InitialDirContext(myEnv);
```

Since the LDAP SPI was used, this would create a new connection to the LDAP server. Since no authentication data was given, the connection will be anonymous with access rights for anonymous users determined by the LDAP server.

Now that a connection is established, the LDAP server can be searched for specific information. For example, looking for the e-mail address of Manny Hegepoupre, could use these commands:

```
Attributes matchAttrs = new BasicAttributes(true);
matchAttrs.put(new BasicAttribute("cn",
"Manny Hegepoupre"));
matchAttrs.put(new BasicAttribute("mail"));

NamingEnumeration results =
ctx.search("ou=People", matchAttrs, "cn", "mail");
```

What is LDAP?

Lightweight Directory Access Protocol (LDAP) is a common directory service used by many large companies. It's derived from the older directory service standard X.500.

Over the last few years LDAP started to replace many older "flat file" or "hashed file" systems that were used to store user information. LDAP provides a single data store of information about a user, where in the past there may have been dozens of separate different files where data was kept.

In addition, LDAP is designed specifically to handle directory services. It is hierarchical and heavily tuned for directory access, so it tends to be very fast for reading data but slow on writing data. While it is not nearly as flexible as an RDBMS, it usually has better performance for directory-based information.

Since LDAP is used in many companies for authentication, this is what the example JavaBean will accomplish.

The LDAPAuthBean

Listing 8.3 shows the actual JavaBean that verifies a user's password against the password on the LDAP server.

In LDAP authentication occurs by logging in to the server. The process appears a little convoluted, but the JavaBean first needs to find the user's specific entry, known as a *distinguished name*, by doing an anonymous search. After the JavaBean knows what the unique ID of the user is, it attempts to login using the password that was provided. In this particular case, the connection is closed immediately after it has been established that this is indeed the proper user.

It's also important to note that this JavaBean is not thread-safe. It should only be used in the page or request scope. Since JavaBeans can really only accept arguments via the accessor methods it becomes difficult to synchronize around the user's name, so the problem is simply avoided by staying in the request scope.

Listing 8.3 LDAPAuthBean.java

```
package com.javadesktop.ldap;

import java.util.*;
import javax.naming.*;
import javax.naming.directory.*;

public class LDAPAuthBean {

  private static final String CTXINIT =
                "com.sun.jndi.ldap.LdapCtxFactory";

  private static final String CTXURL =
                "ldap://ldap.corporatdesktop.com:389";

  private static final String CTXBASE =
                "o=CorporateDesktop";

  private static final String CTXAUTH =
                "DIGEST-MD5 CRAM-MD5";

  private Hashtable ldapEnv;
  private transient String userLogin;
```

Listing 8.3 LDAPAuthBean.java (continued)

```
private transient String userPassword;

public LDAPAuthBean() {
    ldapEnv = new Hashtable();

    ldapEnv.put(Context.INITIAL_CONTEXT_FACTORY,
    CTXINIT);
    ldapEnv.put(Context.PROVIDER_URL, CTXURL);
}

public void setUserLogin(String uid) {
  this.userLogin = uid;
}

public void setUserPass(String password) {
  this.userPassword = password;
}

public boolean isAuth() {
  String userDN = grabDN(this.userLogin);
  boolean auth = false;

  try {
    ldapEnv.put(Context.SECURITY_AUTHENTICATION,
    CTXAUTH);
    ldapEnv.put(Context.SECURITY_PRINCIPAL, userDN);
    ldapEnv.put(Context.SECURITY_CREDENTIALS,
    this.userPassword);

    DirContext ctx = new InitialDirContext(ldapEnv);
    ctx.close();

    auth = true;
  } catch (AuthenticationException e) {
    auth = false;
  } catch (NamingException e) {
    // do some legitimate error checking here.
  }

  return (auth);
```

Listing 8.3 LDAPAuthBean.java (continued)

```
  }

  private String grabDN(String name) {
    String filter = "(uid=" + name + ")";
    String firstDN = null;

    try {
      ldapEnv.put(Context.SECURITY_AUTHENTICATION, "none");

      DirContext ctx = new InitialDirContext(ldapEnv);

      SearchControls constraints = new SearchControls();
 constraints.setSearchScope(SearchControls.SUBTREE_SCOPE);

      NamingEnumeration results =
              ctx.search(CTXBASE, filter, constraints);

      if (results.hasMoreElements()) {
        firstDN = (String)results.nextElement();
      }

      ctx.close();
    } catch (NamingException e) {
    }

    return (firstDN);
  }
}
```

In order to actually use this LDAP JavaBean it needs to be properly packaged. First, it needs to be compiled:

```
javac LDAPAuthBean.java
```

Then a manifest needs to be created showing that this is a JavaBean. The manifest is simply a text file describing the contents of the jar file. In this case the filename myManifest.txt will be used and it will look like this:

```
Manifest-Version: 1.0
Name: com/javadesktop/ldap/LDAPAuthBean.class
Java-Bean: true
```

Now a jar file needs to be created for the JavaBean. Make sure your classes are in the right directory for your package, and then jar the files like this:

```
jar cfm LDAPAuthBean.jar myManifest.txt com/javadesktop/
ldap/*
```

Finally, the JavaBean needs to be placed in the server's `CLASSPATH`. (The specific details of your `CLASSPATH` depend on your environment. Note: some JSP engines have a separate `CLASSPATH` than the default system `CLASSPATH`.) Once that has been done the JavaBean will be accessible from any JSP page.

With the JavaBean complete, the login page itself will need to include some hooks to actually use the LDAP login. Listing 8.4 shows the `login.jsp` page from the previous chapter with modifications to support the new authentication.

It is important to notice the abstraction between the login page and the JavaBean. As far as the login page is concerned, the JavaBean is simply a black box the data goes in, and the user is either approved or is not approved. This means that if the authentication database changes to a different type of naming service, or the URL of the LDAP database changes, the JSP page does not have to be modified.

Listing 8.4 login.jsp

```
<%@ page errorPage="errorPage.jsp" %>
<jsp:useBean id="auth" class="LDAPAuthBean"
scope="request"/>

<%
  auth.setUserName(request.getParameter("loginname"));
  auth.setUserPass(request.getParameter("userPassword"));

  if (!auth.isAuth()) {
%>
<!DOCTYPE HTML PUBLIC "-//W3C//DTD HTML 4.0 Final//EN">
<HEAD>
<TITLE>Login Page</TITLE>
<STYLE>
<!--
font.loginform {
  font-family: Arial,Helvetica,sans-serif;
```

Listing 8.4 login.jsp (continued)

```
  font-size:10pt; font-weight: 600; color: #000000;
}
-->
</STYLE>

</HEAD>
<BODY>
<jsp:include page="debug.jsp" flush="true" />

<CENTER>
<FONT CLASS="loginform">
LOGIN REQUIRED:
</FONT>
<BR>

<FORM NAME="loginform" METHOD=post>
<TABLE BGCOLOR=#990022 BORDER=0 CELLPADDING=5
CELLSPACING=0>

<TR><TD ALIGN=right>
<FONT CLASS="loginform">
Login Name:
</FONT>
</TD><TD ALIGN=left>
<FONT CLASS="loginform">
<INPUT TYPE=text NAME="loginname" SIZE=10>
</FONT>
</TD></TR>

<TR><TD ALIGN=right>
<FONT CLASS="loginform">
Password:
</FONT>
</TD><TD ALIGN=left>
<FONT CLASS="loginform">
<INPUT TYPE=password NAME="loginpassword" SIZE=10>
</FONT>
</TD></TR>

<TR><TD COLSPAN=2 ALIGN=center>
<FONT CLASS="loginform">
```

Listing 8.4 login.jsp (continued)

```
<INPUT TYPE=SUBMIT VALUE="Login">
</FONT>
</TD></TR>
</TABLE>

</FORM>
</CENTER>

</BODY>
</HTML>
<%
  } else {
    String login
    = (String)request.getParameter("loginname");

    session.putValue("login", login);
    session.setMaxInactiveInterval(600);

    String loginpoint
    = (String)session.getValue("loginpoint");
    if (loginpoint == null) {
      StringBuffer defaultpoint = new StringBuffer();
      defaultpoint.append(request.getScheme())
                  .append("://")
                  .append(request.getServerName())
                  .append("/");

      loginpoint = defaultpoint.toString();
    } else {
      session.removeValue("loginpoint");
    }

    response.sendRedirect(loginpoint);
  }
%>
```

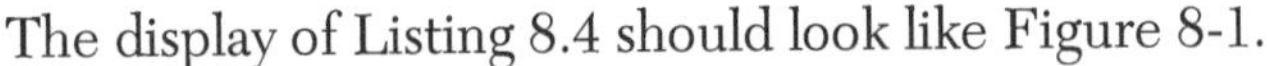

The display of Listing 8.4 should look like Figure 8-1.

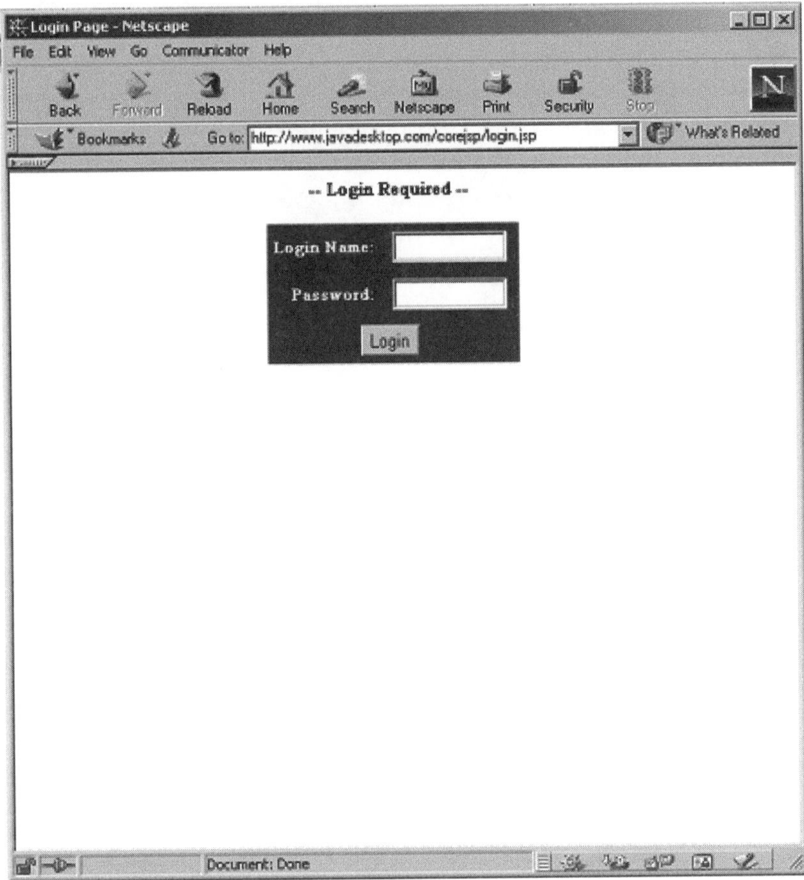

Figure 8-1 Login.jsp

8.4 Components and Component Frameworks

A component is a packaged set of code that communicates with other components through a set of methods called interfaces. Developers simply examine the interfaces of different components and connect them to form applications. Newer technologies allow components to be created on different platforms with different programming languages, as well as allowing components on remote computers to be tied together to form a single application.

The software that ties the components together to form an application is called the component framework. Component frameworks are a major part of enterprise programming: There are three major component frameworks available today: Microsoft has created a component framework called Component Object Model (COM) or Distributed Component Object Model (DCOM); the Open Software Foundation (OSF) developed the Common Object Request Broker Architecture (CORBA); and the third component framework is Enterprise JavaBeans.

8.5 Enterprise JavaBeans

Enterprise JavaBeans are server components written in Java that are distributed across a network. In the simplest sense, they are JavaBeans that can be distributed across a network using Java's distributed object model RMI.

Enterprise JavaBeans are much more complex than normal JavaBeans. They have a set of additional concepts and restrictions that help define them as Enterprise JavaBeans.

Since Enterprise JavaBeans are fairly complex, they typically require a special application server that knows how to handle the Enterprise JavaBeans container. Several of the more advanced JSP engines directly support Enterprise JavaBeans, but it's by no means a standard feature.

Because of the complexity of Enterprise JavaBeans—and the additional requirement of a specialized server—they are outside of the scope of this book. It is helpful to understand how Enterprise JavaBeans differ from normal JavaBeans and the advantages of one versus the other.

Session Beans vs. Entity Beans

Enterprise JavaBeans basically come in two basic types: Session Beans and Entity Beans.

A Session Bean represents a client to the application. The client communicates with the application server by invoking methods that belong to the Enterprise JavaBean. A Session Bean can be thought of as an extension of the client, as far as the application server is concerned it is the client. Each Session Bean can have only one client. When the client terminates, its corresponding Session Bean also terminates. Therefore, a Session Bean is transient, or nonpersistent.

An Entity Bean represents an object in some persistent storage. This persistent storage could be a database, a file, or any other storage mechanism. An Entity Bean might represent a customer, whose information is stored as a row in a relational database table. The persistence of an Entity Bean can either be managed by the EJB container or the Entity Bean itself. However, if the Entity Bean manages its own state then it will need to include code on how to access its data, which removes a significant layer of abstraction and could violate Enterprise JavaBean rules.

Programming Restrictions for Enterprise Beans

Enterprise JavaBeans work by making use of the services provided by the EJB container in the application server. This container and application server is responsible for life-cycle management and interaction between Beans.

To avoid conflicts with these services, Enterprise Beans are explicitly restricted from performing operations involving managing threads, using any file services in `java.io`, listening on sockets, or using native libraries.

Also, since Enterprise JavaBeans are typically used to represent business logic and processes, it's very common for an Enterprise JavaBean to have restrictions on the type of presentation it can make. For example, Enterprise JavaBeans are explicitly restricted from manipulating AWT components.

JavaBeans are a powerful programming addition to Java, and their use in JSP pages helps migrate Web programming to a component model. JavaBeans serve as the business logic layer while JSP pages act as presentation logic. In this way more scaleable and powerful Web applications can be built.

DATABASE CONNECTIVITY

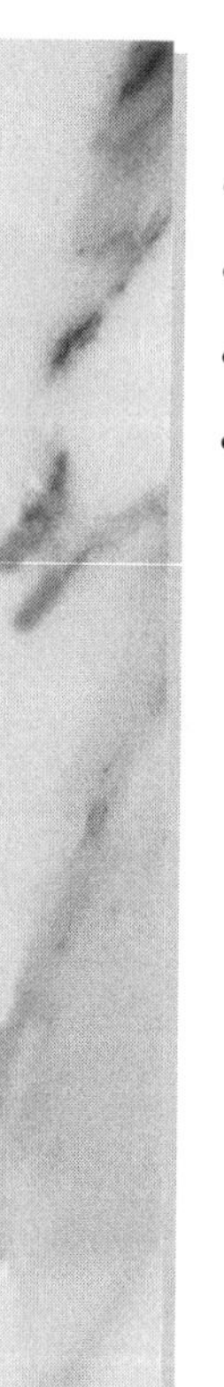

Topics in this Chapter:

- Relational vs. Object-Oriented Databases
- Structured Query Language
- Optimizing JDBC Database Connections
- Connection Pooling

Chapter 9

One of the most powerful features of JSP pages, as well as a great advantage over other scripting languages, is its ability to utilize the full Java API. Specifically, the Java 2 Enterprise Edition (J2EE) comes with many supporting APIs that allow access to external data sources. One example of this was seen in Chapter 8; the JNDI API allows access to external directory services such as Lightweight Directory Access Protocol (LDAP) and Novell Directory Services (NDS). This chapter will focus on one specific API from the J2EE called Java DataBase Connectivity (JDBC).

9.1 What is JDBC?

JDBC can be thought of as a Java interface between database applications and databases. The JDBC developers intended JDBC to become a universal way to access database data. The desired effect was to create a single set of Java objects that could be used to access any database. For the most part, JDBC is very successful at this task.

JDBC is structured around a set of Java interfaces called *drivers*. Each database that supports JDBC has a different set of these drivers tailored specifically to their database engine. The power of JDBC comes from the fact that the programmer does not have to know the specifics of a given database to create an application. JDBC hides the database-specific issues and gives the JSP author a single interface for talking to any JDBC supported database.

To achieve its single interface to multiple sets of databases, JDBC was built on three important principals. The first and foremost principle is that of simplicity. Simple and common tasks are implemented in simple interfaces. Less common or abstract tasks are achieved by extra interfaces.

Second, JDBC is built on the structured query language (SQL). SQL is by far the most common language used to manipulate information in a database. By using a standard such as SQL, JDBC is able to support many different database architectures.

Third, JDBC capitalizes on the experience of existing database APIs. It takes a similar, if less complex, model as that of ODBC. It also is heavily influenced by the X/OPEN SQL Call Level Interface (CLI). This eases the acceptance of JDBC to database vendors and sells the traditional ideal of building on existing tried and tested technologies.

ODBC

ODBC, or Open DataBase Connectivity, was created to provide universal access to databases on Microsoft Windows platforms. While JDBC drew on the successful aspects of OBDC, the two APIs are very different. ODBC is built in C and requires intermediate APIs to connect to other languages. Many developers believe that ODBC never extended beyond the Windows platform because of its overly complex design. Transitioning ODBC outside of the rigidly controlled Windows environment proves to be extremely difficult.

Nonetheless, the Java 1.2 JDK comes with an ODBC bridge that maps JDBC calls to OBDC calls, giving Java access to database management systems (DBMS) that supports ODBC.

Object vs. Relational

Today there are two common models of databases, relational and object-oriented. They are delineated by the method utilized to organize data. By far the most prolific type of database is the relational database. Relational databases can conceptually be visualized as groups of spreadsheets in which rows from a given spreadsheet could be associated with rows in another spreadsheet. In relational database lingo the spreadsheet is called a table, which is further broken up into rows and columns. SQL, which is based on the concept of rows and columns, is most often associated with databases stored in a relational format. Relational databases are sometimes referred to as Relational Database Management Systems (RDBMS).

Object-oriented databases are much newer, but are rapidly increasing in popularity. In an object-oriented database, data is represented in objects and classes, extremely similar to the object-oriented design of Java programs. Java concepts such as encapsulation, inheritance, and polymorphism apply to data modeled in object-oriented databases. Object-oriented databases are often referred to as Object Database Management Systems (ODBMS).

A third type of database model is also emerging. It is called an object-relational database, and describes a traditional relational database that has evolved to include object-oriented capabilities. This model is becoming popular as the vendors of the large relational databases are striving to meet the needs of today's object-oriented programming languages. Object-relational databases are commonly referred to as Object Relation Database Management Systems (ORDBMS).

The value of object-oriented databases is uncovered when examining the methods utilized to store and retrieve information in the database. Java stores data internally in an object-oriented format. To use a relational database, data must be mapped from a table, column, and row format into Java objects. This must be done every time data is retrieved or stored in the database.

With an object-oriented database, data is stored in the same format as the Java application. There is no data-mapping layer. Objects in Java can simply be stored directly into the database. While most object databases support SQL, the preferred method for utilizing an object-oriented database is utilizing database-specific Java APIs. For this reason, JDBC is more often used with databases using a relational model. Since most JDBC drivers are primarily concerned with relational databases, from this point on consider our references to databases to be to *relational databases*.

9.2 Understanding the Relational Model

Understanding how data is organized in a relational database is the first step in connecting database information to a JSP page. All data in a database is stored in a two-dimensional format called a table. Most databases are made up of many tables, each holding particular sets of data. All tables are made up of a fixed number of rows and columns, very much like a spreadsheet. Each column has a particular name and data type. Each row is called an *entry*, as it holds a set of data for each column. It is sometimes helpful to think of columns as *fields* and rows as *records*. A *cell* is where a row meets a column to store a particular piece of data.

An address book is a good analogy to a database table. Each set of names and addresses is an entry, and the categories (or fields) for each entry is a column. Take a look at Figure 9.1 to see an address book in table format.

Remember that most databases are composed of many tables. There might be separate tables for user contact information, product catalogs, and sales records. One of the powerful features of a relational database is its ability to combine data sets from different tables into a single set of information. Think of a database as a spreadsheet where information can be accessed in single cells, rows, columns, sets of cells matching certain criteria, or cells from multiple tables matching certain criteria. Unlike a spreadsheet, cells in a table can only contain certain data types, and not formulas or programs. Databases are only for storage of information, keeping an abstraction layer between data storage and program logic.

Name	Phone	eMail
Damon Hougland	555-1112	damon@javadesktop.com
Aaron Tavistock	555-1105	aaron@javadesktop.com
Gibson Charles	555-1007	gibson@notreal.net
Abigail Nora	555-0306	anora@daughter.com
Julie Alisa	555-1029	Julie@damonandjulie.com
Barbara Wells	555-0321	bwell@goodfortune.org
Christine Gollery	555-1218	chrisg@bigal.net
Adam Reese	555-0701	adam@adamone.org
Allison Marie	555-1002	allison@goldencurls.com

Figure 9–1 Simple Table from Address Book

SQL

So, if there are no functions or formulas in table entries, how is information retrieved from a database? The answer is the Structured Query Language (SQL). While there are some minor differences in syntax and usage, most major database vendors support SQL. JDBC utilizes SQL to retrieve, store, or manipulate information in a database.

Using Java code in scriplets, expressions, or JavaBeans, an SQL query is sent across the network via the JDBC API. If the SQL query returns data from the database the format is that of a table, similar to the original format of the data in the database. The returned table is not necessarily in the same format of the original table, as the SQL query can specify a specific subset of data from one or more tables.

Unlike most common programming languages, SQL appears more like formal English than code. Just like JDBC, it is based on simplicity. In fact, the majority of SQL statements boil down to four basic commands: SELECT, INSERT, UPDATE, and DELETE. Table 9.1 lists the purpose behind these four basic commands.

Table 9.1 SQL Common Commands

SQL Command	***Purpose***
INSERT	Add rows of data to a table
DELETE	Delete rows of data from a table
UPDATE	Change rows of data in a table
SELECT	Retrieve rows of data from a table

The SELECT Statement

The SELECT statement is the most common form of SQL statement, and is used to retrieve columns of data from a database. The syntax for the SELECT statement is:

```
SELECT <column(s)> FROM <table(s)>
```

More than one column and table can be selected. Imagine Figure 9.1 is an actual database table called `address_book` and contains the columns: `Name`, `Phone`, and `eMail`. If a table similar to the one shown in Figure 9.1 is desired, the SQL query might be:

```
SELECT * FROM address_book
```

In this case the "*" character represents a wildcard character that describes "all columns."

There are also several modifiers that can specify specific subsets of data to retrieve. For example, the ORDER BY modifier describes the column by which to order data, the default being alphabetical order. The following SQL statement asks for only the `Name` and `eMail` fields sorted by e-mail address:

```
SELECT Name,email from address_book ORDER BY email
```

The table that results should look similar to Figure 9.2.

Another common modifier is the WHERE modifier. The WHERE modifier is placed before a condition and is used to narrow the query. It can be used to search for a specific value or range of values within a column or multiple columns. Given the `address_book` table, what if only entries where the `Name` equals "Gibson Charles" was desired? This can be specified by the WHERE clause:

```
SELECT * FROM address_book WHERE Name = 'Gibson Charles'
```

Name	eMail
Aaron Tavistock	aaron@javadesktop.com
Adam Reese	adam@adamone.org
Allison Marie	allison@goldencurls.com
Abigail Nora	anora@daughter.com
Barbara Wells	bwell@goodfortune.org
Christine Gollery	chrisg@bigal.net
Damon Hougland	damon@javadesktop.com
Gibson Charles	gibson@notreal.net
Julie Alisa	Julie@damonandjulie.com

Figure 9–2 Subset of Table from Address_Book

This SQL query will return all columns from any entry where the column `Name` is equal to "Gibson Charles." This should return a table that matches Figure 9.3.

A note here on SQL syntax: the SQL commands themselves are not case-sensitive, but in general the table and column names are. As a formatting guideline the SQL commands are often listed in all caps. Also, string literals are enclosed in single quotes, rather than double quotes. Number based fields need no quotation.

Name	Phone	eMail
Gibson Charles	555-1007	gibson@notreal.net

Figure 9–3 Subset of Table from Address_Book

WHERE is not limited to equals conditions. In fact there are several different operators for a WHERE clause, some of which are listed in Table 9.2. One of the most powerful is the LIKE operator, which allows the "`%`" wildcard. The "`%`" wildcard character matches any single character or set of characters in place of its current position. For example:

```
SELECT * FROM address_book WHERE Name LIKE 'G%'
```

would return any entry in the table `address_book` that has a value in the column `Name` that begins with a "`G`".

Table 9.2 WHERE Clause Operators

Operator	*Purpose*	*Example*
=	Equality Test	`SELECT * FROM state WHERE st_init = 'CA'`
!=	Inequality Test	`SELECT * FROM state WHERE st_init != 'TX'`
<	Less than	`SELECT * FROM sales WHERE cost < 100`
>	Greater than	`SELECT * FROM sales WHERE cost > 200`

Table 9.2 WHERE Clause Operators (continued)		
<=	Less than or equal to	`SELECT * FROM sales WHERE cost <= 300`
>=	Greater than or equal to	`SELECT * FROM sales WHERE cost >= 400`
BETWEEN *A AND B*	>= A and <= B	`SELECT * FROM sales WHERE cost BETWEEN 200 AND 300`
LIKE	Contains text	`SELECT * FROM state WHERE name LIKE '%forni%'`

All in all, the SELECT statement is very versatile. Multiple conditions can be combined with AND or OR. Another type of search is called SOUNDEX, which searches for matches that have the same phonetic sound as the specified criteria. One powerful feature is the fact that conditional searches can be done on data that is not to be returned. For example:

```
SELECT Email from address_book WHERE Name LIKE "%Charles"
```

returns the values in the `Email` column that end in "`Charles`" in the `Name` column. SELECT statements can also be nested to create more advanced queries. Along with these features, SELECT statements can join data from more than one table. The clearest way to do this is to prefix the table name to column names for clarity. This is done by specifying *`table_name.column_name`*.

Imagine two tables, one called `system_users` listing basic user information. It would contain the first name, last name, phone number, location, and state initial of each user. Imagine another table that only contains two columns: the state name and the state initial. This table is called `state`. How could these tables be joined? For example:

```
SELECT system_users.first_name, state.state_name
  FROM system_users, state
  WHERE system_users.state_init = state.state_init
```

finds all rows where the column `state_init` is the same in two different tables, `state` and `system_users`. It then returns a two column result that contains the `first_name` field from the `system_users` table and the `state_name` field from the `state` table.

While SQL appears quite simple at first, it is an extremely flexible tool for retrieving information from a relational database. Of course, retrieving information is only one of the functions of SQL.

The INSERT Statement

The INSERT statement is very straightforward: it inserts information into the database. As information is stored in a freeform way, there is no need to specify WHERE the information should be stored in a particular column. Thus, the format of the INSERT statement is very simple:

```
INSERT INTO <table(s)> VALUES <values(s)>
```

Given the previous `address_book` table, a new row could be added with the following INSERT statement:

```
INSERT INTO system_users (Name, Phone)
  VALUES ('Bill Guru', '555-1234')
```

This would create a new row in the table so that it appears something like Figure 9.4. Notice that the column names are listed in a set of parenthesis after the table name. This is to designate which columns to insert the data into. This is not required, as the data will be inserted into the table in the order it was created if the column names are left out. While this might be a convenience, it is never recommended. If a new column is created in the future, all of your code that does not explicitly define the column names in INSERT statements might have to be changed. This brings up another point: INSERT statements can only insert data in rows. This statement does not support inserting new columns.

Name	Phone	eMail
Damon Hougland	555-1112	damon@javadesktop.com
Aaron Tavistock	555-1105	aaron@javadesktop.com
Gibson Charles	555-1007	gibson@notreal.net
Abigail Nora	555-0306	anora@daughter.com
Julie Alisa	555-1029	Julie@damonandjulie.com
Barbara Wells	555-0321	bwell@goodfortune.org
Christine Gollery	555-1218	chrisg@bigal.net
Adam Reese	555-0701	adam@adamone.org
Allison Marie	555-1002	allison@goldencurls.com
Bill Guru	555-1234	

Figure 9–4 Address Book table with new INSERT.

The UPDATE Statement

Notice in Figure 9.4 that the value of e-mail address for Bill Guru is blank. This is because the previous INSERT statement did not specify it. If there is already an existing row that needs to be changed the UPDATE statement is used. The basic syntax of the UPDATE statement is:

```
UPDATE <table> SET <column=value, column=value, …> WHERE
<condition>
```

For example, to add Bill Guru's e-mail address, and to correct his phone number, the following UPDATE statement might be used:

```
UPDATE address_book
  SET Phone=555-4321,eMail='bill@notreal.net'
  WHERE Name='Bill guru'
```

In this case, the WHERE clause is targeted to the specific row that is to be changed. It can also specify multiple rows that all would be set with the same value. This might be valuable if a whole range of data needed to change.

The DELETE Statement

The DELETE statement is used to remove a row or multiple rows from the database. The syntax is extremely similar to that of the SELECT statement, as they both are used to choose specific rows of data.

```
DELETE FROM <table> WHERE <condition>
```

Using the Address Book table as an example, if the recently added Bill Guru entry needed to be deleted the SQL statement would look like:

```
DELETE FROM address_book WHERE Name='Bill Guru'
```

Again, just as with the UPDATE command, multiple rows can be selected through the WHERE clause. Also similar to the UPDATE statement, the DELETE statement only works on rows and not on columns.

More on SQL

SQL is a very simple to read programming language, but it is also very powerful. The four statements discussed here are by far the most common, they but only scratch the surface of SQL commands. In addition there are many advanced techniques such as inner joins, outer joins, unions, self joins, cross joins, and subqueries. While the previous examples give a basic understanding of SQL with which to "hit the ground running," to learn more about SQL and it's advanced features read SQL Fundamentals, by John J. Patrick (Prentice Hall/PTR, 1999).

9.3 JDBC

Built on a strong understanding of relational databases and SQL, the syntax and usage of JDBC itself is not that complicated. The JDBC classes themselves are a part of the `java.sql` package, which are a part of most standard Java distributions. Additionally there are optional extensions to JDBC 2.0, which are maintained under the `javax.sql` package.

JDBC itself cannot access databases directly. This is done by an interface that is created specifically for your database, called a JDBC driver. Most popular databases have JDBC drivers available, although same databases only support JDBC 1.0. If a JDBC driver is not available, check to see if an ODBC driver is available. Sun provides a free ODBC driver for JDBC that can communicate to any ODBC compliant database.

To install a driver, first download the Java classes, usually in a Java Archive File (jar). Then the file must be placed in a directory that is included in your CLASSPATH. Be wary, some JSP engines have their own CLASSPATH that needs to be set different than the default system CLASSPATH.

CORE Note: The JDBC 2.0 API

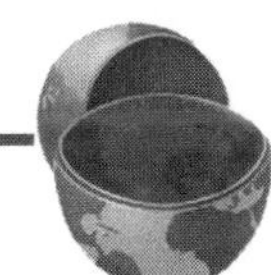

The JDK 1.1 release included the JDBC 1.0 API. With the JDK 1.2 release the JDBC 2.0 API was introduced. The JDBC 2.0 is backward compatible with JDBC 1.0, and shares the package name of `java.sql`. *JDBC 2.0 introduces several new features, including:*

- *The ability to scroll forward or backward in a set of results*
- *The ability to move to a specific row*
- *Sending multiple SQL requests to the database in a batch*
- *Using the new SQL 3 data types in columns*
- *Updating tables using Java methods instead of SQL commands*

Beyond these core enhancements there are optional packages built-in to JDBC 2.0 that may be implemented by the database driver. Two of the most interesting packages are connection pooling and distributed transactions.

The JDK 1.2 and the 2.0 version of a JDBC driver for a specific database must be used to utilize the features of JDBC 2.0. As JDBC 2.0 is relatively new, drivers for a specific database may not be available.

Step 1: Specifying the Driver

The first step in utilizing JDBC is specifying the specific driver needed for a database. This can be done in three different ways. The first way is simplest to code, but the least often used. Within the properties file of your Java runtime environment the JDBC drivers that might be called can be specified with the "`jdbc.drivers`" system property.

A second method is to explicitly load the JDBC driver when needed. This is simply done in a single line of code:

```
Class.forName("sun.jdbc.odbc.JdbcOdbcDriver");
```

This example loads the Sun JDBC/ODBC driver into the Java run-time environment. When the JDBC driver class is loaded it invokes the `registerDriver()` method of the `DriverManager` class, which handles JDBC driver instances. As a side note, this method can throw a `ClassNotFoundException`, so it is prudent to enclose it in a try/catch block.

The third, and most commonly used method of specifying a JDBC driver involves calling the `registerDriver()` function of the `DriverManager` class directly. For example:

```
DriverManager.registerDriver(new oracle.jdbc.driver.Ora-
cleDriver());
```

Here the Oracle JDBC driver is loaded. This is seen as the least efficient method, as the `registerDriver()` function itself is called twice, once by the code itself and once by the driver class as part of it's instantiation.

The next step involves calling the `getConnection()` method of the `DriverManager` class. Whatever method was used to load the driver class, the `DriverManager` will attempt to locate the correct driver from those loaded either during initialization or explicitly.

Step 2: Establishing the Database Connection

Once a database driver is loaded, the second step is to establish a connection to the database. This is done through the `Connection` object. A sample connection might look like:

```
Connection conn =
      DriverManager.getConnection(DB_URL, "Login_Name",
      "Password");
```

Notice that the connection object is created by the `getConnection()` method of the `DriverManager` object. In general `getConnection()` takes three arguments, but this may vary depending on your database and database driver. The first argument is the database URL. In general, the Java standard method of connecting to a data source is through a URL. The database URL usually follows one of the following formats:

```
jdbc:driver_name:database_name
jdbc:driver_name://host/database_name
```

The first section is always `jdbc`. The next section tells JDBC which driver to use. After this section the URL is specific to the individual database driver. Sometimes there is a section describing a specific sub-driver or other information specific to your database. Here are a couple of real examples:

```
jdbc:oracle:thin:@localhost:1521:JSP
jdbc:mysql://localhost/javadesktop?user=dbuser&password=jsp-
book
```

The first example describes a connection to an Oracle database. Oracle's JDBC driver comes in two different flavors, `oci` and `thin`. `thin` specifies a native Java connection, rather than using an OCI interface. Next comes the name of the local machine, the UNIX port the server is listening on, and the database security identifier (SID). The second example is for a connection to a mySQL database. `localhost` again specifies the hostname, and `javadesktop` specifies the database name. In addition the name and password for this connection are specified in this URL, so they are not needed as arguments to the `getConnection()` object.

Now put the database driver specification and the creation of the connection object together:

```
String url  =
"jdbc:oracle:thin:@www.javadesktop.com:1521:JSPBOOK";
String id   = "jsp";
String pass = "book";
Class.forName("oracle.jdbc.driver.OracleDriver");
Connection conn = DriverManager.getConnection(url, id,
pass);
```

Note: all JDBC functions have the ability to throw an `SQLException`. It is a good idea to catch these exceptions or provide an error page that can produce good debugging information.

Step 3: Making a Statement

Now that there is a database driver loaded and a connection to the database, there needs to be a way to send an SQL statement to the database. This is done by creating a `Statement` object that is created with the `createStatement()` method of the `Connection` object. For example:

```
Statement stmt = conn.createStatement();
```

By now the elegant simplicity of JDBC should be apparent. The database driver is loaded into the `DriverManager`. Next a method of the `DriverManager` creates a connection to the database. Then a method of the `Connection` object creates a `Statement` object.

Step 4: Sending the Query

The next step, once a `Statement` object has been created, it to send the SQL to the database. To do this the `Statement` object has two main methods. Knowing which one to use depends on whether or not an SQL query will return any results. The SELECT statement returns a set of data. For SELECT statements there is the `executeQuery()` method. It takes a `String` of SQL that returns data, in the form of a JDBC `ResultSet` object.

The INSERT, UPDATE, and DELETE functions do not return data, and use the `executeUpdate()` method. The `executeUpdate()` method also takes an SQL statement in the form of a `String`, but returns an `int`. This `int` is either zero for SQL statements that return nothing, or the number of rows affected by the INSERT, UPDATE, or DELETE statements. Here is an example of both:

```
String sql  = "SELECT * FROM system_users";
ResultSet rset = stmt.executeQuery(sql);

String sql
= "DELETE FROM address_book WHERE Name='Bill Guru'";
int returnValue = stmt.executeUpdate(sql);
```

Step 5: In Closing

While it isn't always necessary, it is always a good idea to call the close methods of the JDBC objects. This ensures that database connections are closed and resources are freed. JDBC's `Statement` and `Connection` objects each have a `close()` method for just this purpose:

```
stmt.close();
conn.close();
```

The ResultSet Object

The ResultSet object is returned when the SQL statement returns the value of a SELECT statement. It contains the columns and rows of data that were returned. Within the data there is a cursor that can be moved row by row. It begins before the first row, and can be moved forward a single row at a time using the next() method. In JDBC 1.0 the cursor can only be moved forward. With JDBC 2.0 new methods are available to traverse the data set in many different ways.

The next() method returns a boolean value that indicates whether or not there is a current row of data. It should be called at least once, as it is placed before the first row when data is inserted in the ResultSet object.

As each row is traversed, the data in each column is accessible through get methods. There is a get method for several different data types that map to SQL data types. Some examples are getString(), getDate(), and getInt(). Each of these methods takes either an int corresponding to the column number or a String representing the name of the column. Important note: the int value of the column starts at 1, not 0. Additionally the column name String is case-insensitive. Columns with the same name are evaluated left to right. JDBC gets the data from the column and attempts to convert it to the appropriate data type.

Given the next() and get methods each cell of data in a ResultSet table can be cycled through. For example, for a ResultSet of four integer columns each data value can be evaluated with the following while/for construct:

```
int rowNum = 0;
out.print("<PRE>");
ResultSet rset
     = stmt.executeQuery("SELECT * FROM dummy_table");
while(rset.next()) {
  rowNum++;
  out.print("Row number " + rowNum + ";\n");
  for (int colNum=1; colNum <= 4; colNum++) {
    out.print(\tCol " + colNum + " value = " +
    rset.getInt(colNum) + "\n");
  }
}
out.print("</PRE>");
```

The while loop walks through every row, while the for loop walks through every column. Notice that this is a fairly simple interface. While database concepts and knowledge of the SQL language are prerequisites, JDBC itself is not very complicated.

9.4 JDBC and JSP

Now that the basic syntax of a JDBC query is known they can be integrated into JSP pages. For the most part this is pretty straightforward. As HTML and XML are text-based languages, the `getString()` method of the `ResultSet` object is the most heavily utilized. Also, for displaying the data set the HTML table structure naturally comes to mind. Take a look at Listing 9.1. It is a simple search form that finds address book entries in a table called system_users. There is also a second table called state, which serves as a lookup table for state names and their initials.

Listing 9.1 SimpleJDBC.jsp

```
<!DOCTYPE HTML PUBLIC "-//W3C//DTD HTML 4.0 Final//EN">
<%@ page import="java.sql.*" %>

<HTML>
<BODY BGCOLOR="white">
<FORM ACTION="<%=request.getRequestURI() %>"
METHOD="POST">
<INPUT TYPE="text" name="query" size="15" MAXLENGTH="30"
      VALUE="<% if (request.getParameter("query") != null)
               out.print(request.getParameter("query"));
%>" >
<INPUT TYPE="submit" VALUE="Search">
</FORM>
<TABLE BORDER="1" CELLPADDING="3" CELLSPACING="0">
   <TR><TD><B>First Name</B></TD>
       <TD><B>Last Name</B></TD>
       <TD><B>Title</B></TD>
       <TD><B>Phone</B></TD>
       <TD><B>Building</B></TD>
       <TD><B>State</B></TD>
       <TD><B>Start Date</B></TD></TR>
<%
 if (request.getParameter("query") != null) {
     String url  =
"jdbc:oracle:thin:@www.javadesktop.com:1521:JSPBOOK";
     String id   = "jsp";
     String pass = "book";
```

Listing 9.1 SimpleJDBC.jsp

```
      String query
       = request.getParameter("query").toLowerCase();
      String sql
       = "SELECT * FROM system_users,state where " +
                   "(LOWER(first_name) LIKE '%" + query +
                  "%' OR LOWER(last_name) LIKE '%" + query +
                   "%') AND system_users.state_init " +
                   "= state.state_init ORDER BY first_name";

      Class.forName("oracle.jdbc.driver.OracleDriver");
      Connection conn
       = DriverManager.getConnection(url, id, pass);
      Statement stmt = conn.createStatement();
      ResultSet rset = stmt.executeQuery(sql);

      while (rset.next()){
        String phNum
        = "(" + rset.getString("phone").substring(0,3) +
          ")" + rset.getString("phone").substring(3,6) +
          "." + rset.getString("phone").substring(6,10);
      %>
       <TR><TD><%= rset.getString("first_name") %>
       </TD><TD><%= rset.getString("last_name") %>
       </TD><TD><%= rset.getString("title") %>
       </TD><TD><%= phNum %>
       </TD><TD><%= rset.getString("building") %>
       </TD><TD><%= rset.getString("state_name") %>
       </TD><TD><%= rset.getDate("entry_date") %>
       </TD></TR>
      <%
      }
      stmt.close();
      conn.close();
  }
%>
</TABLE>
</BODY>
</HTML>
```

This is a simple JSP page. Notice first that the standard Java JDBC libraries are loaded:

```
<%@ page import="java.sql.*" %>
```

Next is a simple form that takes a single text input field named "query." The form takes the current URI as an action, guaranteeing that this same JSP page will be called even if the location or name of the JSP file changes. The input box takes a value of its own parameter if it is not null (a null value actually prints the word "null" in the text box). This means that once a search is completed the text box will continue to display the last query. Note that this form is shown whether or not a search takes place:

```
<FORM ACTION="<%=request.getRequestURI() %>" METHOD="GET">
<INPUT TYPE="text" name="query" size="15" MAXLENGTH="30"
       VALUE="<% if (request.getParameter("query") != null)
              out.print(request.getParameter("query")); %>" >
<INPUT TYPE="submit" VALUE="Search">
</FORM>
```

This is followed by a fairly simple HTML table declaration, which serves as a header row for search results. Note that this will be displayed whether or not a search takes place.

This is followed by the main processing block. This entire block is enclosed by the following `if` statement:

```
if (request.getParameter("query") != null) {
```

This determines if a parameter of the name "query" was received by the JSP page. The next section sets up some `Strings` that contain the necessary information for making a database connection, as well as the SQL query. `url`, `id`, and `pass` stand for the database URL, login name, and password respectively. `query` is set to the value of the request parameter of the same name, and is made all lowercase.

`sql` is the SQL query. While it appears complex, it is really very simple. It is searching for all column values in two tables: `system_users` and `state`. The first WHERE clause is searching for two things: it is trying to find a match of either the `first_name` column or the `last_name` column against the `query` string. An SQL function called `lower()` is used here to convert the column values to lower case before the comparison. Percent signs are used as wildcard characters and are tacked on to each end of the `query` string. As the `query` string was also made lowercase it is known that the comparison will be case-insensitive. All of this is enclosed in parenthesis to keep it separate from the second WHERE clause.

Next there is an AND, which denotes a second WHERE clause. This clause is asking for rows in the `state` table and the `system_users` table that each have a common field: `state_init`. It is known that each data value in the `system_users state_init` field have a corresponding value in the `state` table `state_init field`, so in effect this WHERE clause joins the two tables. The real-world function here is to make the full name of the state available for display.

To end the statement there is the ORDER BY clause asking for results sorted by the `first_name` field. If this page was hit with a query value of "Damon" the SQL statement would be:

```
SELECT * FROM system_users,state where (LOWER(first_name)
LIKE '%Damon%' OR LOWER(last_name) LIKE '%Damon%') AND
system_users.state_init = state.state_init ORDER BY
first_name
```

Notice that a huge amount of business logic is completed in the SQL statement. This makes the program somewhat modular. An alternate method of completing this logic would be to return the entire table and read the `ResultSet` object into a Java data object that could be repeatedly operated on. Not only would the Java object be hard to navigate, but bringing the entire table across the wire might be extremely slow. By using the above method, the processing time is divided between the remote server and the JSP page, leaving the database search function to the database itself.

Next comes a straightforward set of JDBC methods that load a driver, establish a connection, create a statement, and execute the SQL query. The result of these processes is a JDBC `ResultSet` object.

```
Class.forName("oracle.jdbc.driver.OracleDriver");
Connection conn = DriverManager.getConnection(url, id,
pass);
Statement stmt = conn.createStatement();
ResultSet rset = stmt.executeQuery(sql);
```

This is followed by a while loop that prints the specified columns for each row of the `ResultSet`. Included here is also some data manipulation. The phone `String`, which consists of ten simple digits, is modified to a more recognizable format with parenthesis and a period.

```
     while (rset.next()){
String phNum = "(" + rset.getString("phone").substring(0,3) +
```

```
            ")" + rset.getString("phone").substring(3,6) +
            "." + rset.getString("phone").substring(6,10);
%>
 <TR><TD><%= rset.getString("first_name") %>
 </TD><TD><%= rset.getString("last_name") %>
 </TD><TD><%= rset.getString("title") %>
 </TD><TD><%= phNum %>
 </TD><TD><%= rset.getString("building") %>
 </TD><TD><%= rset.getString("state_name") %>
 </TD><TD><%= rset.getDate("entry_date") %>
 </TD></TR>
<%
}
```

Finally, the `close()` methods of the `Statement` and `Connection` objects are called, the HTML table is closed, as well as the HTML page itself. The output of the page would look similar to Figure 9.5.

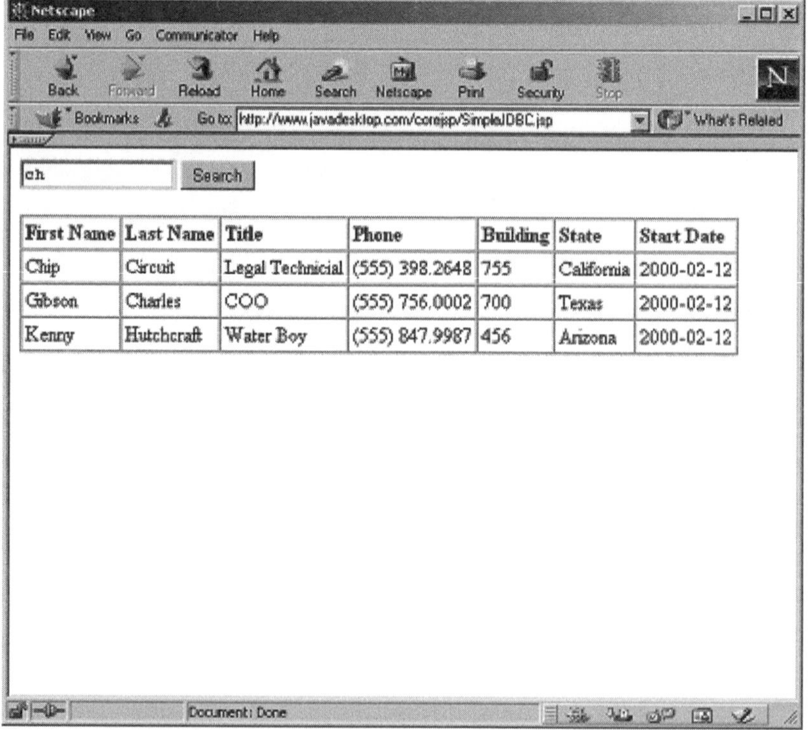

Figure 9–5 SimpleJDBC.jsp

Prepared Statements

While Listing 9.1 is a fairly good example of JDBC use, there are definitely some obvious areas for improvement. First and foremost there is a new `Connection` and `Statement` object created for every single query hit on the page. Additionally the creation of the SQL string seems very chaotic. Fortunately, both JSP pages and JDBC have some features that allow these drawbacks to be overcome, and the above example to be optimized.

The SQL statement in Listing 9.1 is fairly long, and only a very small part of the statement actually changes between each hit on the page. This can be a large resource problem. The database engine must parse the SQL string in a very exacting manner, as it has to convert values in the string format to the native data types used in the database. This has to be done each time the page is hit, as the SQL statement might change each time.

This is actually a common problem with SQL itself, not just with JSP pages. To solve this issue, SQL and relational databases support an extension of the `Statement` object called a `PreparedStatement`. Prepared statements work on the idea that the majority of the SQL query can be sent ahead to the database engine to be parsed and compiled, while the parts of the SQL query that will change can be sent to the server "just in time." Furthermore, the parts of the SQL query that change are also sent in their native data type, allowing the database to insert them directly into the query.

To utilize a prepared statement the `PreparedStatement` interface—a subinterface of the `Statement` object—is used. The formats of the two are very similar, but differ in a few key areas. First, the SQL statement is modified so that question marks are inserted where data values might change. Second, the SQL query is used in the construction of the `PreparedStatement` object itself, instead of within the `executeQuery()` method. Third, there are special set methods that must be used to substitute values in the SQL query before the `executeQuery()` method is called. The names of these methods are very similar to the get methods of the `ResultSet` object, as there is one for each data type that maps into the database. Some common methods are `setString()`, `setInt()`, and `setDate()`. Each of these functions take two arguments: the `int` value designating the order in which to substitute values for question marks, and the data itself. Thus, a sample `PreparedStatement` call might look like:

```
Class.forName("oracle.jdbc.driver.OracleDriver");
conn = DriverManager.getConnection(url, id, pass);
stmt = conn.prepareStatement(sql);
stmt.setString(1, "%Aaron%");
stmt.setString(2, "%Aaron%");
ResultSet rset = stmt.executeQuery();
```

Prepared statements do two things: first, they optimize SQL queries; and second, they give an added abstraction layer to SQL query creation that enables code to be cleaner and easier to read. But alone these do not solve all of the issues with Listing 9.1. By substituting a `PreparedStatement` call instead of a `Statement` call there still exists the problem of making a new `Connection` and `PreparedStatement` for each query hit.

To solve this problem, the power of JSP pages must be called in. Because JSP pages are multithreaded a single database `Connection` and `Prepared-Statement` can be created in the `jspInit()` function and utilized by every hit to the page. Establishing a database connection is generally the most resource-intensive part of a database query. By performing this only once tremendous resource gains can be made. Listing 9.2 rewrites Listing 9.1 utilizing the `jspInit()` and `jspDestroy()` functions, as well as a `Prepared Statement` object.

Listing 9.2 PreparedStatement.jsp

```
<!DOCTYPE HTML PUBLIC "-//W3C//DTD HTML 4.0 Final//EN">
<%@ page import="java.sql.*" %>

<%! Connection conn;
    PreparedStatement stmt;
%>
<%! public void jspInit(){
      try{
       String url  =
      "jdbc:oracle:thin:@www.javadesktop.com:1521:JSPBOOK";
       String id   = "jsp";
       String pass = "book";
       String sql
       = "SELECT * FROM system_users,state where " +
                 "(LOWER(first_name) LIKE ? OR " +
                  "LOWER(last_name) LIKE ?) " +
                  "AND system_users.state_init " +
                  "= state.state_init ORDER BY first_name";

       Class.forName("oracle.jdbc.driver.OracleDriver");
       conn = DriverManager.getConnection(url, id, pass);
       stmt = conn.prepareStatement(sql);
     }catch(SQLException e){}
      catch(ClassNotFoundException e){}
  }
```

Listing 9.2 PreparedStatement.jsp (continued)

```
%>
<%! public void jspDestroy(){
     try{
        stmt.close();
        conn.close();
     }catch(SQLException e){}
  }
%>
<HTML>
<BODY BGCOLOR="white">
<FORM ACTION="<%=request.getRequestURI() %>" METHOD="GET">
<INPUT TYPE="text" name="query" size="15" MAXLENGTH="30"
      VALUE="<% if (request.getParameter("query") != null)
                out.print(request.getParameter("query"));
%>" >
<INPUT TYPE="submit" VALUE="Search">
</FORM>
<TABLE BORDER="1" CELLPADDING="3" CELLSPACING="0">
   <TR><TD><B>First Name</B></TD>
       <TD><B>Last Name</B></TD>
       <TD><B>Title</B></TD>
       <TD><B>Phone</B></TD>
       <TD><B>Building</B></TD>
       <TD><B>State</B></TD>
       <TD><B>Start Date</B></TD></TR>
<%
  if (request.getParameter("query") != null) {
     String query
       = request.getParameter("query").toLowerCase();
       stmt.setString(1, "%" + searchVar + "%");
       stmt.setString(2, "%" + searchVar + "%");
       ResultSet rset = stmt.executeQuery();

     while (rset.next()){
      String phNum
          = "(" +  rset.getString("phone").substring(0,3) +
            ") " + rset.getString("phone").substring(3,6) +
             "." + rset.getString("phone").substring(6,10);
     %>
      <TR><TD><%= rset.getString("first_name") %>
      </TD><TD><%= rset.getString("last_name") %>
      </TD><TD><%= rset.getString("title") %>
      </TD><TD><%= phNum %>
```

Listing 9.2 PreparedStatement.jsp (continued)

```
        </TD><TD><%= rset.getString("building") %>
        </TD><TD><%= rset.getString("state_name") %>
        </TD><TD><%= rset.getDate("entry_date") %>
        </TD></TR>
      <%
      }
  }
%>
</TABLE>
</BODY>
</HTML>
```

First, notice that in a declaration tag two global variables are created:

```
<%! Connection conn;
    PreparedStatement stmt;
%>
```

The `Connection` and `PreparedStatement` objects are used throughout the JSP page body as well as within both `jspInit()` and `jspDestroy()`.

The `jspInit()` method is next. It is extremely similar to the JDBC statements made in Listing 9.1. There are two notable differences. First, the SQL query is much easier to read now that the sections that change have been replaced with question marks. Second, the `sql` string is passed in the creation of the `PreparedStatement` object, unlike the `Statement` object syntax.

```
<%! public void jspInit(){
      try{
        String url  =
        "jdbc:oracle:thin:@www.javadesktop.com:1521:JSPBOOK";
        String id   = "jsp";
        String pass = "book";
    String sql   = "SELECT * FROM system_users,state where " +
          "(LOWER(first_name) LIKE ? OR " +
          "LOWER(last_name) LIKE ?) " +
          "AND system_users.state_init " +
          "= state.state_init ORDER BY first_name";

        Class.forName("oracle.jdbc.driver.OracleDriver");
        conn = DriverManager.getConnection(url, id, pass);
        stmt = conn.prepareStatement(sql);
      }catch(SQLException e){}
```

```
      catch(ClassNotFoundException e){}
  }
%>
```

The `jspDestroy()` method is very simple. It simply closes the `PreparedStatement` and `Connection` objects:

```
<%! public void jspDestroy(){
      try{
         stmt.close();
         conn.close();
      }catch(SQLException e){}
       catch(ClassNotFoundException e){}
  } %>
```

Note that in both `jspInit()` and `jspDestroy()` the exceptions are caught. This is because since they are overriding the standard `jspInit()` and `jspDestroy()` methods the default class constructor signature is required to be kept intact.

Again the main body of the program is reached, and not much has changed. The two `setString()` functions have been added to insert the query string into the SQL statement. As they change the `PreparedStatement` object, which is shared by every thread in the JSP page, they are enclosed in a `synchronized()` block. Additionally, the `executeQuery()` method no longer sends the `sql` string, as it is now belongs to the `PreparedStatement` object.

```
<%
  if (request.getParameter("query") != null) {
     String query = request.getParameter("query")
                    .toLowerCase();

     ResultSet rset = null;
     synchronized(stmt){
       stmt.setString(1, "%" + searchVar + "%");
       stmt.setString(2, "%" + searchVar + "%");
       rset = stmt.executeQuery();
     }

     while (rset.next()){
      String phNum = "(" +  rset.getString("phone")
                      .substring(0,3) +
                      ") " + rset.getString("phone")
                      .substring(3,6) +
                       "." + rset.getString("phone")
                      .substring(6,10);
     %>
      <TR><TD><%= rset.getString("first_name") %>
```

```
            </TD><TD><%= rset.getString("last_name") %>
            </TD><TD><%= rset.getString("title") %>
            </TD><TD><%= phNum %>
            </TD><TD><%= rset.getString("building") %>
            </TD><TD><%= rset.getString("state_name") %>
            </TD><TD><%= rset.getDate("entry_date") %>
            </TD></TR>
          <%
          }
    }
%>
```

By far this is a much better program. It utilizes the multithreading features of JSP pages to create only a single connection to the database. It also utilizes the power of prepared statements to reuse a single compiled database query, without having to create the costly database connection or parse and compile the query string each time the page is hit. The actual speed of the searches increases exponentially. When viewed it will look exactly like Figure 9.1 (but runs noticeably faster).

But for all of its increases in speed and efficiency there is still a potential problem: scalability. There is only one database connection, which can only sustain a certain amount of traffic. If usage grows beyond this amount performance will suffer.

There are actually many different ways of solving this problem. One way is to utilize the features of Enterprise JavaBeans, which commonly deals with these issues. Another idea is to refine the program further, and possibly create a new connection for a certain known number of requests. A third idea is to use a `ConnectionPool` object from JDBC 2.0. It is a very efficient way to deal with database connection overhead, as well as being very scaleable.

Connection Pooling

Connection pooling is a process that allows connection to be recycled instead of destroyed when an application releases it. Reusing connections can increase performance exponentially because establishing a connection is an expensive operation

This technique is relatively new, so not many databases currently support its features. It requires JDBC 2.0 (and therefore Java 1.2 or above) as well as an extension to JDBC 2.0.

The ConnectionPool.jsp example demonstrates how connection pooling mechanism can be used to recycle connections. Here the JSP Page will create a connection pool object in the `jspInit()` method. With each request, the pool will allocate a connection. When the JSP page has completed processing, it will return the connection to the pool.

Listing 9.3 ConnectionPool.jsp

```
<!DOCTYPE HTML PUBLIC "-//W3C//DTD HTML 4.0 Final//EN">
<%@ page
import="java.sql.*, javax.sql.*, oracle.jdbc.pool.*,
javax.naming.*" %>

<%! PooledConnection  pool;

    public void jspInit() {
     try{
       OracleConnectionPoolDataSource ocpds =
               new OracleConnectionPoolDataSource();
ocpds.setURL("jdbc:oracle:thin:@localhost:1521:JSPBOOK");
       ocpds.setUser("jsp");
       ocpds.setPassword("book");
       pool = ocpds.getPooledConnection();
     }catch(SQLException e){}
  }

  public void jspDestroy() {
     try{
       pool.close();
     } catch(SQLException e) {}
  }
%>
<HTML>
<BODY BGCOLOR="white">
<FORM ACTION="<%=request.getRequestURI() %>" METHOD="GET">
<INPUT TYPE="text" name="query" size="15" MAXLENGTH="30"
       VALUE="<% if (request.getParameter("query") != null)
                  out.print(request.getParameter("query"));
%>" >
<INPUT TYPE="submit" VALUE="Search">
</FORM>
<TABLE BORDER="1" CELLPADDING="3" CELLSPACING="0">
   <TR><TD><B>First Name</B></TD>
       <TD><B>Last Name</B></TD>
       <TD><B>Title</B></TD>
```

Listing 9.3 ConnectionPool.jsp (continued)

```
       <TD><B>Phone</B></TD>
       <TD><B>Building</B></TD>
       <TD><B>State</B></TD>
       <TD><B>Start Date</B></TD></TR>
<%
  if (request.getParameter("query") != null) {
       String searchVar = request.getParameter("query")
              .toLowerCase();
       Connection conn = null;
  try{
    String sql
       = "SELECT * FROM system_users,state where " +
         "(lower(first_name) LIKE ? OR lower(last_name) " +
         "LIKE ?) AND system_users.state_init " +
         "= state.state_init ORDER BY first_name";
    conn = pool.getConnection();
    PreparedStatement stmt = conn.prepareStatement(sql);
    stmt.setString(1, "%" + searchVar + "%");
    stmt.setString(2, "%" + searchVar + "%");
    ResultSet rset = stmt.executeQuery();

    while (rset.next()){
      String phNum
      = "(" +  rset.getString("phone").substring(0,3) +
      ") " + rset.getString("phone").substring(3,6) +
      "." +  rset.getString("phone").substring(6,10);
     %>
      <TR><TD><%= rset.getString("first_name") %>
      </TD><TD><%= rset.getString("last_name") %>
      </TD><TD><%= rset.getString("title") %>
      </TD><TD><%= phNum %>
      </TD><TD><%= rset.getString("building") %>
      </TD><TD><%= rset.getString("state_name") %>
      </TD><TD><%= rset.getDate("entry_date") %>
      </TD></TR>
     <%
     }
     stmt.close();
     conn.close();
   } catch(SQLException e){}
     finally {
        if (conn != null) {
```

Listing 9.3 ConnectionPool.jsp (continued)

```
            try{
            conn.close(); }

    catch(SQLException e){}
}
        }
  }
%>
</TABLE>
</BODY>
</HTML>
```

Again, this example has the same functionality as Listing 9.1 and Listing 9.3, but is implemented in a different way. The first thing that is significantly different is the page directive import attributes. Besides the standard `java.sql` package, the `javax.sql`, `oracle.jdbc.pool`, and `javax.naming` packages are all imported. The `javax.sql` package contains the standard extensions to JDBC 2.0, of which connection pooling is a part.

The `javax.naming` package is the Java Naming and Directory Interface (JNDI) API. JNDI was utilized in Chapter 8 in a JavaBean example. The `PooledConnection` object is instantiated with an override of the `Connection-PoolDataSource` interface specific to the database driver that is being used. This object utilizes the JNDI API to create a standard way of referring to a database connection called a DataSource. The package `oracle.jdbc.pool` gives access to Oracle's override of this interface, called `OracleConnection-PoolDataSource`.

Next, the declaration section of the JSP page is also very different. First, only the `PooledConnection` object is in a declaration. Also, the `jspInit()` function is very different. It consists of the creation of a `OracleConnection-PoolDataSource` interface. This object has set methods to pass in the database URL, login name, and password that will be needed by the connection pool to create the database connections. Once these parameters are set the `getPooledConnection()` method of the `OracleConnectionPoolDataSource` interface is called to create the `PooledConnection` object.

```
      OracleConnectionPoolDataSource ocpds =
              new OracleConnectionPoolDataSource();
  ocpds.setURL("jdbc:oracle:thin:@localhost:1521:JSPBOOK");
```

```
ocpds.setUser("jsp");
ocpds.setPassword("book");
pool = ocpds.getPooledConnection();
```

This process might seem complex, but adds a necessary layer of abstraction for using connection pools. Also note that this example uses Oracle's implementation of the JDBC 2.0 API `PooledConnection` extension. Other database implementations will be extremely similar, but have their own object to override the `ConnectionPoolDataSource` interface.

In the main body of the JSP page, the processing is so similar to the last two examples a detailed explanation is not necessary. However, there are a couple of items worthy of note. First, a `PreparedStatement` is used instead of a `Statement` object. While the benefit of reusing a `PreparedStatement` is not available in this example, it is still used because of the layer of abstraction it gives to the code. The `sql` string stays the same, while variables are inserted with the `setString()` object.

Also note the `finally()` clause at the end of the `try` block. This is here to ensure that any connections to the database will be returned in case there is a processing problem. Without calling the `close()` method the `Connection` object remains checked out of the pool.

This example looks just like Figure 9.1, as it has the same functionality as Listing 9.1 and 9.2. It is not as fast as Listing 9.2, but can scale much more efficiently. In the end it is best to choose the solution that best supports the requirements of the application.

9.5 JDBC and JavaBeans

Coding JDBC in JavaBeans has several advantages. JDBC code itself is often very complex. Separating it into a JavaBean adds an abstraction layer and gives the program a better component-centric organization. Additionally, a large number of JDBC JSP programs return HTML tables as an output. A JavaBean that takes a generic SELECT SQL statement and returns an HTML table would be a reusable tool. Listing 9.4 is a JavaBean that takes several Strings as parameters and returns an HTML table based on the `ResultSet`.

Listing 9.4 JDBCBean.java

```
package com.javadesktop.jdbc;

import java.sql.*;
import java.io.*;
import java.util.*;

public class JDBCBean implements Serializable{
      protected transient String tableName, url;
      protected transient String query, columnNames;
      protected transient String resultTable, condn;
      protected transient String userid, password;
      protected transient Connection conn;

      public JDBCBean(){
        tableName = null;
        resultTable = null;
        condn = null;
        columnNames = null;
        resultTable = null;
        query = null;
        conn = null;
        userid = null;
        password = null;
      }

      public void setTableName(String tableName){
        this.tableName = tableName;
      }

      public String getTableName(){
        return tableName;
      }

      public void setURL(String url){
        this.url = url;
      }

      public String getURL(){
        return url;
      }
```

Listing 9.4 JDBCBean.java (continued)

```
public void setCondn(String condn){
  this.condn = null;
  this.condn = condn;
}

public String getCondn(){
  return condn;
}

public void setUserid(String userid){
  this.userid = userid;
}

public String getUserid(){
  return userid;
}

public void setPassword(String password){
  this.password = password;
}

public String getPassword(){
  return password;
}

public void setColumnNames(String columnNames){
  this.columnNames = columnNames;
}

public String getColumnNames(){
  return columnNames;
}

public void setResultTable(String resultTable){
  this.resultTable = resultTable;
}

public String getResultTable(){
  this.readTable();
  return resultTable;
}
```

Listing 9.4 JDBCBean.java (continued)

```
  public void readTable(){
    int i = 0;
    String condition = "";

    if(columnNames == null){
      columnNames = "*";
    }

    if(condn == null){
      condition = "";
    }
    else{
      condition = " WHERE " + condn;
    }

    query = "SELECT ";

   if (columnNames.charAt(0) == '*') {
     query += "* FROM " + tableName;
   } else {
        query += columnNames + " FROM " + tableName;
     }

   if((!condition.equals(""))){
     query += condition;
   }

   executeQuery(query);
  }

  private void executeQuery(String query){

    if(conn == null){
      initialize();
    }

    try{
      Statement stmt = conn.createStatement();
      ResultSet rset = stmt.executeQuery(query);
      ResultSetMetaData rsmd = rset.getMetaData();
      StringBuffer returnBuffer = new StringBuffer();

        int colNum = rsmd.getColumnCount();
```

Listing 9.4 JDBCBean.java (continued)

```
        returnBuffer.append("\n\n<TABLE BORDER=\"1\" " +
      "CELLSPACING=\"0\" CELLPADDING=\"3\">\n\t<TR>\n");

           for (int i=1; i <= colNum; i++){
               returnBuffer.append("\t\t<TD>");
               returnBuffer.append("<B>" +
                 rsmd.getColumnName(i) + "</B></TD>\n");
           }
           returnBuffer.append("\t</TR>\n");

           while (rset.next()){
             returnBuffer.append("\t<TR>\n");
             for (int i=1; i <= colNum; i++)
               returnBuffer.append("\t\t<TD>" +
               rset.getString(i) + "</TD>\n");
               returnBuffer.append("\t</TR>\n");
               }

               returnBuffer.append("</TABLE>");

               resultTable = returnBuffer.toString();

               stmt.close();
                done();

            }catch(SQLExceptionse){se.printStackTrace();}
           }

         private void initialize(){
           try{
      Class.forName("oracle.jdbc.driver.OracleDriver");
  conn =
          DriverManager.getConnection(url, userid,
        Password);
     }catch(SQLException se){se.printStackTrace();}
     catch(ClassNotFoundException cnfe)
             {cnfe.printStackTrace();}
   }
   public void done(){
```

Listing 9.4 JDBCBean.java (continued)

```
            if(conn != null){
              try{
                 conn.close();
            }catch(SQLException se)
              {se.printStackTrace();}
            }
        }
}
```

The structure of JDBCBean.java is very simple. It has several set and get methods to access `protected` values, each of which is a `String`. `url`, `userid`, and `password` are used to create the database connection object. `query` represents the SQL query itself, while `tableName`, `columnNames`, and `condn` are used to construct `query`. `resultTable` is the HTML table in `String` format that is used to display the result of the SQL query. Each of these methods, excluding `resultTable`, follows the standard method of accessing protected JavaBean variables:

```
public void setPassword(String password){
   this.password = password;
}

public String getPassword(){
   return password;
}
```

A `String` is the chosen return type for two reasons. First, eventually HTML or XML will be created, which both are character-based formats. Second, by using all `Strings` it guarantees the `jsp:setProperty` and `jsp:getProperty` tags can be used, without having to reference methods of the JavaBean directly. This adds clarity and abstraction to any JSP page that will call this JavaBean.

In addition to the set and get methods for the protected values, there are four other methods that complete the query itself: `readTable()`, `executeQuery()`, `initialize()`, and `done()`. `ReadTable()` is called by the get method of `resultTable`. `ReadTable()` creates the SQL query and calls `executeQuery()`. `executeQuery()` called `initialize()` to open the database, creates the statement and receives the `ResultSet`, converts the `ResultSet` to an HTML table and then applies it to `resultTable`. `executeQuery()` then calls `done()` which closes the database connection.

For the most part these methods are very similar to the ones used in Listings 9.1, 9.2, and 9.3. There is an added complexity due to the fact that the column names are specified as a `String`. Since `columnNames` is simple placed into the SQL statement `query`, it can take the form of a comma-delimited list. While this is efficient for creating SQL statements, it does not tell the program the names or number of columns that will be in the `ResultSet`. In order for the JavaBean to return a variable number of columns, it would have to know information about the data itself.

MetaData

Listing 9.4, JDBCBean.java, introduces a new object in JDBC: the `ResultSetMetaData` object. Metadata can be thought of as data about data. In other words, `ResultSet` holds the columns and rows, while `ResultSetMetaData` hold information like number of columns and column names. This object is used to gather information about the `ResultSet` object itself. Some of the methods of the `ResultSetMetaData` object can be seen in Table 9.3.

To create a `ResultSetMetaData` object the `getMetaData()` method of the `ResultSet` object is called. In Listing 9.4 the HTML table is created by both a `for` loop, and nesting a `for` loop within a `while` loop. The first `for` loop is for creating the column titles. It is constrained by the number of columns, and prints the name of the current column as it loops through each column number. Both of these methods are supplied by the `ResultSetMetaData` object..

Table 9.3 ResultSetMetaData Methods

Method	***Functionality***
`getColumnCount()`	Returns a int whose value is the number of columns in the ResultSet.
`getColumnName(int)`	Returns the name of column int. NOTE: the numbering starts with 1 not 0.
`getColumnType(int)`	Returns the SQL type of column int. NOTE: the numbering starts with 1 not 0.

Following the column titles comes the table data itself. The `while` loop is constrained by the `next()` method of the `ResultSet`, and the `for` loop is constrained by the number of columns from the `ResultSetMetaData` object. In other words, the `while` loop accounts for each row, as the `for` loop accounts for each column in a row.

```
ResultSet rset = stmt.executeQuery(query);
ResultSetMetaData rsmd = rset.getMetaData();
StringBuffer returnBuffer = new StringBuffer();

            int colNum = rsmd.getColumnCount();

            returnBuffer.append("\n\n<TABLE BORDER=\"1\" " +
          "CELLSPACING=\"0\" CELLPADDING=\"3\">\n\t<TR>\n");

        for (int i=1; i <= colNum; i++){
            returnBuffer.append("\t\t<TD>");
            returnBuffer.append("<B>" +
            rsmd.getColumnName(i) + "</B></TD>\n");
        }
        returnBuffer.append("\t</TR>\n");

        while (rset.next()){
          returnBuffer.append("\t<TR>\n");
          for (int i=1; i <= colNum; i++)
            returnBuffer.append("\t\t<TD>" +
            rset.getString(i) + "</TD>\n");
            returnBuffer.append("\t</TR>\n");
            }

            returnBuffer.append("</TABLE>");

      resultTable = returnBuffer.toString();
```

JDBCBean.java is a very simple example, and does not utilize advanced JDBC features like prepared statements and connection pools. It also is not guaranteed thread-safe, so it should be called with a scope of request. Listing 9.5 is a simple JSP page that utilizes the JDBCBean JavaBean in a very simple way.

Listing 9.5 JDBCBean.jsp

```
<!DOCTYPE HTML PUBLIC "-//W3C//DTD HTML 4.0 Final//EN">

<HTML>
<BODY BGCOLOR="white">

<jsp:useBean class="com.javadesktop.jdbc.JDBCBean"
             scope="page"
       id="example" >
   <jsp:setProperty name="example"
       property="URL"
       value="jdbc:oracle:thin:localhost:1521:JSP" />
   <jsp:setProperty name="example"
                    property="Userid"
           value="jsp" />
   <jsp:setProperty name="example"
                    property="Password"
           value="thePassword" />
   <jsp:setProperty name="example"
                    property="TableName"
           value="system_users" />
   <jsp:setProperty name="example"
                    property="ColumnNames"
           value="*" />
   <jsp:setProperty name="example"
                    property="Condn"
           value="first_name != 'Bill'" />
   <jsp:getProperty name="example"
                    property="ResultTable" />
</jsp:useBean>

</BODY>
</HTML>
```

A `<jsp:useBean>` action encloses the entire JavaBean block. Several `<jsp:setProperty>` actions are used to set the required values: `userid`, `password`, `url`, and `tableName`. Additionally, the optional values of `condn` and `columnNames` are set. A final `<jsp:getProperty>` action is used to execute the search, and return the HTML table.

Notice how clean the JSP page appears. It contains no actual Java code, but rather uses JSP tags to connect presentation logic to program logic. JavaBeans are an excellent way to create JSP programs that have a well-organized, component design.

Insert and Update

Listings 9.1 through 9.5 all gave good examples of using a SELECT SQL statement to retrieve data from a database. Listing 9.6 goes a step further, integrating both UPDATE and INSERT SQL statements with a SELECT statement in a single application. The program utilizes a single database connection and prepared statements for fast response times. It also ties three separate HTML pages into one JSP page. By tying multiple pages to a single JSP page the database connection can be reused as needed.

The first page displayed by Listing 9.5 is a simple search form to find a particular entry in the database to edit. It also gives a "New Entry" button to facilitate adding a new entry to the database. The second page is a more complex form based on the database itself. It lists all fields that the user can edit. The third and final page is a result page that returns whether or not the INSERT or UPDATE was successful.

Listing 9.6 Update.jsp

```
<!DOCTYPE HTML PUBLIC "-//W3C//DTD HTML 4.0 Final//EN">
<%@ page import="java.sql.*" %>

<%! Connection conn;
    PreparedStatement stmtSelect;
    PreparedStatement stmtInsert;
    PreparedStatement stmtUpdate;

  public void jspInit() {
     try{
       String url
= "jdbc:oracle:thin:@localhost:1521:JSPBOOK";
       String id   = "jsp";
       String pass = "theBook";
       String sqlSelect
= "SELECT * FROM system_users WHERE (LOWER(first_name) " +
"LIKE ? OR LOWER(last_name) LIKE ?) ORDER BY first_name";
 String sqlInsert
 = "INSERT INTO system_users (system_id, first_name, " +
 "last_name, title, phone, building, state_init, " +
 "entry_date) VALUES (?, ?, ?, ?, ?, ?, ?, ?)";
 String sqlUpdate
 = "UPDATE system_users SET system_id = ?, first_name = " +
```

Listing 9.6 Update.jsp (continued)

```
"?, last_name = ?, title = ?, phone = ?, building = ?," +
" state_init = ?, entry_date = ? WHERE system_id = ?";

      Class.forName("oracle.jdbc.driver.OracleDriver");
      conn = DriverManager.getConnection(url, id, pass);
      stmtSelect = conn.prepareStatement(sqlSelect);
      stmtInsert = conn.prepareStatement(sqlInsert);
      stmtUpdate = conn.prepareStatement(sqlUpdate);
    }catch(SQLException e){}
    catch(ClassNotFoundException e){}
  }

  public void jspDestroy() {
    try {
       stmtSelect.close();
       stmtInsert.close();
       stmtUpdate.close();
       conn.close();
    } catch(SQLException e) {}
  }
%>
<% if (request.getParameter("action") == null) { %>
  <HTML>
  <HEAD><TITLE>Add/Update Database</TITLE></HEAD>
  <BODY bgcolor="#FFFFFF" TEXT="#000000" LINK="#000066"
  VLINK="#000066" ALINK="#000066">

  <TABLE BORDER=0 WIDTH=100% HEIGHT=90% CELLSPACING=0
     CELLPADDING=0>
   <TR>
    <TD VALIGN="center" ALIGN="center">
     <TABLE BORDER=0 WIDTH=300 CELLSPACING=0 CELLPADDING=0>
      <TR>
       <TD BGCOLOR="#000000">
        <TABLE BORDER=0 WIDTH="100%" CELLSPACING=1
          CELLPADDING=4>
         <TR>
          <TD BGCOLOR="#003399">
         <FONT FACE="MS Sans Serif" COLOR="#FFFFFF" SIZE=2>
          <B>Enter Name</B></FONT>
         </TD>
         </TR>
         <TR>
```

Listing 9.6 Update.jsp (continued)

```
          <TD BGCOLOR="#EEEEEE" ALIGN="center"><BR>
          <FORM METHOD="post"
                ACTION="<%= request.getRequestURI() %>">
            <INPUT TYPE="textbox" NAME="query" VALUE=""
              SIZE=20>
          <INPUT TYPE="hidden" NAME="action" VALUE="form">
            <INPUT TYPE="submit" VALUE=" Search  "><BR>
         </FORM><NOBR>
         <FORM METHOD="post"
                ACTION="<%= request.getRequestURI() %>">
         <INPUT TYPE="hidden" NAME="action" VALUE="form">
            <INPUT TYPE="submit" VALUE="New Entry"><BR>
        </FORM>
          </TD>
         </TR>
        </TABLE>
       </TD>
      </TR>
     </TABLE>
    </TD>
   </TR>
  </TABLE>
  </BODY>
  </HTML>

<% } else if (request.getParameter("action")
.equals("form")) { %>

  <%
   String phone="", first_name="", last_name ="",
entry_date="";
 String title="", building="", state_init="", system_id="";

   if (request.getParameter("query") != null) {

       String searchVar = request.getParameter("query");
                          .toLowerCase();
     try{
       ResultSet rset = null;
       synchronized(stmtSelect){
         stmtSelect.setString(1, "%" + searchVar + "%");
         stmtSelect.setString(2, "%" + searchVar + "%");
         rset = stmtSelect.executeQuery();
```

Listing 9.6 Update.jsp (continued)

```
        }

if (rset.next()) {
  if (rset.getString("phone") != null) phone =
    rset.getString("phone");
  if (rset.getString("first_name") != null) first_name =
    rset.getString("first_name");
  if (rset.getString("last_name") != null) last_name =
    rset.getString("last_name");
  if (rset.getString("title") != null) title =
    rset.getString("title");
  if (rset.getString("building") != null) building =
    rset.getString("building");
  if (rset.getString("state_init") != null) state_init =
    rset.getString("state_init");
  if (rset.getString("system_id") != null) system_id =
    rset.getString("system_id");
  if (rset.getDate("entry_date") != null) entry_date =
    rset.getDate("entry_date").toString();
}
if (rset.next())
out.print("<SCRIPT>alert(\"The search you made has more " +
   "than one result! Use your browser's back button to " +
          "refine search.\");</SCRIPT>");

     } catch(SQLException e){}
   }
  %>
  <HTML>
  <HEAD>
  <TITLE>Database Entry</TITLE>
  </HEAD>
  <BODY BGCOLOR="#FFFFFF">
  <H2>Database Entry:</H2>
  <% if (entry_date != "") out.print("Last Modified: " +
entry_date);   %>
  <FORM METHOD="post"
ACTION="<%= request.getRequestURI() %>">
    <TABLE WIDTH="400" BORDER="0">
      <TR>
        <TD WIDTH="100">
          <DIV ALIGN="right">System ID:</DIV>
        </TD>
        <TD WIDTH="300">
          <INPUT TYPE="text" NAME="system_id"
```

Listing 9.6 Update.jsp (continued)

```
    MAXLENGTH="6" SIZE="6" VALUE="<%= system_id %>">
   </TD>
  </TR>
  <TR>
   <TD WIDTH="100">
     <DIV ALIGN="right">First Name:</DIV>
   </TD>
   <TD WIDTH="300">
     <INPUT TYPE="text" NAME="first_name"
   MAXLENGTH="30" SIZE="30" VALUE="<%= first_name %>">
   </TD>
  </TR>
  <TR>
   <TD WIDTH="100">
     <DIV ALIGN="right">Last Name:</DIV>
   </TD>
   <TD WIDTH="300">
     <INPUT TYPE="text" NAME="last_name"
    MAXLENGTH="30" SIZE="30"
     VALUE="<%= last_name %>">
   </TD>
  </TR>
  <TR>
   <TD WIDTH="100">
     <DIV ALIGN="right">Title:</DIV>
   </TD>
   <TD WIDTH="300">
     <INPUT TYPE="text" NAME="title"
    MAXLENGTH="30" SIZE="30" VALUE="<%= title %>">
   </TD>
  </TR>
  <TR>
   <TD WIDTH="100" HEIGHT="34">
     <DIV ALIGN="right">Phone:</DIV>
   </TD>
   <TD WIDTH="300" HEIGHT="34">
     <INPUT TYPE="text" NAME="phone"
    MAXLENGTH="10" SIZE="10" VALUE="<%= phone %>">
   </TD>
  </TR>
  <TR>
   <TD WIDTH="100">
     <DIV ALIGN="right">Building:</DIV>
   </TD>
   <TD WIDTH="300">
```

Listing 9.6 Update.jsp (continued)

```
          <INPUT TYPE="text" NAME="building"
         MAXLENGTH="3" SIZE="3" VALUE="<%= building %>">
        </TD>
      </TR>
      <TR>
        <TD WIDTH="100">
          <DIV ALIGN="right">State:</DIV>
        </TD>
        <TD WIDTH="300">
          <INPUT TYPE="text" NAME="state_init"
         MAXLENGTH="2" SIZE="2" VALUE="<%= state_init %>">
        </TD>
      </TR>
      <TR>
        <TD WIDTH="100">
          <INPUT TYPE="submit" NAME="Submit"
          VALUE="Submit">
        </TD>
        <TD WIDTH="300">
          <INPUT TYPE="reset" NAME="Reset" VALUE="Reset">
  <% if (system_id != ""){ %>
     <INPUT TYPE="hidden" NAME="action" VALUE="update">
  <% } else { %>
     <INPUT TYPE="hidden" NAME="action" VALUE="insert">
  <% } %>
        </TD>
      </TR>
    </TABLE>
  </FORM>
  </BODY>
  </HTML>
<% } else if (request.getParameter
("action").equals("insert")) { %>

  <%
  try{
      synchronized(stmtInsert){
        stmtInsert.setString(1, request.
        getParameter("system_id"));
        stmtInsert.setString(2, request.
        getParameter("first_name"));
        stmtInsert.setString(3, request.
        getParameter("last_name"));
        stmtInsert.setString(4, request.
        getParameter("title"));
```

Listing 9.6 Update.jsp (continued)

```
        stmtInsert.setString(5, request.
        getParameter("phone"));
        stmtInsert.setString(6, request.
        getParameter("building"));
        stmtInsert.setString(7, request.
        getParameter("state_init"));
        stmtInsert.setDate(8, new java.sql.Date(new
                              java.util.Date().getTime()));
        stmtInsert.executeUpdate();
      }
    out.print("Record Successfully Entered. <BR>" +
          "<A HREF=\"" + request.getRequestURI() +
          "\">Return</A>");
    } catch (SQLException e){
      out.print("Record Entry Failed! <BR>" +
          "<A HREF=\"" + request.getRequestURI() +
          "\">Return</A>");
      out.print("<br>" + e.getMessage());
    }

} else if (request.getParameter("action")
.equals("update")) {

   try{
      synchronized(stmtUpdate){
        stmtUpdate.setString(1, request.
        getParameter("system_id"));
        stmtUpdate.setString(2, request.
        getParameter("first_name"));
        stmtUpdate.setString(3, request.
        getParameter("last_name"));
        stmtUpdate.setString(4, request.
        getParameter("title"));
        stmtUpdate.setString(5, request.
        getParameter("phone"));
        stmtUpdate.setString(6, request.
        getParameter("building"));
        stmtUpdate.setString(7, request.
        getParameter("state_init"));
        stmtUpdate.setDate(8, new java.sql.Date(new
                              java.util.Date().getTime()));
        stmtUpdate.setString(9, request.
        getParameter("system_id"));
        stmtUpdate.executeUpdate();
      }
```

Listing 9.6 Update.jsp (continued)

```
    out.print("Record Successfully Updated. <BR>" +
            "<A HREF=\"" + request.getRequestURI() +
            "\">Return</A>");
    } catch (SQLException e){
      out.print("Record Update Failed! <BR>" +
            "<A HREF=\"" + request.getRequestURI() +
            "\">Return</A>");
      out.print("<br>" + e.getMessage());
    }
  %>
<% } %>
```

The page begins with a declaration of a `Connection` object as well as three `PreparedStatement` objects, one for the SELECT, one for the UPDATE, and one for the INSERT.

```
Connection conn;
PreparedStatement stmtSelect;
PreparedStatement stmtInsert;
PreparedStatement stmtUpdate;
```

The `jspInit()` and `jspDestroy()` methods that follow are almost exactly the same as in the prepared statement example (Listing 9.2), except for the fact that three `PreparedStatements` are initialized. The SELECT statement is similar to the SELECT statements in recent examples, taking two variables that both represent the string to be compared to the first and last name database fields. The INSERT and UPDATE statements each take eight variables that represent the seven fields from the database form, as well as a date of entry/change field. Additionally, the UPDATE statement takes a ninth variable that represents the understood key value of `system_id`.

```
public void jspInit() {
   try{
  String url  = "jdbc:oracle:thin:@localhost:1521:JSPBOOK";
     String id   = "jsp";
     String pass = "thePass";
     String sqlSelect
= "SELECT * FROM system_users WHERE (LOWER(first_name) " +
"LIKE ? OR LOWER(last_name) LIKE ?) ORDER BY first_name";
     String sqlInsert
```

```
    = "INSERT INTO system_users (system_id, first_name, " +
  "last_name, title, phone, building, state_init, " +
  "entry_date) VALUES (?, ?, ?, ?, ?, ?, ?, ?)";
      String sqlUpdate
 = "UPDATE system_users SET system_id = ?, first_name = " +
  "?, last_name = ?, title = ?, phone = ?, building = ?," +
     " state_init = ?, entry_date = ? WHERE system_id = ?";
      Class.forName("oracle.jdbc.driver.OracleDriver");
      conn = DriverManager.getConnection(url, id, pass);
      stmtSelect = conn.prepareStatement(sqlSelect);
      stmtInsert = conn.prepareStatement(sqlInsert);
      stmtUpdate = conn.prepareStatement(sqlUpdate);
    }catch(SQLException e){}
    catch(ClassNotFoundException e){}
 }

  public void jspDestroy() {
    try {
       stmtSelect.close();
       stmtInsert.close();
       stmtUpdate.close();
       conn.close();
    } catch(SQLException e) {}
}
```

The next section describes the main body of the JSP page. It is contained in a single `if` control-flow statement that determines which page to present based on a request parameter called "action." If action has no value it draws the search form page. If action is equal to "form" it displays the entry for adding or editing a database entry. If action is equal to "insert" or "update" it processes the appropriate SQL statement and returns a page that notifies the user whether or not the action was successful. In a condensed version:

```
if (request.getParameter("action") == null) {

  // Display Search Page

} else if (request.getParameter("action").equals("update")) {

  // Display Database Form

} else if (request.getParameter("action").equals("insert"))
```

```
{
  // Run SQL INSERT statement and return result
} else if (request.getParameter("action").equals("update"))
{
  // Run SQL UPDATE statement and return result
}
```

The first section, processed if the request parameter "action" is null, simply displays an HTML page with a form. The only JSP element is the form tag action, which utilized the `request.getRequestURI()` method. This guarantees that the JSP page will work if it is renamed or moved. The whole page is listed here for simplicity. In an actual production environment this would be better served by a `<jsp:include>` action. Not only would this produce a more readable and more component-oriented design, but the `request.getRequestURI()` method would still work as the `include` action simply forwards the page request to the included page. The result of the JSP page would appear similar to Figure 9.6.

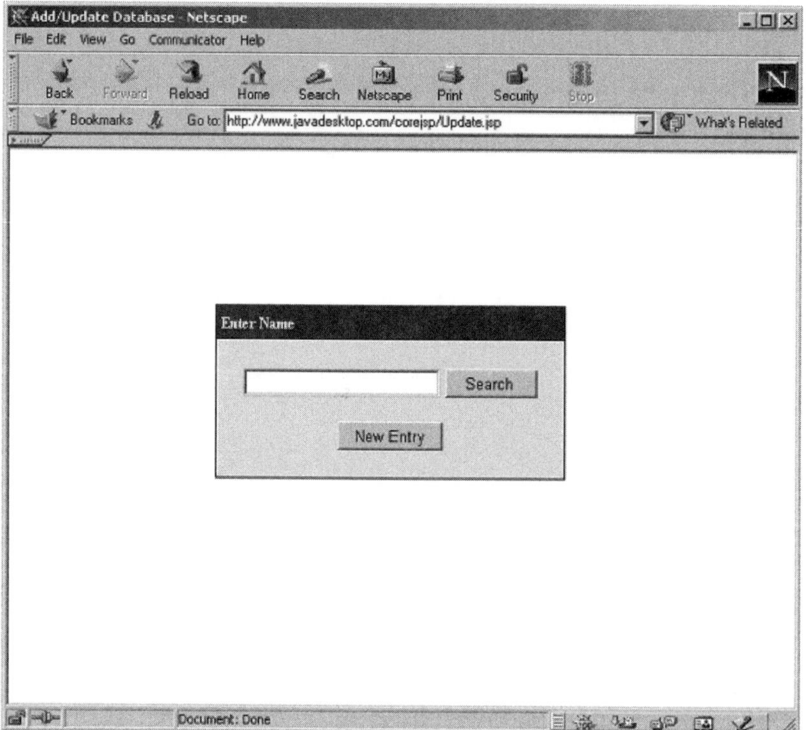

Figure 9–6 Update.jsp View 1

The second page is displayed when the request parameter action is equal to "form." It begins by creating a `String` for each value that exists in the database. Each of these `Strings` is initialized to an empty value.

```
String phone="", first_name="", last_name ="", entry_date="";

String title="", building="", state_init="", system_id="";
```

Next there is an `if` control-flow statement that determines whether or not there was a request parameter named query. If there was this indicates that the "Search" button was entered, and the database should be searched for a record. If the value of the request parameter query is null the "New Entry" button was pressed, and the database should not be searched.

With a query value the SELECT prepared statement is used to return a `ResultSet`. There is no `while` loop for the `ResultSet` as only one entry is desired. Instead an `if` statement is used, as processing does not need to occur unless there is at least one row found. Inside the `if` statement is a series of `if` statements that determine if the database fields are null or if they contain data. This is important because a null value and an empty string in Java are two different things. With a null value the form field would actually print the word "null." If a field is empty it is desired to have an empty `String`. If they are not null the string corresponding to the database field is filled with the database value.

```
if (request.getParameter("query") != null) {

    String searchVar = request.getParameter("query");
                         .toLowerCase();
  try{
    ResultSet rset = null;
    synchronized(stmtSelect){
      stmtSelect.setString(1, "%" + searchVar + "%");
      stmtSelect.setString(2, "%" + searchVar + "%");
      rset = stmtSelect.executeQuery();
    }

    if (rset.next()) {
      if (rset.getString("phone") != null)
                  phone = rset.getString("phone");
      if (rset.getString("first_name") != null)
      first_name = rset.getString("first_name");
      if (rset.getString("last_name") != null)
      last_name = rset.getString("last_name");
      if (rset.getString("title") != null) title
```

```
  = rset.getString("title");

         if (rset.getString("building") != null)
building = rset.getString("building");

         if (rset.getString("state_init") != null)
state_init = rset.getString("state_init");

         if (rset.getString("system_id") != null)
system_id = rset.getString("system_id");

         if (rset.getDate("entry_date") != null)
entry_date = rset.getDate("entry_date").toString();

       }
if (rset.next())
out.print("<SCRIPT>alert(\"The search you made has more " +
   "than one result! You can use your browser's back " +
   "button to refine your search, or accept the first " +
           "entry\");</SCRIPT>");

     } catch(SQLException e){}
  }
```

At the end of the `if` statement is another `if` statement that checks to see if there is a second value in the `ResultSet`. If this is true, a short JavaScript function is printed to the page. This would cause a popup window to be displayed warning the user that there was more than one record found. Another way of handling this problem would be to display another intermediate list of records found from which the user could select one. The output of the second view would look like Figure 9.7.

The last two sections are almost identical, with two distinctions: the `PreparedStatement` object used, and an additional `setString()` method that inserts the value of the system_id field. First the set methods are called for the variable values. For the date field a `java.sql.Date` object is constructed by calling the `getTime()` function of the `java.util.Date` object. Then the executeUpdate() method is called. If there is no exception thrown, the page returns a successful response, else the `catch` statement returns an unsuccessful one.

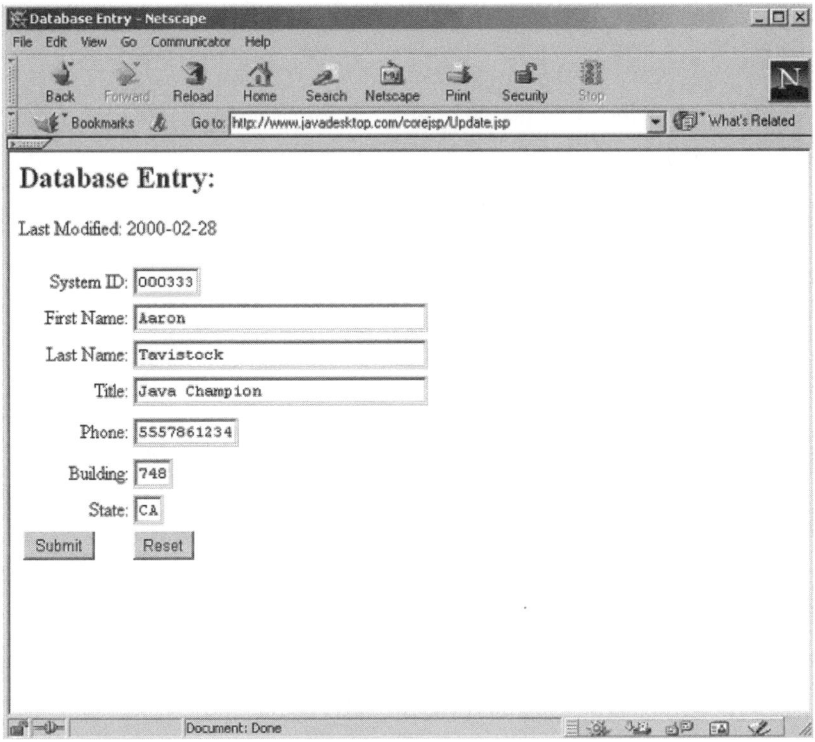

Figure 9-7 Update.jsp View 2

```
try{
   synchronized(stmtUpdate){
     stmtUpdate.setString(1, request
     .getParameter("system_id"));
     stmtUpdate.setString(2, request
     .getParameter("first_name"));
     stmtUpdate.setString(3, request
     .getParameter("last_name"));
     stmtUpdate.setString(4, request
     .getParameter("title"));
     stmtUpdate.setString(5, request
     .getParameter("phone"));
     stmtUpdate.setString(6, request
     .getParameter("building"));
     stmtUpdate.setString(7, request
     .getParameter("state_init"));
     stmtUpdate.setDate(8, new java.sql.Date(new
```

```
java.util.Date().getTime()));
        stmtUpdate.setString(9, request
        .getParameter("system_id"));
        stmtUpdate.executeUpdate();
      }
    out.print("Record Successfully Updated. <BR>" +
            "<A HREF=\"" + request.getRequestURI() +
            "\">Return</A>");
    } catch (SQLException e){
      out.print("Record Update Failed! <BR>" +
            "<A HREF=\"" + request.getRequestURI() +
            "\">Return</A>");
      out.print("<br>" + e.getMessage());
    }
```

On a successful update the JSP page appears like Figure 9.8.

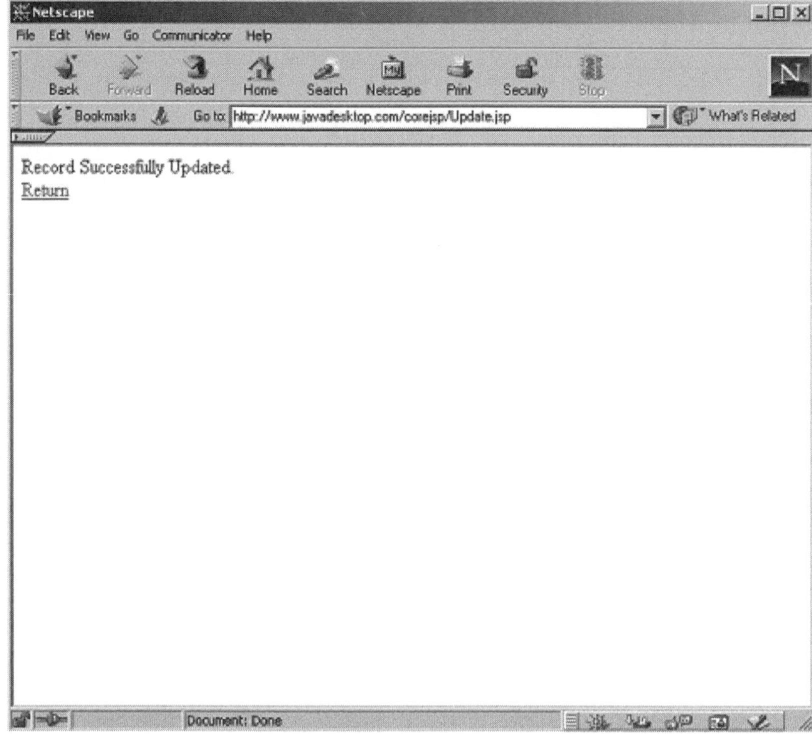

Figure 9-8 Update.jsp View 3

JDBC remains the standard for connecting Java programs to relational databases. With the release of the JDBC 2.0 API the core set of methods have been expanded to provide better speed and functionality. As JSP provides a better separation of presentation data and business logic, it seems consistent to utilize JDBC to separate data from other program elements. These few examples give a good overview of man common features of JDBC, but they only scratch the surface of its capabilities. For an in-depth look at the JDBC API get the JDBC Developer's Resource (2nd Edition) by Art Taylor (Prentice Hall/PTR, 1999).

JSP AND XML

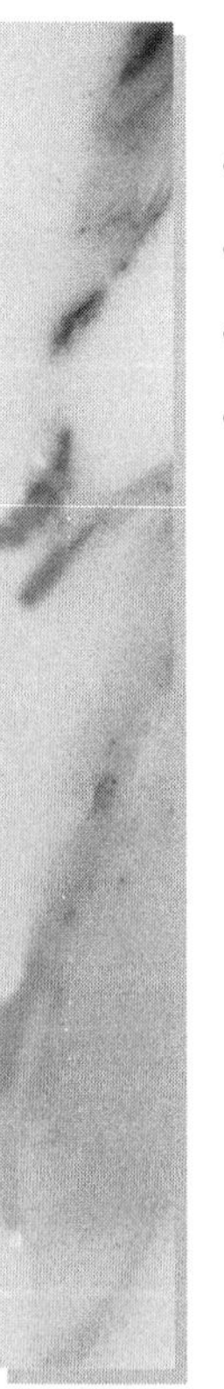

Topics in this Chapter:

- XML Overview
- JSP as XML Documents
- Transforming XML with XSLT
- Fetching Database Data as XML

Chapter 10

Just what is this phenomenon sweeping the software development industry called XML? How can it help in designing enterprise applications? What is its relationship to Java? These questions can be answered in one simple phrase: Java is cross-platform code, and XML is cross-platform data. While XML is much more than this, it cuts to the chase and describes XML's inherent value.

XML is less like a markup language, and more like a meta-language for defining markup languages. Beyond that, XML itself can be used to define XML applications, such as XSL and XSLT. In fact, the power of XML goes well beyond the realm of Web-based applications. It has the potential to one day become the de facto standard format for data transfer.

More important for this book, JSP and XML have a unique relationship. JSP pages can be written as valid XML documents. This means that JSP pages can be thought of as an XML application. In addition, JSP pages are not just tuned to producing HTML pages, but XML pages as well. Add to this mix the fact that Java has a large set of XML libraries and tool available, and the inherent value XML has to add to JSP page programming is obvious.

10.1 XML 101

XML stands for Extensible Markup Language, a markup language similar to HTML. Unlike HTML, which was designed to describe presentation, XML was designed to describe data. The "Extensible" part of XML means that tags are not predefined in XML. Tags must be defined for each XML page. In other words, XML is self-describing. XML is both a language to store data, as well as a language to describe languages. XML uses a DTD (Document Type Definition) to formally describe the data.

XML is different from HTML in many ways. Each was created to solve different problems. A common misconception is that XML is a replacement for HTML. XML was designed to describe data and to store data. HTML was designed to display data and to focus on how the data should look. In other words, XML is about describing information, while HTML is about *displaying* information.

One of the greatest drawbacks of HTML is that all of the HTML tags are predefined. This means that HTML authors are only able to use tags that are defined in the HTML standard. XML allows authors to define their own tags and their own document structure.

In many ways XML can be seen as a compliment to HTML. XML can be used to structure and describe Web data, while HTML can be used to format and display the same data.

It must also be realized that utilizing XML for the Web is just the tip of the iceberg. Software has to utilize common formats to transfer data between different components, programs, or systems. This format can be thought of as a language. The problem arises that each side of these data transfers must understand the specific data format used in order for the transfer to be successful. The power of XML allows this problem to be solved. The definition of the language (a DTD) is portable and understandable. As long as each side of the data transfer understands XML, any XML language desired can be used.

XML Structure

At first glance XML seems very similar to HTML. While this is true, XML is much stricter in the format of tags and data. An example XML file might look like:

```
<?xml version="1.0"?>
<!DOCTYPE book SYSTEM "http://www.javadesktop.com/
cbook.dtd">
```

```
<book>
<title>CORE JSP Programming</title>
<chapter>Introduction</chapter>
<heading>The history of the web application</heading>
<body>JSP is apart of the evolution of the web application</
body>
</book>
```

The first line in the document is known as the XML declaration—required to be the first line in the page, and it can have no white space preceding it. It defines the XML version of the document. In this case the document conforms to the 1.0 specification of XML:

```
<?xml version="1.0"?>
```

The next line is called the document type declaration, abbreviated DOCTYPE. It is important to note that this is different from a document type definition (abbreviated DTD). The HTML examples in this book all have a DOCTYPE listed:

```
<!DOCTYPE HTML PUBLIC "-//W3C//DTD HTML 4.0
Final//EN">
```

The format of the DOCTYPE is fairly simple. It contains the DOCTYPE keyword, the name of the root element (case-sensitive), and the document's DTD. The XML DOCTYPE either contains or points to markup declarations that provide a grammar for a class of documents. This grammar is known as a document type definition, or DTD.

While this sounds complex, it is actually a simple idea. A grammar or DTD can be thought of as instructions or rules on how to format a document. In the real world everyone knows how to format a letter. A letter is a grammar. If one wrote down the rules of how to write a letter, such as "The body begins with the word Dear followed by the recipient's name and a comma" this would be a part of the "letter" DTD.

The DOCTYPE can point to an external location containing markup declarations, contain the markup declarations directly, or can do both. The DTD for a document consists of both taken together.

Both the HTML DOCTYPE, as well as the DOCTYPE in the XML example, contain pointers to external locations. There are two types of these pointers, SYSTEM and PUBLIC. PUBLIC identifiers have a special URI format, as they point to accepted XML DTDs. The SYSTEM identifier points to a URL that contains a DTD file. In the XML example, the SYSTEM identifier "cbook.dtd" gives the URI of a DTD for the document.

The format of a DTD fragment or DTD file is outside of the scope of this book, but understanding their value is important. DTDs provide a formal declaration of the elements, attributes, and entities allowed in a document of a specified type. An important concept here is validity. A document is considered valid if it both declares that it conforms to a specific DTD, as well as actually conforming to the DTD. A DOCTYPE declaration is actually optional. If left out, the XML document is not *invalid*, but rather *not valid*.

Most XML parsers offer the ability to validate XML documents based on their given DTD specification. This is a major step forward compared to HTML, where it is common to deviate from the specification, especially among different browsers.

Moving on, the next line defines the first element of the document, known as the root element. If a DOCTYPE is listed, this element must match the one listed in the DOCTYPE declaration.

```
<book>
```

The next lines defines four child elements of the root (title, chapter, heading, and body):

```
<title>CORE JSP Programming</title>
<chapter>Introduction</chapter>
<heading>The history of the web application</heading>
<body>JSP is apart of the evolution of the web application</
body>
```

The last line defines the end of the root element. All XML documents must contain a single tag pair to define the root element:

```
</book>
```

All XML elements must have a closing tag. This is different from HTML where some elements do not have to have a closing tag. The following code is legal in HTML:

```
<li>This is a list item
<li>This is another list item
```

In XML all elements must have closing tags:

```
<li>This is a list item</li>
<li>This is another paragraph</li>
```

Another caveat to XML is that all tags are case-sensitive. The tag `<Book>` is different from the tag `<book>`. Opening and closing tags must therefore be written with the same case. The following example would be invalid:

```
<Chapter>Chapter 1: Introduction</chapter>
```

Additionally, all XML elements must be properly nested. In HTML some elements can be improperly nested within each other like this:

```
<b><i>This text is bold and italic</b></i>
```

This would cause an XML document to be invalid! The proper XML format would be:

```
<b><i>This text is bold and italic</i></b>
```

XML elements, just like HTML elements, can have attributes. In XML attribute values must always be quoted:

```
<book name=COREJSP> <!-- Invalid! -->
<book name="COREJSP"> <!-- Valid. -->
```

In general, it is a good idea to avoid using attributes. Attributes are handy in HTML, but in XML attributes can easily be substituted by elements. The following example contains exactly the same information as the one above, but with the name stored in a `<name>` element:

```
<book><name>COREJSP</name>
```

Problems with attributes include the inability to contain multiple values, as well as the fact that attributes are not expandable.

CDATA and PCDATA

All XML documents consist of characters, which are generally referred to as character data, or CDATA. There are actually two flavors of CDATA, data that should be parsed and data that shouldn't be parsed. Within XML data that is to be parsed is referred to as PCDATA, and data that should not be parsed is simply referred to as CDATA. Escaping characters in XML is complicated, so by defining text as CDATA it removes them from the parser and the need for escaping.

In general it is safe to consider all data in an XML document as PCDATA, except for any sequence designated as CDATA within a CDATA declaration. A CDATA declaration begins with `<![CDATA[` and ends with `]>`. For example:

```
<book>
<![CDATA[
I am text that is not parsed; I am surrounded by a CDATA
declaration
]>
</book>
```

While this might be uncommon in the majority of XML pages, it is very common in automatically generated XML pages where it is not known whether or not included data will need to be escaped. This is especially true in JSP pages that are written as XML.

All in all, the XML document format is extremely similar to that of HTML, but has much stricter rules for data organization. In fact, many believe that in the future HTML will be evolving into a new standard called XHTML, which is the merge of the HTML format into XML. In any case, while there are some specific caveats to XML formatting, it will in no way seem unfamiliar to the HTML coder.

10.2 JSP as XML Documents

As mentioned in Chapters 2 and 3, JSP pages have two different formats: the JSP syntax and the XML standard syntax. While both can be used to describe the same JSP page, each has its own inherent advantages and disadvantages.

The authors of the JSP specification felt that the hand-authoring friendliness of JSP pages is very important for its initial adoption. They also believed that tool manipulation of JSP pages would play a strong role in the future. To support tool manipulation the authors of the specification chose XML, due to growing collection of tools and APIs that support XML.

In fact, search through the directories of your favorite JSP 1.1-compliant engine. There is a good chance there will be files named `*.xml` that contain JSP pages converted to the complementary XML format.

The JSP Format to XML Format Transformation

Converting a JavaServer Page in JSP format to a JavaServer page in XML format is fairly straightforward. It involves certain known processing steps. Take a look at Listing 10.1. It is a very simple JSP page that utilizes a directive, declaration, scriptlet, and expression.

To convert this example to an XML formatted JSP page begins with adding the XML declaration. After this portion would normally come the DOCTYPE. The JSP specification does not require a DOCTYPE. Next comes the JSP root element. Having a single root element might seem counter intuitive, as JSP pages are organized as a sequence of template text and JSP elements.

However, a root element is required. The JSP 1.1 Specification defines a standard root element that is utilized at the top of any XML format JSP page. Thus the top two entries would look like this:

```
<?xml version="1.0" ?>
```

```
<jsp:root xmlns:jsp="http://java.sun.com/products/jsp/dtd/
jsp_1_0.dtd" name="example">
```

Listing 10.1 Example.jsp

```
<!DOCTYPE HTML PUBLIC "-//W3C//DTD HTML 4.0 Final//EN">
<%@ page session="true" %>

<%! public java.util.Date PrintDate() {
       return(new java.util.Date());
    }

    int counter;
%>

<HTML>
<HEAD>
<TITLE>Current Date</TITLE>
</HEAD>
<BODY>

The current date is:
<%= PrintDate() %>
<br>
This page has been accessed
<% counter++;
   out.print(counter);
 %>
times since last restarted.

</BODY>
</HTML>
```

Here the root element has two parameters. One is a `name` parameter, which matches the name of the JSP file. The second parameter is `xmlns:jsp`. This defines the XML namespace.

XML namespaces are somewhat complex to understand. In fact, namespaces are separated from the XML 1.0 recommendation into their own. The important thing to know is that namespaces exist so that element and attribute names are not duplicated. Colons are used in XML to delineate namespaces, and here the colon signifies that the top level of the JSP namespace is `jsp`. Thus, this tag is named `jsp:root` to signify that the name `root` resides under the `jsp` namespace. In the case where there is a `taglib` directive used in the JSP page the root element would be further changed to include the namespace of the new tag library.

After the XML declaration and root element comes the rest of the JSP page. For the most part, the conversion consists of converting expressions, scriptlets, directives, and declarations to their XML format. Table 10.1 lists the JSP and XML formats of these tags.

Table 10.1 JSP and XML formats

JSP Format	***XML Format***
`<%@ page ... %>`	`<jsp:directive.page ... />`
`<%@ taglib ... %>`	`jsp:root element is annotated with namespace information.`
`<%@ include ... %>`	`<jsp:directive.include .../>`
`<%! ... %>`	`<jsp:declaration> .... </jsp:declaration>`
`<% ... %>`	`<jsp:scriplet> .... </jsp:scriplet>`
`<%= .... %>`	`<jsp:expression> .... </jsp:expression>`

Actions are already in the XML format. Everything within the XML tags, as well as all template data, is then enclosed in CDATA element tags. Additionally, there might be a few quoting changes necessary, as the quoting rules of XML are more formal that that of JSP. To close things out the `root` tag is closed at the end of the file. Listing 10.2 is a rewrite of Listing 10.1 in XML format.

Listing 10.2 Example.jsp XML Version

```
<?xml version="1.0" ?>
<jsp:root xmlns:jsp="http://java.sun.com/products/jsp/dtd/
jsp_1_0.dtd" name="example">
<![CDATA[ <!DOCTYPE HTML PUBLIC \"-//W3C//DTD HTML 4.0
Final//EN\">]]>
<jsp:directive.page session="true" />
<jsp:declaration>
  <![CDATA[
      public java.util.Date PrintDate() {
            return(new java.util.Date());
      }
      int counter;
  ]]>
</jsp:declaration>

<![CDATA[
<HTML>
<HEAD>
<TITLE>Current Date</TITLE>
</HEAD>
<BODY>
The current date is:
]]>

<jsp:expression>
  <![CDATA[ PrintDate()]]>
</jsp:expression>

<![CDATA[
<br>
This page has been accessed
]]>

<jsp:scriptlet>
  <![CDATA[
    counter++;
    out.print(counter);
  ]]>
</jsp:scriptlet>

<![CDATA[
```

Listing 10.2 Example.jsp XML Version (continued)

```
times since last restarted.
</BODY>
</HTML>
]]>
</jsp:root>
```

There are some times where there is not a good mapping from JSP pages to XML. The best example of this is the use of request-time parameters as the attribute of another tag. For example:

```
<% String footer = request.getParameter("footer"); %>
<jsp:include page="<%= footer %>" />
```

In XML there is no valid way of inserting a subelement into an attribute. In this case, the less-than and greater-than characters are removed so they can be properly parsed, and the JSP engine is programmed in such a way that it will look for JSP tags within the parameters of elements:

```
<jsp:scriptlet>
<![CDATA[String footer = request.getParameter("footer"); ]]>
</jsp:scriptlet>
<jsp:include  page="%= footer %" />
```

Not a great solution, but necessary to include the needed functionality.

All in all, the XML format of JSP pages makes the manipulation of XML pages easy to implement with a wide variety of XML tools. Unfortunately, it does not add any real value to the JSP programmer. However, it is a good example of the close relationship JSP and XML have.

To really see the value of XML to JSP pages, XML has to be made available to the end user. XML itself does not have any presentation logic. It is for describing and storing data. Fortunately, there are a large number of cooperative technologies that surround XML to provide this functionality. The most commonly used is called XSL, which stands for Extensible Style Language.

10.3 XSL 101: XSL, XSLT, and XPath

The Extensible Style Language (XSL) is really two different languages. One is a transformation language and the other is a formatting language. Both of these are actually applications written in XML. The transformation language is called XSLT, and it provides rules of how one language can be transformed into another. The new document may use the markup and DTD of the original XML document or it may use a completely different set of tags. In particular, it may use the tags defined by the second part of XSL, the formatting objects. XSLT is completely independent of the XSL formatting language, and can function on its own. XSLT became a formal specification in November of 1999, although there have been many different implementations that have supported earlier working drafts.

The formatting language itself, called simply XSL, is still in a working draft state. It is similar to Cascading Style Sheets (CSS). An easy way to think of XSL is as a vocabulary for formatting documents.

While both languages can be utilized for transforming XML documents to HTML documents, XSLT is emphasized here. Not only because of it is a standard, but because XSLT is powerful. It not only has control over how elements are displayed, but what gets displayed and in what order.

Beyond XSL and XSLT there is a third specification that is important to understand when transforming XML documents into HTML. It is called XPath. XPath is a language for addressing parts of an XML document. It is designed to be used by XSLT, as well as other technologies.

The primary purpose of XPath is to address parts of an XML document. Beyond its primary purpose, it also provides basic facilities for manipulation of strings, numbers, and Booleans. XPath uses a compact, non-XML syntax to facilitate its use within URIs and XML attribute values.

In addition to its use for addressing, XPath is also designed so that it has a natural subset that can be used for matching; in other words, testing whether or not a node matches a pattern. For example, a common use of Xpath in an XSLT transformation is the use of "/", which is the XPath symbol notation for the root element.

Learning XSLT

To have a complete understanding of XSLT is outside of the scope of this book. It is a very robust programming language. The goal here is to give a basic understanding of the language, and how it can be useful in transforming XML files into HTML.

During an XSL transformation, a program called an XSL processor reads both an XML document and an XSL style sheet. The XSL processor then outputs a new document based on the instructions the processor finds in the XSL style sheet.

The following is a very simple XSLT style sheet:

```
<?xml version="1.0"?>
<xsl:stylesheet version="1.0"
          xmlns:xsl="http://www.w3.org/1999/XSL/Transform">
 <xsl:template match="book">
   <html>
     <xsl:apply-templates/>
   </html>
 </xsl:template>
</xsl:stylesheet>
```

Again note that XSLT is an XML application. The XML declaration and root element are very similar to the format of a JSP document. There are actually two different root elements than can be used in XSLT: `xsl:transform` and `xsl:stylesheet`. They are interchangeable, both taking the same set of attributes.

After the root element comes a `xsl:template` tag. This tag specifies matching criteria for XML elements, as well as the text to replace the element with. In this example the `book` element is identified with the match attribute of the `xsl:template` tag. Within the body of the `xsl:template` tag the text to replace both the open and close `book` tag is listed, separated with the `xsl:apply-templates` tag.

Note that what replaces each tag does not have to be uniform. It can be anything. It simply must be placed between the `xsl:template` and `xsl:apply-templates` tags. Also, the replacement for the open tag and the close tag do not have to be the same or correlate.

While there are many other XSLT tags, this example gives a good example of how XSL is formed. Combined with XML and JSP pages XML can represent the data, XSL can represent the presentation logic, and JSP can represent the business logic. This adds an abstraction layer and gives the overall program a more component-base design.

XML Parsers and XSLT Processors

To use XML and XSLT in JSP pages there must be an XML parser and an XSLT processor. Fortunately there are many different offerings of both. Deciding on which packages to use should be determined by your programming needs, as well as the specific features offered by each package.

For Java XML parsers there are three that seem to be extremely popular: Sun's JAXP (Java API for XML Parsing), which was formerly known as Project X; the Apache Group's Xerces Java Parser, which is the basis for IBM's next generation XML4J parser; and Oracle's XML Parser. All three are available for free and can be redistributed. Table 10.2 gives an overview of each of these XML parsers.

Table 10.2 Java XML Parsers

Xerces Java Parser: *http://xml.apache.org/xerces-j/index.html*

Xerces (named after the Xerces Blue butterfly) provides XML parsing and generation. The parser has full-validation parsers capabilities, implementing the W3C XML and DOM (Level 1 and 2) standards, as well as the de facto SAX (version 2) standard. The Apache Group's goal was to make the parsers highly modular and configurable. Initial support for XML Schema (draft W3C standard) is also provided.

JAXP - Java API for XML Parsing: *http://java.sun.com/xml/*

The JAVA API for XML Parsing (JAXP) is an optional Java package that provides basic functionality for reading, manipulating, and generating XML documents. It is a thin and lightweight API that provides a standard to integrate any XML-compliant parser with a Java application. This means that programmers can swap between XML parsers without making application code changes. Included in the distribution is the Java Project X XML parser, although any XML conformant parser can be used. JAXP offers 100% conformance to the XML 1.0 Specification, SAX 1.0, DOM Level 1 Core, and XML namespaces.

Oracle XML Parser for Java: *http://technet.oracle.com/tech/xml/parser_java2/*

The Oracle XML Parser for Java is a standalone XML component that parses an XML document or a standalone DTD so that it can be processed by a Java application. It supports the DOM (Document Object Model) Level 1.0 and SAX (Simple API for XML) 1.0 APIs, as well as XML namespaces. It also has an integrated XSLT 1.0 processor.

There are also several XSLT processors on the market. Each has it's own abilities and functionality, but for the following examples the Apache Group's Xalan will be used. Xalan (named after a rare musical instrument) fully implements the XSL Transformations (XSLT) Version 1.0 and the XML Path Language (XPath) Version 1.0. Xalan can interface to Xerces, which is also used in the following examples. Xalan can also interface with any XML parser that supports the Document Object Model (DOM).

The real advantage Xalan offers is its integration with the Document Table Model (DTM). Parsing XML data often has high overhead. Many of the features of parsing XML are not utilized by XSLT, and therefore processing them is wasted cycles. Xalan uses a method called the DTM, which uses integer arrays in place of a larger data model. For larger input and output XML files, the performance improvements can be very significant.

10.4 Combining XML and XSLT

Now that XML and XSLT are understood, a simple example can be made that combines the two to output HTML. Before hitting the JSP page, an XML file and XSLT file must be identified. Listing 10.3 is a simple XML example that has no DTD. The XML file describes data about a book. The root element is `<book>` . It contains various tags, such as `<title>`, `<section>`, `<para>`, and `<note>`.

Listing 10.3 Book.xml

```
<?xml version="1.0" ?>
<book>
  <title>CORE JSP Programming</title>
  <chapter>
     <title>Chapter One: Introduction</title>
     <section>
        <title>A History of the Web</title>
        <para>JavaServer Pages (JSP) is an exciting new
      technology that provides powerful and efficient
      creation of dynamic content.  JSP is a
      presentation layer technology that allows
      static web content to be mixed with Java code.
      JSP allows the use of standard HTML, but adds
      the power and flexibility of the Java programming
      lan-guage.</para>
```

Listing 10.3 Book.xml (continued)

```
        <note>This is is just a small piece of section
        one.</note>
      </section>
      <section>
        <title>JavaServer Pages</title>
        <para>JSP is an <emph>extremely</emph> powerful
        choice
      for web development.  JSP is a technology using
      server side scripting that is actually translated
      into Servlets and compiled be-fore they are run.
      This gives developers a scripting interface to
      create powerful Java Servlets.</para>
        <note>Remember to insert images.</note>
      </section>
    </chapter>
</book>
```

To accompany the XML file, Listing 10.4 lists an XSLT file that is specifically created for `book.xml`. Besides using the `xsl:template` tags seen in the above XSL examples, it uses two new tags. The `xsl:strip-space` tag takes an `element` attribute that lists elements from the XML page. Each of these elements is then stripped of any unnecessary whitespace characters. The `xsl:output` tag has several attributes that define the output XML page (in this case HTML). In Listing 10.4, `xsl:output` is used to set the output type to XML, the encoding to iso-8859-1, and turns on formatting tags with indenting.

Listing 10.4 Book.xsl

```
<xsl:stylesheet version="1.0"
 xmlns:xsl="http://www.w3.org/1999/XSL/Transform">

<xsl:strip-space elements="book chapter section"/>
<xsl:output
   method="xml"
   indent="yes"
   encoding="iso-8859-1"
/>
 <xsl:template match="book">
 <html>
   <head>
```

Listing 10.4 Book.xsl (continued)

```
      <title>
        <xsl:value-of select="title"/>
      </title>
    </head>
    <body>
      <xsl:apply-templates/>
    </body>
  </html>
</xsl:template>
 <xsl:template match="book/title">
  <h1>
    <xsl:apply-templates/>
  </h1>
</xsl:template>
 <xsl:template match="chapter/title">
  <h2>
    <xsl:apply-templates/>
  </h2>
</xsl:template>
 <xsl:template match="section/title">
  <h3>
    <xsl:apply-templates/>
  </h3>
</xsl:template>
 <xsl:template match="para">
  <p>
    <xsl:apply-templates/>
  </p>
</xsl:template>
 <xsl:template match="note">
  <p class="note">
    <b>NOTE: </b>
    <xsl:apply-templates/>
  </p>
</xsl:template>
 <xsl:template match="emph">
  <em>
    <xsl:apply-templates/>
  </em>
</xsl:template>
 </xsl:stylesheet>
```

Once the XML and XSLT files are created, the JSP page itself is very short. It simply involves creating an instance of the `XSLTProcessor` class and passing it the URLs of the XML and XSL files. Listing 10.5 gives an example of a JSP page that combines the XML and XSL files to output HTML. It utilizes the Xerces XML parser and the Xalan XSLT Processor, so these archives have been downloaded from Apache.org and installed in the CLASSPATH.

Listing 10.5 xml2html.jsp

```
<%@ page import="org.xml.sax.*" %>
<%@ page import="org.apache.xalan.xslt.*" %>

<%
String xmlFileName = request.getParameter("XML");
String xslFileName = request.getParameter("XSL");

if (xmlFileName != null && xslFileName != null){
  try{
    XSLTProcessor processor
    = XSLTProcessorFactory.getProcessor();
    processor.process(new XSLTInputSource(xmlFileName),
                      new XSLTInputSource(xslFileName),
                      new XSLTResultTarget(out));
  } catch(SAXException e){}
} else {
     %>
       <HTML>
         <HEAD><TITLE>Mistake in Request</TITLE></HEAD>
         <BODY><H1>Mistake in using xml2html</H1>
         XML and XSL are both required parameters to the
         servlet
 </BODY>
       </HTML>
     <%
}
%>
```

The first two lines import the Xerces and Xalan packages:

```
<%@ page import="org.xml.sax.*" %>
<%@ page import="org.apache.xalan.xslt.*" %>
```

After they are loaded two HTML parameters are put into `Strings`. If those the `Strings` are not null then the `XSLTProcessor` is created and passed the parameters. The two strings that represent the XML and XSL file are passed into new instances of the `XSLTInputSource` object.

The `XSLTInputSource` object is extremely versatile. In fact, either the URL or the local file path can be sent as the parameter and `XSLTInputSource` will determine the source and utilize it. To print the output of the `XSLTProcessor` a new `XSLTResultTarget` is created taking the `out` object in its constructor. This causes the output of the `XSLTProcessor` to be written directly to `out`.

```
try{
  XSLTProcessor processor =
   XSLTProcessorFactory.getProcessor();
  processor.process(new XSLTInputSource(xmlFileName),
                    new XSLTInputSource(xslFileName),
                    new XSLTResultTarget(out));
} catch(SAXException e){}
```

If the two required parameters were not sent, the page simply returns an error page. Given the previous XML and XSL files as input, the output of Listing 10.5 would look like Figure 10.1. All in all, this is a very simple example, and demonstrates the component benefits of using JSP with XML and XSLT. The JSP file holds the business logic, the XML files holds the data, and the XSL file holds the presentation logic. Each file is short, and easy to read because it is tailored to its specific function.

Given that Listing 10.5 takes URLs for parameters also opens up a whole new set of possibilities. In addition to parsing XML and transforming it with XSLT, JSP pages can generate XML pages directly.

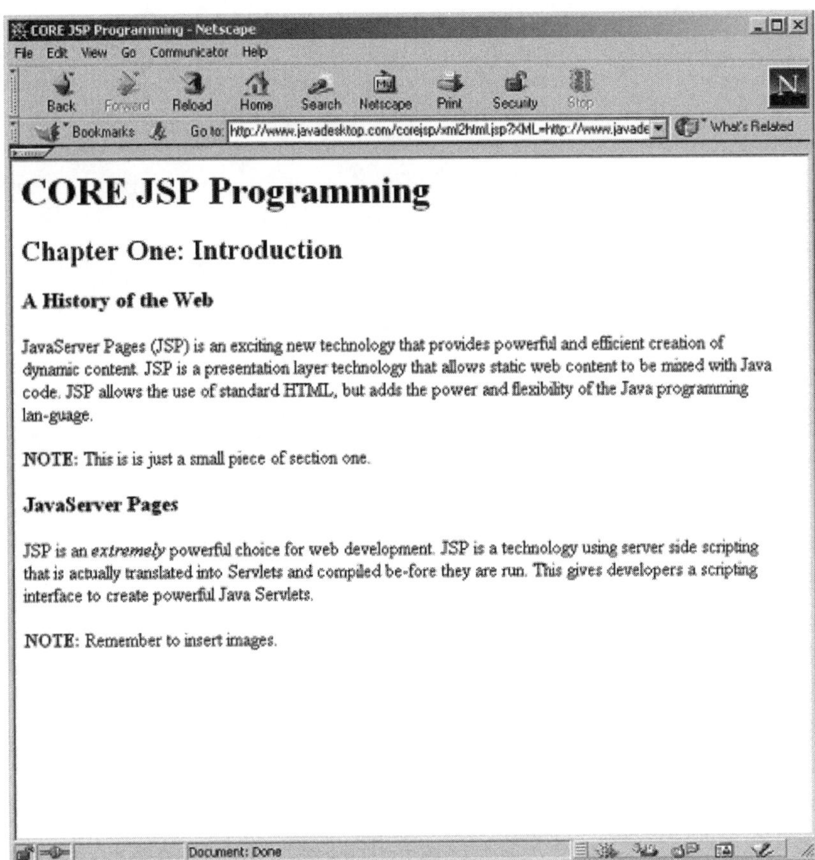

Figure 10–1 Output of xml2html.jsp

10.5 Generating XML from JSP

Generating XML from JSP pages is nothing complex. The one key thing involved it setting the correct content type in the page directive. This is done with:

```
<%@ page contentType="text/xml" %>
```

After this point it is up to the JSP author to create output that matches the given XML language definition.

One of the problems that came up in Chapter 9 was the cumbersome way the rows and columns of relational databases have to be converted manually to a format Java can understand. One solution for this problem is to convert the data directly to XML. This makes the program more portable, as it does not need to have the row numbers or names hard-coded into it. It also creates a very clean set of Java code.

Listing 10.6 does an SQL search on a database and converts the `ResultTable` returned into XML. The XML file has a root element of `<dataset>`. Each row is contained in a `<row>` tag, and each set of data is encapsulated in a tag that is dynamically created from the column name.

Listing 10.6 jdbc2xml.jsp

```
<%@ page import="java.sql.*" contentType="text/xml" %>
<%
  String url  = "jdbc:oracle:thin:@localhost:1521:JSPBOOK";
  String id   = "jsp";
  String pass = "thePass";
  String sql  = "SELECT * FROM system_users";

  Class.forName("oracle.jdbc.driver.OracleDriver");
  Connection conn
     = DriverManager.getConnection(url, id, pass);
  Statement stmt = conn.createStatement();
  ResultSet rset = stmt.executeQuery(sql);
  ResultSetMetaData rsmd = rset.getMetaData();
  int cols = rsmd.getColumnCount();
  out.println("<?xml version=\"1.0\" ?>");
%>

<dataset>
<% while (rset.next()){
     out.println(" <row>");
     for(int i=1; i<=cols; i++){
       String colName = rsmd.getColumnLabel(i);
       out.println("    <"+colName.toLowerCase()+">"+
                    rset.getString(i)+
                    "</"+colName.toLowerCase()+">");
       }
     out.println(" </row>");
   }
%>
</dataset>
```

Listing 10.6 is so straightforward it does not need any explanation. When run against the test database used in Chapter 9 it produces output similar to Listing 10.7:

Listing 10.7 Output of jdbc2xml.jsp

```
<?xml version="1.0" ?>
<dataset>
 <row>
    <system_id>000121</system_id>
    <first_name>Damon</first_name>
    <last_name>Hougland</last_name>
    <title>Mattress Tester</title>
    <phone>5557868945</phone>
    <building>745</building>
    <state_init>TX</state_init>
    <entry_date>2000-02-12 19:43:47.0</entry_date>
 </row>
 <row>
    <system_id>000333</system_id>
    <first_name>Aaron</first_name>
    <last_name>Tavistock</last_name>
    <title>Java Champions</title>
    <phone>5557861234</phone>
    <building>748</building>
    <state_init>CA</state_init>
    <entry_date>2000-03-07 00:00:00.0</entry_date>
 </row>
 <row>
    <system_id>000345</system_id>
    <first_name>Joseph</first_name>
    <last_name>Blow</last_name>
    <title>Mail Supervisor</title>
    <phone>5557864567</phone>
    <building>710</building>
    <state_init>CA</state_init>
    <entry_date>2000-02-12 19:43:47.0</entry_date>
 </row>
 <row>
    <system_id>000234</system_id>
    <first_name>Bill</first_name>
    <last_name>Marketing</last_name>
    <title>Finance Engineer</title>
    <phone>5559257440</phone>
    <building>635</building>
    <state_init>TX</state_init>
```

Listing 10.7 Output of jdbc2xml.jsp (continued)

```
    <entry_date>2000-02-12 19:43:47.0</entry_date>
  </row>
  <row>
    <system_id>000234</system_id>
    <first_name>Lawrence</first_name>
    <last_name>Paydirt</last_name>
    <title>Company Nurse</title>
    <phone>5559257777</phone>
    <building>936</building>
    <state_init>CA</state_init>
    <entry_date>2000-02-12 19:43:47.0</entry_date>
  </row>
  <row>
    <system_id>001847</system_id>
    <first_name>Nancy</first_name>
    <last_name>Jungle</last_name>
    <title>Recruiter</title>
    <phone>5558472057</phone>
    <building>145</building>
    <state_init>TX</state_init>
    <entry_date>2000-02-12 19:43:48.0</entry_date>
  </row>
  <row>
    <system_id>001848</system_id>
    <first_name>Kenny</first_name>
    <last_name>Hutchcraft</last_name>
    <title>Water Boy</title>
    <phone>5558479987</phone>
    <building>456</building>
    <state_init>AZ</state_init>
    <entry_date>2000-02-12 19:43:48.0</entry_date>
  </row>
  <row>
    <system_id>001841</system_id>
    <first_name>Chip</first_name>
    <last_name>Circuit</last_name>
    <title>Legal Technicial</title>
    <phone>5553982648</phone>
    <building>755</building>
    <state_init>CA</state_init>
    <entry_date>2000-02-12 19:43:48.0</entry_date>
  </row>
  <row>
    <system_id>000124</system_id>
```

Listing 10.7 Output of jdbc2xml.jsp (continued)

```
    <first_name>Shaoping</first_name>
    <last_name>Lee</last_name>
    <title>Master Chef</title>
    <phone>5559551245</phone>
    <building>756</building>
    <state_init>TX</state_init>
    <entry_date>2000-02-12 19:43:48.0</entry_date>
  </row>
  <row>
    <system_id>000001</system_id>
    <first_name>Abigail</first_name>
    <last_name>Nora</last_name>
    <title>CEO</title>
    <phone>5557560001</phone>
    <building>700</building>
    <state_init>TX</state_init>
    <entry_date>2000-02-12 19:43:48.0</entry_date>
  </row>
  <row>
    <system_id>000002</system_id>
    <first_name>Gibson</first_name>
    <last_name>Charles</last_name>
    <title>COO</title>
    <phone>5557560002</phone>
    <building>700</building>
    <state_init>TX</state_init>
    <entry_date>2000-02-12 19:43:48.0</entry_date>
  </row>
</dataset>
```

The problem now is: What to do with the XML? If viewed in Netscape 4.x it will prompt the user to save the file to disk. In Internet Explorer 5 the XML is viewable in a standard format, but this is presentation logic supplied by the program, not by the JSP author.

The answer, quite simply enough, is to use Listing 10.5, `xml2html.jsp`, to display the data. As Listing 10.5 simply takes two URLs as its XML and XSL file, the XML parameter can be pointed to Listing 10.6. While this may seem complex, it is actually fairly straightforward. Figure 10.2 outlines the flow of the page. Listing 10.6 creates an XML page dynamically. This dynamically created data and the static XSL stylesheet are the two parameters given to Listing 10.5, which transforms the files into a HTML page for output.

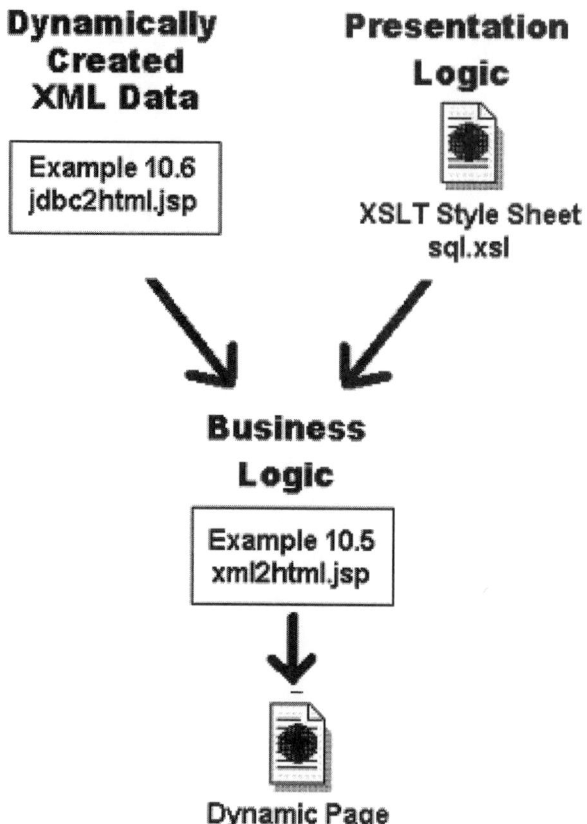

Figure 10–2 Application Flow of Listing 10.6

To do this a new XSL file is needed that will correspond to the XML tags in the dynamically created XML file. Listing 10.8 is an XSLT template that converts the XML tags in the XML file to an HTML table. Its structure is no different than that of the previous XSL examples.

One difference is the use of pipes (|) in the `match` attribute of the `xsl:template` tags. The value of this field is actually a part of XPath. The pipe symbol represents the logical "or" clause. In this way all possible tags of the XML file are covered.

Listing 10.8 sql.xsl

```
<?xml version="1.0"?>
<xsl:stylesheet
     xmlns:xsl="http://www.w3.org/XSL/Transform/1.0"
     version="1.0"
     xmlns="http://www.w3.org/TR/REC-html40">

<xsl:output method="html" indent="yes"/>
<xsl:strip-space elements="*"/>

<xsl:template match="dataset">
  <HTML>
   <BODY>
    <TABLE BORDER="1" CELLPADDING="3">
      <TR>
       <TD><B>System ID</B></TD>
       <TD><B>First Name</B></TD>
       <TD><B>Last Name</B></TD>
       <TD><B>Title</B></TD>
       <TD><B>Phone Number</B></TD>
       <TD><B>Building</B></TD>
       <TD><B>State</B></TD>
       <TD><B>Entry Date</B></TD>
      </TR>
<xsl:apply-templates/>
    </TABLE>
   </BODY>
  </HTML>
</xsl:template>

<xsl:template match="row">
    <tr>
      <xsl:apply-templates/>
    </tr>
</xsl:template>

<xsl:template match="title|first_name|last_name|phone">
    <td>
<xsl:apply-templates/>
```

Listing 10.8 sql.xsl (continued)

```
    </td>
</xsl:template>

<xsl:template
match="entry_date|system_id|state_init|building">
    <td>
<xsl:apply-templates/>
    </td>
</xsl:template>
</xsl:stylesheet>
```

Given the output of Listing 10.6 and the new XSL stylesheet in Listing 10.8, the output of Listing 10.7 should look like Figure 10-3.

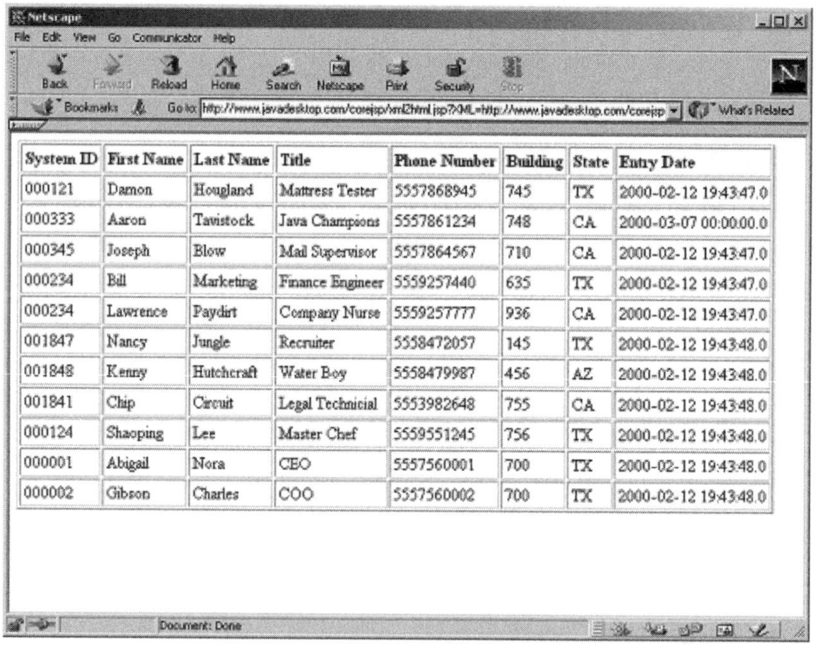

System ID	First Name	Last Name	Title	Phone Number	Building	State	Entry Date
000121	Damon	Hougland	Mattress Tester	5557868945	745	TX	2000-02-12 19:43:47.0
000333	Aaron	Tavistock	Java Champions	5557861234	748	CA	2000-03-07 00:00:00.0
000345	Joseph	Blow	Mail Supervisor	5557864567	710	CA	2000-02-12 19:43:47.0
000234	Bill	Marketing	Finance Engineer	5559257440	635	TX	2000-02-12 19:43:47.0
000234	Lawrence	Paydirt	Company Nurse	5559257777	936	CA	2000-02-12 19:43:47.0
001847	Nancy	Jungle	Recruiter	5558472057	145	TX	2000-02-12 19:43:48.0
001848	Kenny	Hutchcraft	Water Boy	5558479987	456	AZ	2000-02-12 19:43:48.0
001841	Chip	Circuit	Legal Technicial	5553982648	755	CA	2000-02-12 19:43:48.0
000124	Shaoping	Lee	Master Chef	5559551245	756	TX	2000-02-12 19:43:48.0
000001	Abigail	Nora	CEO	5557560001	700	TX	2000-02-12 19:43:48.0
000002	Gibson	Charles	COO	5557560002	700	TX	2000-02-12 19:43:48.0

Figure 10–3 Output of Listing 10.7:

The added value that XML pages can give to JSP applications is obvious. They allow an extra abstraction layer that separates data from both presentation logic and business logic. The examples above give a glimpse of the world of possibilities XML and JSP offers; this is only a small fraction of XML's capabilities. To learn more about XML read *The XML Handbook* (2nd *Edition*) by Charles F. Goldfarb (Prentice Hall/PTR, 1999).

CUSTOM TAGS

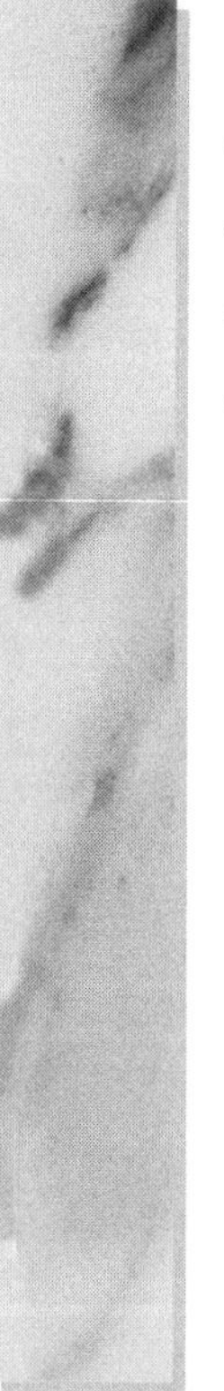

Topics in this Chapter:

- Custom Tag Basics
- The Custom Tag API
- Creating a new Custom Tag
- Creating Composite Tags

Chapter 11

When it comes to design strategy there have been two different themes in this book: first, try to write code in a component-based design; and second, try and separate presentation logic from business logic. One method of doing this is the JavaBean, which allows the JSP page to serve as a front end for presentation while the JavaBean itself is used for business logic.

Other examples have made use of including JSP files using the include action (`<jsp:include ... />`) and include directive (`<%@ include ... %>`). Each of these methods works in different ways, but both present significant problems for scalability and portability.

In the end, the JSP specification authors realized that there needed to be a way to create custom JSP actions, or custom tags. Not only would this provide a portable way of defining and creating JSP libraries, but it would also provide an interface for JSP tools to share these libraries.

11.1 Custom Tag Basics

Tag libraries are extremely powerful, and thus fairly complex. They incorporate all of the tag features of JSP actions, such as supporting nested actions, scripting elements, and the creation of scripting variables. They can be used to instantiate objects, and are scripting-language neutral. Probably their most powerful feature is that the JSP author can develop a component and never need to understand the inner workings of the tag library, or even the calling methods.

While they are an advanced technique for the JSP author, they are a major step toward separation of business logic and presentation logic. Defined from the start to be portable, they are also an excellent mechanism for creating and distributing functions from JSP page to JSP page.

Custom Tag Syntax

The custom tag syntax is exactly the same as the syntax of JSP actions. The JSP action prefix is `jsp`, while a custom tag prefix is determined by the `prefix` attribute of the `taglib` directive used to instantiate a set of custom tags. The prefix is followed by a colon and the name of the tag itself.

The actions tag does not have separate JSP and XML formats because it already is in the XML format. It is the same with custom tags. The colon delimited tag name is actually part of the XML namespaces standard. The format of a standard custom tag looks like:

```
<utility:repeat number="12">Hello World!</utility:repeat>
```

Here a tag library named `utility` is referenced. The specific tag used is named `repeat`. The tag has an attribute named `number`, which is assigned a value of "12." The tag contains a body that has the text "Hello World!", and then the tag is closed.

Besides being able to define its own attributes, custom tags can have an `id` attribute, which allows the tag to create new objects and assign them a scripting variable.

```
<htmltool:table id="tabletag" border="0" />
<% tabletag.setCols(5); %>
```

In the above example the tag `table` is used from the `htmltool` tag library. The `id` attribute creates a scripting element called `tabletag`, which refers to the new object created by this custom tag. In the following line this new scripting element is used to call the `setCols()` method of the custom tag instance.

Hopefully, these examples show that custom tags have an almost identical structure to the JSP action tags. They should also show the complex number of variations that the custom tags can have. This becomes important when programming new custom tags, as they will have to possibly account for attributes, body data, and new scripting elements within their classes.

The Players

Tag extensions are very complex. Beyond the custom tags themselves, there are actually several different components that are all necessary for custom tags to work. First there is the tag library, which are the classes that make up the Java program called by the custom tags. Next is the `taglib` directive, which is used to identify the tag library as well as associate it with a tag namespace prefix. Finally there is the tag library descriptor, an XML document that describes the tag library. Each of these components must be in place before custom tags can be used.

The Tag Library and Tag Handlers

The tag library is a collection of actions that add functionality to a JSP page. They are classes that provide the functionality of the custom tag. While tag libraries can be distributed several ways, it is common for them to be contained in a jar file. When distributed in a jar file, the tag lib descriptor must be included in the META-INF directory and named `taglib.tld`.

Tag libraries can also be distributed in a special format called a Web Application Archive (WAR file). Creating and using WAR files are discussed in great detail in Chapter 12.

Tag libraries are tied to the `taglib` directive by the `uri` attribute of the `taglib` directive. It can be any valid URI as long as can be used to identify the semantics of the tag library.

At the heart of the tag library is the tag handler. The tag handler is a server-side object that is created to evaluate actions during the execution of a JSP page. Every tag library extends one of the tag handler classes. It supports a protocol that handles the passing of information between the JSP page and the custom tag.

Tag handlers are simply JavaBeans. There are two interfaces to tag handlers, `Tag` and `BodyTag`. `Tag` is used for simple constructs that are not interested in manipulating the body content of the custom tag. `BodyTag` is an extension of `Tag` and gives the tag handler access to what is between the open and close tags. Two classes, `TagSupport` and `TagBodySupport` can be used as base classes when creating new tag handlers.

The `taglib` *Directive*

The `taglib` directive is the mechanism that ties the tag library descriptor to the JSP page, as well as set the tag namespace prefix to be used in the JSP page. It has two attributes, both of which are required.

The `uri` attribute contains a Universal Resource Identifier (URI) that points to the location of the Tag library. In the case of a jar file distribution of a tag library, the URI points to the jar file itself, which contains the tag library descriptor in the form of a `taglib.tld` file.

The `prefix` attribute identifies the XML namespace prefix that will identify tags that are a part of the new tag library. The namespaces available to a JSP page is limited to the default `jsp` namespace as well as any namespace created by the `taglib` directive. An example taglib directive might look like:

```
<%@ taglib
       uri="http://www.javadesktop.com/taglib/htmltool.jar"
       prefix="tool"
%>
```

The `uri` attribute here tells the JSP engine that the tag specified is located in the file at: `http://www.javadesktop.com/taglib/htmltool.jar`. The prefix attribute tells the JSP engine that all tags beginning with `<tool:tag-name>` should be routed to the tag handler associated with `htmltool.jar`.

The Tag Library Descriptor

The tag library descriptor (TLD) is an XML document that describes a tag library. It is used by the JSP container to interpret pages that contain `taglib` directives. It can also be used by JSP authoring tools that generate JSP pages using tag libraries.

The TLD is basically a set of metadata about a tag library. It describes the tag library as a whole, as well as describing its individual tags, attributes, version numbers, and other information. Each action in the tag library is listed in the TLD. Information contained for each action includes its name, the class that contains its tag handler, and all of its attributes.

The distinct advantage of having a TLD file is that tools can find out information about a tag library without having to instantiate objects or load libraries. This is a standard approach that is used in many parts of the Java 2 Enterprise Edition (J2EE).

TLD documents, as they are XML, follow an XML DTD. The official DTD is described at: `http://java.sun.com/j2ee/dtds/web-jsptaglibrary_1_1.dtd`.

Custom Tag Types

There are many different types of custom tags. Some tags interpret the tag body, while others do not. Some tags instantiate new objects while many do not. Each of these custom tag types has to be approached differently from the custom tag programmer's perspective. Table 11.1 takes a look at the different type of custom tags as well as the differences between them.

Table 11.1 Different Actions

No Body or Objects

`<mytag:tag myattr="foo" />`

The simplest type of custom tag has no body and creates no new objects. Without processing the body the custom tag would extend the TagSupport class.

A Body with No Objects

`<mytag:tag myattr="foo">Hello!</mytag:tag>`

A custom tag that evaluates the body of its tag but does not create any objects is more difficult. Instead of extending TagSupport it extends TagBodySupport. A processing loop is created to iterate through the body of the tag until all processing is complete. This can be especially complicated when the tag body contains subtags.

No Body with New Objects

`<mytag:tag myattr="foo" id="mytag"/>`

Again, without processing the body, the custom tag would extend the TagSupport class. In this case a new object is created and assigned to a scripting element called "mytag." Having a new object that relates to a scripting element is somewhat of a complicated task. The key is to synchronize the value of the new scripting element with the object. This is done through the TagExtraInfo class. Each time a new object and scripting element is created this class must be created. The information that the TagExtraInfo class contains is all of the names and types of scripting elements that will be assigned objects. It is the custom tag author's responsibility to make sure this class is created and has the right information.

A Body with New Objects

`<mytag:tag id="mytag"/>Hello!</mytag:tag>`

This is the most difficult type of custom tag, as both the complexity of extending the TabBodySupport class as well as the creation of a TagExtraInfo class is necessary. This type of custom tag implements all of the possible specifications of a custom tag, including attributes, evaluating the body, and creating new objects and scripting elements.

It is also important to note that a custom tag can have any number of parameters, and can even have no parameters at all. This also plays a significant role in the programming complexity of a custom tag.

11.2 The Custom Tag API

Before reviewing an example custom tag, it is a good idea to take a look at the interfaces and methods used by tag libraries.

Special Methods and Constants for Custom Tags

The tables below are listed from the assumption that tags will be created to extend `BodyTagSupport`. Information on the methods for other extensions can be found in the API reference in Appendix C.

One of the most significant features that custom tags have is their ability to change the behavior of the page. This is done by simply changing the value that the tag returns.

Every custom tag should return a known value, or a predefined constant. Table 11.2 shows the static return constants that dictate how the JSP page should process.

Table 11.2 Static Constants

Constant	Description
`static int SKIP_BODY`	Skip body evaluation.
`static int EVAL_BODY_TAG`	Request the creation of new BodyContent on which to evaluate the body of this tag.
`static int EVAL_BODY_INCLUDE`	Evaluate body into existing out stream.
`static int EVAL_PAGE`	Continue evaluating the page.
`static int SKIP_PAGE`	Skip the rest of the page.

A method summary is provided in table 11.3:

Table 11.3 Method Signatures

`int doEndTag()`
Process the end tag. This method will be called on all tag objects. All instance state associated with this instance must be reset.

`int doStartTag()`
Process the start tag for this instance. The doStartTag() method assumes that all setter methods have been already invoked and that the body has not yet been invoked.

`static Tag findAncestorWithClass(Tag from, java.lang.Class classnm)`
Find the nearest instance of a given class type that is closest to a given instance. This class is used for coordination among cooperating tags.

`java.lang.String getId()`
The value of the ID attribute of this tag; or null.

`Tag getParent()`
The tag instance enclosing this tag instance.

`java.lang.Object getValue(java.lang.String name)`
Get a value.

`java.util.Enumeration getValues()`
Enumerate the values.

`void release()`
release() called after doEndTag() to reset state.

`void removeValue(java.lang.String name)`
Remove a value.

`void setId(java.lang.String id)`
Set the ID attribute.

`void setPageContext(PageContext pageContext)`
Set the page context.

Table 11.3 Method Signatures (continued)

`void setParent(Tag someTag)`
Set the nesting tag of this tag.

`void setValue(java.lang.String name, java.lang.Object value)`
Set a value.

`JspWriter getPreviousOut()`
Get surrounding out.

`int doAfterBody()`
Actions after some body has been evaluated. Not invoked in empty tags or in tags returning SKIP_BODY in doStartTag(). This method is invoked after every body evaluation. The pair "BODY" and "doAfterBody()" is invoked initially if doStartTag() returned EVAL_BODY_TAG, and it is repeated as long as the doAfterBody() evaluation returns EVAL_BODY_TAG. The method reinvocations may lead to different actions because there might have been some changes to shared state, or because of external computation.

`void doInitBody()`
Prepare for evaluation of the body. It will be invoked at most once per action invocation. Will not be invoked if there is no body evaluation. Frequently it is not redefined by tag author.

`BodyContent getBodyContent()`
Get current bodyContent.

`void setBodyContent(BodyContent someBody)`
Prepare for evaluation of the body. It will be invoked at most once per action invocation. Will not be invoked if there is no body evaluation. Frequently it is redefined by tag author.

Understanding the Tag Library Descriptor File

The tag library descriptor (TLD) file is used to describe everything about a tag library. Everything the JSP page knows about the tag is acquired from this file.

In fact, the JSP engine actually builds the method signatures that are available by reading this file. Minor errors in this file can cause some interesting errors that a state that the constructors signature does not match the method call.

The TLD file follows an XML style of syntax, so it includes nested structures. Fortunately, its a fairly simple file and is relatively easy to break down into logical blocks.

Table 11.4 Tag Library Descriptor Entities

`taglib`	Parent class.
`tlibversion`	Version of taglib that should be used.
`jspversion`	Version of JSP that should be used.
`shortname`	Handle for the tag library—this is the first part of the tag name on a JSP page.
`uri`	A unique identifier—this doesn't actually have to point anywhere, in fact it doesn't need to be a URI, but its still good practice to really have it be a URI to the library.
`info`	Description for the tag library.
`tag`	Tag definition (contains subsets: **name**, **tagclass**, **bodycontent**, **info**, and **attribute**) .

`tag subsets {`

`name`	The name of tag. This is the second part of the tag name on a JSP page.
`tagclass`	The name of the class.
`bodycontent`	Type of content ("Empty," "JSP," or "Tag Dependent").
`info`	Description for the tag.
`attribute`	Tag attributes (contains subsets: **name**, **required**, and **rtexpvalue**).

`attribute subsets {`

`name`	Name of the attribute.
`required`	Is required (true/false).
`rtexprvalue`	Value translated by JSP (true/false).

`}`

`}`

Special Packaging Considerations

When a new tag library is created it needs to be packaged in a jar file with the TLD. The TLD needs to be put into the META-INF directory so that the jar file will be used as a tag library.

The jar command does not provide command-line switches to include nonmanifest files in the META-INF directory, so this needs to be done by brute force. A META-INF directory needs to be created in parallel with the source tree. Then when the jar is created the META-INF directory needs to be explicitly added. For example:

```
jar cf taglib.jar com/javadesktop/taglib/* META-INF/*
```

11.3 Creating a New Custom Tag

Listing 11.1 shows the first example of using custom tags. The example creates an new tag that iterates through a section of the JSP page a certain number of times. The functional components will be discussed as after each component has been presented.

Listing 11.1 LoopTag.jsp

```
package com.javadesktop.utiltags;

import javax.servlet.jsp.*;
import javax.servlet.jsp.tagext.*;

public class LoopTag extends BodyTagSupport {
  private int maxCount = 0;
  private int currentCount = 0;

  public void setCount(int count) {
    this.maxCount = count;
  }

  public int doStartTag() {
    if (currentCount < maxCount) {
      return EVAL_BODY_TAG;
    } else {
      return SKIP_BODY;
    }
```

Listing 11.1 LoopTag.jsp (continued)

```
  }

  public int doAfterBody() throws JspException {
    currentCount++;

    if (currentCount < maxCount) {
      return EVAL_BODY_TAG;
    } else {
      return SKIP_BODY;
    }
  }

  public int doEndTag() throws JspException {
    try {
      if(bodyContent != null)
    bodyContent.writeOut(bodyContent.getEnclosingWriter());
    } catch(java.io.IOException e) {
    throw new JspException("IO Error: " + e.getMessage());
    }

    return EVAL_PAGE;
  }

  public void release() {
    super.release();
    currentCount = 0;
  }
}
```

Listing 11.1 is the meat and bones of this custom tag. It does all the work in managing the iterations handling whether the data should be displayed or not.

The class signature and the first method are not really remarkable. They resemble a JavaBean, except the class extends `BodyTagSupport`. The more interesting sections are the other methods in the file.

The `doStartTag()` method will be run when the tag is first called. It checks if there are iterations to do. If there are no iterations to do then the `SKIP_BODY` constant is returned, which says essentially "ignore everything between the start and end tags." If there are iterations to be done, the `EVAL_BODY_TAG` is returned that says "process everything between the start and end tags."

Next in the source code is the `doAfterBody()` method. Each time the body is processed this method is called. This method first increments the iteration counter. Next, it does the same thing the `doStartTag()` method did, if there is more iteration, process the body. Since this method is called after each body is processed, it creates the loop.

Next the `doEndTag()` occurs, this is called when the closing the tags. This tag contains a particularly interesting looking piece of code:

```
try {
  if(bodyContent != null)
     bodyContent.writeOut(bodyContent.getEnclosingWriter());
} catch(java.io.IOException e) {
  throw new JspException("IO Error: " + e.getMessage());
}
```

All this code is doing is printing the content of the body. Unfortunately, this needs to done in this manner because the custom tag does not have access to the `out` object of the JSP page. The writer needs to be found indirectly using `getEnclosingWriter()`, then pushed to the `JspWriter` using `writeOut()`.

Finally, there is the `release()` method that is called when the processing tag is done and needs to clean up. It simply uses the super class provided by the tag interface and resets the counter.

The Tag Library Descriptor

In order to actually create a custom tag there needs to be a tag library descriptor (TLD), `taglib.tld`. Listing 11.2 shows the TLD for the first example of custom tags. The TLD file has a major effect on the how the tags will be exposed to the JSP page. By examining this file it should be fairly easy to figure out the tags that will be made available by this new tag library.

Listing 11.2 taglib.tld

```
<?xml version="1.0" encoding="ISO-8859-1" ?>
<!DOCTYPE taglib PUBLIC
   "-//Sun Microsystems, Inc.//DTD JSP Tag Library 1.1//EN"
   "http://java.sun.com/products/jsp/dtd/web-
jsptaglib_1_1.dtd"
     >

<taglib>
  <tlibversion>1.0</tlibversion>
  <jspversion>1.1</jspversion>
  <shortname>util</shortname>
```

Listing 11.2 taglib.tld (continued)

```
  <uri>http://www.javadesktop.com/taglib/utiltags.jar
</uri>
  <info>Util Tag library</info>
  <tag>
    <name>loop</name>
    <tagclass>com.javadesktop.utiltags.LoopTag</tagclass>
    <bodycontent>JSP</bodycontent>
    <info>Allows looping</info>
    <attribute>
      <name>count</name>
      <required>true</required>
      <rtexprvalue>false</rtexprvalue>
    </attribute>
  </tag>
</taglib>
```

In particular the `<shortname>` tag tells identifies the name of the library, `'util'`. The `<name>` tag identifies the methods that will be made available, in this case there is only one, `'loop'`. Finally, the `<attribute>` tag identifies the arguments for each tag, again in this case only one is available, `'count'`. So the actual tag that will be used from this library will look like this on the JSP page: `<util:loop count="n">` .

Custom Tags in Action

The new library needs to be packaged up as a file with the TLD and put into the CLASSPATH. Now this new tag can be accessed from any JSP page on the server. Listing 11.3 shows a JSP page that uses this new tag library.

Listing 11.3 looptest.jsp

```
<%@ taglib
      uri="http://www.javadesktop.com/taglib/utiltags.jar"
      prefix="util"
%>

<html>
<body>

<table border=0 cellpadding=3 cellspacing=5>
<util:loop count="5">
  <tr>
  <util:loop count="5">
```

Listing 11.3 looptest.jsp (continued)

```
    <td bgcolor=#ccccff align=center>
    <b><%= (int)(Math.random()*9)+1 %></b>
    </td>
  </util:loop>
  </tr>
</util:loop>
</table>

</body>
</html>
```

While the looping feature is very powerful, this specific example is fairly trivial. It generates a grid of random numbers. It's not very complex, but it does show how the tag would be used and even shows that the tag is easily nested.

Figure 11-1 shows the output from looptest.jsp.

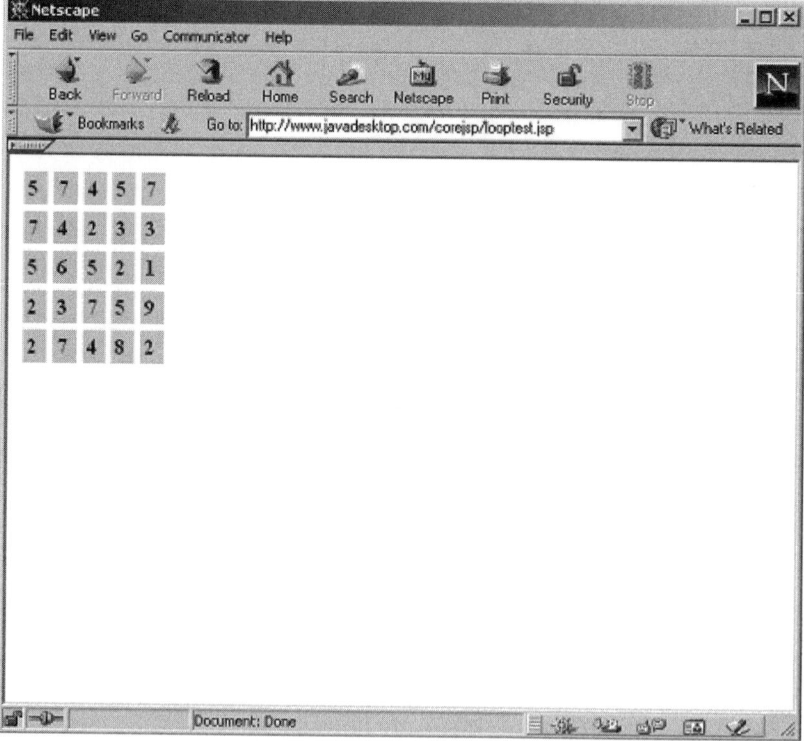

Figure 11-1 Output of looptest.jsp

11.4 Creating Composite Tags

A more complete example of using custom tags involves using composite tags, where one tag contains additional subtags. A composite tag basically takes a custom tag that would normally like this:

```
<my:tag foo="bar" baz="fla"> </my:tag>
```

and makes it into a custom tag set that resembles like this:

```
<my:tag>
  <my:foo> bar </my:foo>
  <my:baz> fla </my:baz>
</my:tag>
```

Using composite tags tends to be extremely useful in a tag library where there are a large number of potential arguments. Composite tags also have the additional benefit of producing human readable tags on the JSP page.

Creating composite tags does not involve a change to the taglib descriptor. Instead this is accomplished by making several parallel tags with different behaviors and designating whether they are an external tag or a child tag.

The external tag set is no different from a normal tag set. However, the child tags are significantly different. A child tag usually begins by finding out its parent. If the parent class does not match what the class is expecting then an exception is thrown. Once the child tag has established the parent tag, the child tag will have the ability to call methods and set properties in the parent.

A Composite Tag Example

This example takes the relatively common task of sending an e-mail from a Web page and creates an extremely easy e-mail tag-based interface.

The example actually uses JavaMail behind the scenes, but insulates the JSP author from the details of JavaMail. Each child tag sets a particular value for JavaMail to use in sending the e-mail.

Listing 11.4 shows the top-level component of this example. This becomes the external tag that will include the child tags.

Listing 11.4 EmailSend.java

```
package com.javadesktop.mailtags;

import java.util.*;
import javax.servlet.jsp.*;
import javax.servlet.jsp.tagext.*;
```

Listing 11.4 EmailSend.java (continued)

```
import javax.mail.*;
import javax.mail.internet.*;
import javax.activation.*;

public class EmailSend extends BodyTagSupport {
  private String emailTo = null;
  private String emailFrom = null;
  private String emailSubject = null;
  private String emailServer = null;

  public EmailSend() {
  }

  public void setEmailTo(String to) {
    this.emailTo = to;
  }

  public void setEmailFrom(String from) {
    this.emailFrom = from;
  }

  public void setEmailSubject(String subject) {
    this.emailSubject = subject;
  }

  public void setEmailServer(String server) {
    this.emailServer = server;
  }

  public int doStartTag() {
    return EVAL_BODY_TAG;
  }

  public int doEndTag() throws JspException {
    BodyContent body = getBodyContent();

    if (emailServer == null) {
      this.emailServer = "localhost";
    }

    if (emailSubject == null) {
      this.emailSubject = "No Subject";
    }

    if (emailFrom == null || emailTo == null) {
```

Listing 11.4 EmailSend.java (continued)

```
      throw new JspException("Missing TO or FROM address");
    } else {
      Properties props = System.getProperties();
      props.put("mail.smtp.host", emailServer);
      Session emailsession =
                   Session.getDefaultInstance(props, null);

      try {
        Message email = new MimeMessage(emailsession);
        email.setFrom(new InternetAddress(emailFrom));
        InternetAddress[] address
        = {new InternetAddress(emailTo)};
     email.setRecipients(Message.RecipientType.TO,address);
        email.setSubject(emailSubject);
        email.setSentDate(new Date());
        email.setHeader("X-Mailer","JSP Mail Tags");
        email.setText(body.getString().trim());
        Transport.send(email);
      } catch (MessagingException e) {
        throw new JspException(e.getMessage());
      }
    }

    return EVAL_PAGE;
  }

  public void release() {
    super.release();
  }
}
```

Like the previous tag library example, the top portion of this class closely resembles a standard JavaBean. This particular component to the tag library acts as a container for the child tags, then attempts to call JavaMail when the tag is closed.

The additional classes represent child tags. It is important to note that these child tags make references to the parent class, so it is important that parent class is compiled and already in the CLASSPATH at this point. If this is not done then the classes for the child tags will not compile.

Each of these child tags represents a single attribute to the parent. The child tags are extremely similar; they each put the body of the tag in as a setter method in the parent tag. As they are very similar, there is no need to have individual comments on each.

There could be many more of child tags in this custom tag example than listed here, but in the interest of preserving space while maintaining functionality, the child tags have been reduced to the most important three. Each additional tag would use a child tag like the ones listed below, an entry would need to be added to the TLD, and a setter method created in the parent tag.

Listing 11.5 EmailTo.java

```
package com.javadesktop.mailtags;

import javax.servlet.jsp.*;
import javax.servlet.jsp.tagext.*;

public class EmailTo extends BodyTagSupport {
  EmailSend myEmail;

  public EmailTo() {
  }

  public int doStartTag() throws JspException {
    myEmail=(EmailSend)getParent();

    if(myEmail==null) {
      throw new JspException("Email not started");
    }

    return EVAL_BODY_TAG;
  }

  public int doAfterBody() {
    BodyContent body = getBodyContent();

    myEmail.setEmailTo(body.getString());

    body.clearBody();

    return SKIP_BODY;
  }
}
```

Listing 11.6 lists the EmailFrom tag:

Listing 11.6 EmailFrom.java

```
package com.javadesktop.mailtags;

import javax.servlet.jsp.*;
import javax.servlet.jsp.tagext.*;

public class EmailFrom extends BodyTagSupport {
  EmailSend myEmail;

  public EmailFrom () {
  }

  public int doStartTag() throws JspException {
    myEmail=(EmailSend)getParent();

    if(myEmail==null) {
      throw new JspException("Email not started");
    }

    return EVAL_BODY_TAG;
  }

  public int doAfterBody() {
    BodyContent body = getBodyContent();

    myEmail.setEmailFrom(body.getString());

    body.clearBody();

    return SKIP_BODY;
  }
}
```

Listing 11.7 is almost the same as Listing 11.6:

Listing 11.7 EmailSubject.java

```
package com.javadesktop.mailtags;

import javax.servlet.jsp.*;
import javax.servlet.jsp.tagext.*;

public class EmailSubject extends BodyTagSupport {
  EmailSend myEmail;

  public EmailSubject() {
  }

  public int doStartTag() throws JspException {
    myEmail=(EmailSend)getParent();

    if(myEmail==null) {
      throw new JspException("Email not started");
    }

    return EVAL_BODY_TAG;
  }

  public int doAfterBody() {
    BodyContent body = getBodyContent();

    myEmail.setEmailSubject(body.getString());

    body.clearBody();

    return SKIP_BODY;
  }
}
```

With all the child classes complete and compiled, a TLD still needs to be created for this tag library. Listing 11.8 shows the new `taglig.tld`. Notice that both the child and parent tags are shown as simple tags; there is no understanding of which is a parent or child.

Listing 11.8 taglib.tld

```
<?xml version="1.0" encoding="ISO-8859-1" ?>
<!DOCTYPE taglib PUBLIC
   "-//Sun Microsystems, Inc.//DTD JSP Tag Library 1.1//EN"
   "http://java.sun.com/products/jsp/dtd/
web-jsptaglib_1_1.dtd"
     >

<taglib>
  <tlibversion>1.0</tlibversion>
  <jspversion>1.1</jspversion>
  <shortname>email</shortname>
  <uri>http://www.javadesktop.com/taglib/mailtags.jar</
uri>
  <info>Email Tag library</info>
  <tag>
    <name>message</name>
    <tagclass>com.javadesktop.mailtags.EmailSend</tagclass>
    <bodycontent>JSP</bodycontent>
    <info>Basic Email Wrapper</info>
  </tag>
  <tag>
    <name>recipient</name>
    <tagclass>com.javadesktop.mailtags.EmailTo</tagclass>
    <bodycontent>JSP</bodycontent>
    <info>Email Recipient</info>
  </tag>
  <tag>
    <name>sender</name>
    <tagclass>com.javadesktop.mailtags.EmailFrom</tagclass>
    <bodycontent>JSP</bodycontent>
    <info>Email Sender</info>
  </tag>
  <tag>
    <name>subject</name>
    <tagclass>com.javadesktop.mailtags.EmailSubject</tag-
class>
    <bodycontent>JSP</bodycontent>
    <info>EmailSubject</info>
  </tag>
</taglib>
```

Now the package needs to be compiled into a jar file in the appropriate way for a tag library. The code shown in Listing 11.9 will show an example of using these new e-mail tags.

Listing 11.9 mailtest.jsp

```
<%@ taglib
      uri="http://www.javadesktop.com/taglib/mailtags.jar"
      prefix="email"
%>

<%@ page errorPage="errorPage.jsp" %>
<%@ include file="confirmLogin.jsp" %>

<!DOCTYPE HTML PUBLIC "-//W3C//DTD HTML 4.0 Final//EN">

<html>
<style>
<!--
font.header {
  font-family: arial,helvetica,sans-serif;
  font-size: 14pt;
}
td.form {
  font-family: arial,helvetica,sans-serif;
  font-size: 10pt; background-color: #ccccff;
  color: #000000;
}
-->
</style>

<body>
<jsp:include page="debug.jsp" flush="true" />
<jsp:include page="navbar2.jsp" flush="true" />

<center>

<%
  String sender = request.getParameter("sender");
  String subject = request.getParameter("subject");
```

Listing 11.9 mailtest.jsp (continued)

```
  String message = request.getParameter("message");

  if ( message != null && sender != null ) {
%>

<email:message>
<email:recipient>support@javadesktop.com</email:recipient>
<email:sender><%= sender %></email:sender>
<email:subject><%= subject %></email:subject>
<%= message %>
</email:message>
<font class="header">
Thank you for your feedback, we try to read and reply to
all our email as soon as posible.
</font>

<%
  }
%>

<font class="header">
Send an email to Customer Support
</font>

<form method=post>
<table border=0 bgcolor=#ccccff cellpadding=8 cellspac-
ing=0>
<tr>
  <td class="form" align=right>sender</td>
  <td class="form" align=left><input type=text
name="sender"></td>
</tr>

<tr>
  <td class="form" align=right>subject</td>
  <td class="form" align=left><input type=text name="sub-
ject"></td>
```

Listing 11.9 mailtest.jsp (continued)

```
</tr>

<tr>
  <td class="form" align=right>message</td>
  <td class="form" align=left>
    <textarea wrap=virtual name="message" rows=10 cols=50>
    </textarea>
  </td>
</tr>

<tr><td class="form" colspan=2>
<center>
<input type=submit value="send email">    
<input type=reset value="cancel email">
</center>
</td></tr>

</table>

</form>
</center>
</body>
</html>
```

Figure 11-2 shows the results of this new page, but the diagram doesn't do justice to the page. Most of the page above is fairly typical, but there is a really interesting section where the new tags are actually used. The e-mail is created and sent by these six lines:

```
<email:message>
<email:recipient>support@javadesktop.com</email:recipient>
<email:sender><%= sender %></email:sender>
<email:subject><%= subject %></email:subject>
<%= message %>
</email:message>
```

Custom tags are one of the most promising features of JSP. It allows a better separation of Java code and HTML presentation, as well as a standard, portable way to distribute software libraries. It allows JSP authors the ability to implement a component without knowledge of the internal layout or method signatures. It relies on a standard XML format for implementation, and is extremely similar to the JSP action tags.

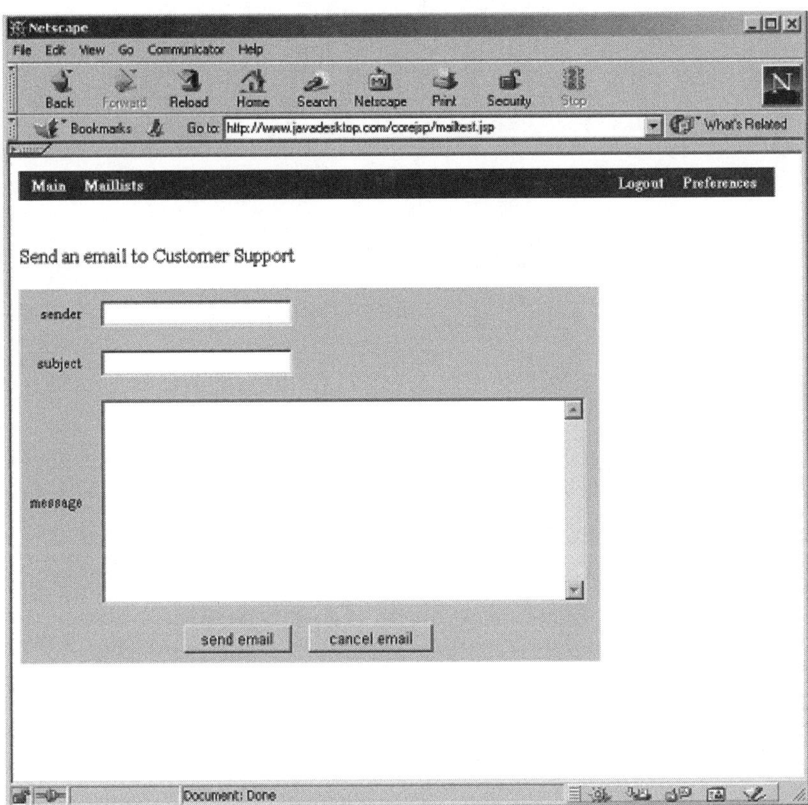

Figure 11-2 Output of Mailtest.jsp

More important, custom tags bring the JSP paradigm closer to the component model. Many Java code purists believe that mixing Java code and HTML code in the same file is a bad model. With custom tags there is a complete separation of HTML presentation logic and Java business logic. While coding custom tags is more complex, it has distinct advantages in scalability, portability, and component design. As JSP continues to evolve, look for the role of custom tags to expand.

DESIGNING AND DEPLOYING JSP APPLICATIONS

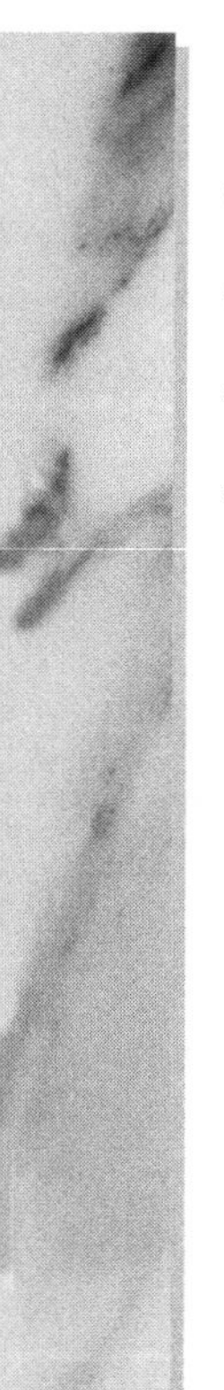

Topics in this Chapter:

- Separating Presentation and Application Logic
- Separating Controller and Presentation Logic
- JSP Application Model 1 and 2
- Web Archive Files (WAR)

Chapter 12

In addition to the need to develop a JSP program is the need to architect a JSP application to suit the production needs of a project. These needs generally fall into two areas, architecture design and program deployment.

Design involves creating a central strategy around which the application is to be developed. This involves many things, including program workflow, message flow, and shared access to outside data sources. A major portion of designing an architecture for an application is similar to laying the foundation of a building. It is the framework on which the entire application must rely. The enterprise application needs of scalability, availability, upgrade-ability, and management all rely on a solid application framework. Is the application composed in such a way that a large development team can work simultaneously? Does minor functionality changes demand a major application change, or simply recoding one component? These questions should be answered by designing the right architecture before development of an application begins.

Application deployment plays an equally important role in the life cycle of software development. By what means is the application to be distributed or released into production? What is the process for moving an application to a testing environment? What is the process for upgrading or patching an application already in production? These decisions should be made during the application design phase to accommodate the development and testing phases of the software development life cycle.

12.1 Reducing Complexity with Decomposition

The most effective way of designing an application architecture is by decomposing an application into separate components. This is the underlying theme in all modern forms of design and is the foundation of object-oriented development. Component based architectures are built on the concept of modules, which can be developed, changed, or upgraded independently of the entire application. This builds a high level of abstraction, and allows applications to be developed in team environments. It also produces code that is more maintainable then applications with a centralized design.

However, application architects should be wary of the amount of granularity used with component-based design. While decomposing an application into separate components has many benefits, separating components into too granular of a framework can actually make an application more complex. The key is to have a sound organization to the separation of components, and to size the level of component granularity with the size of both the application and the development team.

Methods for Architecting JSP Components

There are several methods that can be used to physically separate JSP applications into different components. Each of these has advantages and disadvantages based on the type of application, the size of the application, and the skill level of the application developers.

The first method is the most simple. It involves creating different components in different JSP pages and combining them with dynamic include actions. The second method is by far the most prevalent, and involves connecting the JSP page to external JavaBeans or Enterprise JavaBeans. The third method is rapidly growing in popularity, and involves creating modules in tag libraries.

Each of these different methods has different strengths and weaknesses based on individual situations, and in general it is best to combine these methods and utilize them where they have the most advantages.

Using Dynamic Page Includes

By utilizing include action tags, individual JSP page components can be created as separate JSP files. This is very similar to using dynamic Server Side

Includes (SSI). This method was used in Chapter 7 to add new components to an application as they were developed. While this can be a quick and dirty way of creating reusable code, the inherent problems of this architecture are significant.

There are scalability issues with this method. Another issue is difficulties in sharing information between the pages. Further, there is not standardized interface for connecting the components (JSP pages) together. There is also the inability of one JSP author to work with another's code without large amounts of documentation, detailed comments, and an understanding of general strategy.

Despite all of these drawbacks, using include actions do serve a good purpose and are perfect for many different types of situations. This is especially true with small applications or small components that only provide limited functionality. Used in combination with other component methods they help compose a good component programming "arsenal."

Using JavaBeans and Enterprise JavaBeans

Using JavaBeans is covered in Chapter 8. In the world of Java programming, JavaBeans are considered the defacto standard for component programming. They have come a long way from their original intended use as GUI components. Most Java Servlet and JSP page authors consider them to be the standard method of creating Java components. However, due to their ability to be used in many different situations, there are a few inherent features of JavaBeans that are not perfectly suited for JSP page authoring. In general these disadvantages are seen as a limitation of connecting JSP page and JavaBean technologies together, and not limitations of the JavaBean API itself.

Advantages and Disadvantages of using JavaBeans with JSP

Some of the disadvantages of using JavaBeans with JSP are inherent in the functionality and design of JavaBeans, but they affect JSP programming nonetheless. The advantages all lean toward the benefits of object-oriented programming, with emphasis on code reusability and maintainability as well as component design.

Probably the most common complaint about JavaBeans is the required use of a standard, argumentless constructor. In cases where a single attribute needs to be sent to the JavaBean it is cumbersome to use both the `useBean` and `setProperty` tags.

In addition the JSP-JavaBean syntax is often seen as very cumbersome. For example:

```
<jsp:useBean id="myBean" class="MyBean" scope="session">
<jsp:setProperty  name="myBean" property="prop" value="val">

can easily be replaced with:

<%
   MyBean myBean = (MyBean)session.getAttribute("myBean");
   if (myBean == null) {
     myBean = new MyBean();
     session.setAttribute("myBean", myBean);
   }
   myBean.setProp("val");
%>
```

While the former takes up less space, it is argued that the latter is more readable to the average Java programmer. It also gives better insight to what actions are actually being performed.

Another common criticism of using JavaBeans with JSP is the awkwardness of the `getProperty` and `setProperty` tags. It is cumbersome to set JavaBean properties that are not `Strings`. There is `String` conversion for the basic types such as `int`, `byte`, or `char`. In addition request parameters can be used to set properties. If the JSP author needs to set a property of another type, the only method using the `setProperty` tag is to use a request time computation, such as an expression. This begs the question: Why use an expression within a `setProperty` tag when the property can be set directly within a scriptlet? None of the methods for using a setProperty tag with a non-`String` value are straightforward.

Furthermore, getting objects with the `getProperty` tag forces the data to be formatted within the standard `toString()` method of the object. This is useless in situations where the results of the `toString()` method don't contain usable data. For example, most of the collections classes, such as Vector or HashMap, tend to use `toString()` as a debugging tool. In addition, the JSP-JavaBean action tags do not support indexed (multivalue) properties within JavaBeans. This means that there is no straightforward way to send multiple-value objects to and from JavaBeans using JSP-JavaBean actions.

While there are many difficulties with utilizing JavaBeans in JSP pages, they are still seen as a superior architecture due to their component programming benefits. JavaBeans minimize the amount of code in the JSP pages. This is a definite step forward toward a separation of presentation and application logic. It is generally accepted that it is much easier to maintain a Web application if you keep the code in the JSP pages to a minimum.

JavaBeans also support introspection, which allows an IDE to provide a visual design feature. When moving in "Internet time," there is enormous value in integrating components into Integrated Developer Environments (IDEs) for rapid application development.

Additionally, JavaBeans promote a more reusable, object-oriented design. By using JavaBeans other Java applications, such as Applets or standalone applications, can utilize their functionality.

Finally, and probably most important, the JavaBeans API is simple. JavaBeans can be used to make small, lightweight components that are easy to implement and use. JSP developers can learn the basic concepts of JavaBeans very quickly and begin writing and using simple components with very little effort.

Using Tag Libraries with JSP

Using tag libraries is covered heavily in Chapter 11. Tag libraries are a relatively new technology. In general, developing tag libraries is seen as a large amount of work, but using the custom tags that are created is seen as a straightforward task. Page designers with limited Java skills, as well as visual development environments, should be able to utilize tab libraries easily.

The Advantages and Disadvantages of Using Tag Libraries

By far the biggest disadvantage of using tag libraries is their complexity. Several different components must come together for custom tags to work. Besides the tags themselves, there is the `taglib` directive, the tag library, and the tag library descriptor. Each of these components must be written correctly and stored in specific locations for tag libraries to work.

Due to the complex nature of tag libraries, they are also hard to setup and deploy. Additionally, limited support for tag libraries existed at the time this book was written, making the use of tag libraries dependent on the application platform selected.

Another limitation of tag libraries is their suitability for components outside of JSP pages. While a JavaBean can be created that serves as a back end for both a standalone application as well as a JSP page, tag libraries are specifically limited to JSP page programming.

There are several advantages to using tag libraries. First and foremost is that they are simple to use. The JSP author does not need to understand the inner workings of the custom tag to be able to develop with it. Custom tags are used the exact same way as JSP action tags, making them scripting-language neutral.

Tag libraries can also be extremely useful with visual development environments. It's likely that many standard HTML editors will support the use of custom tags in the near future. Because they are portable in nature and use XML as a configuration language they are perfect for integrating into IDEs.

Tag libraries are an excellent way to separate Java code from the presentation layer. They are the perfect solution for creating templates or for including control-flow operations into JSP pages in a component-based, reusable manner.

Tag libraries, just like JavaBeans and include actions, have their own advantages and disadvantages. Taken together these three methods allow many different types of decomposing JSP pages into reusable components.

JSP Design Models

Having taken a look at the different physical levels that JSP applications can be broken down into, it is important to have an overall strategy or organization for how the different components relate.

Most JSP applications fall into two levels of component organization, separated by the role or responsibility each component plays in the application life cycle. The first level of separation is natural in JSP applications, as it was the foundation on which JSP was developed. This is separation of presentation logic from application logic. Often called page-centric design, this model can be thought of as a typical "JSP only" application. In early JSP specifications this model was called Model 1 (See Figure 12.1).

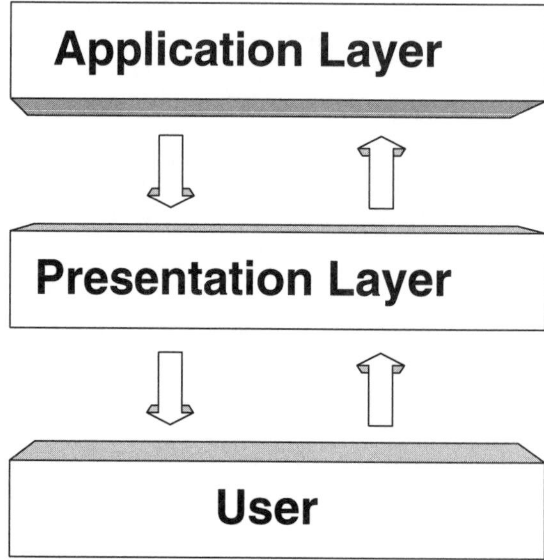

Figure 12–1 Separation of the Application and Presentation Logic

A second level of component organization is to take the existing Model 1 and separate the controller logic from the presentation logic. This model was called Model 2, and is often referred to as a Servlet-oriented design, due to the fact that it is almost always implemented with both JSP pages and Java Servlets. Model 2 has separate components to deal with the user interface, application, and user interaction (see Figure 12.2).

To further understand these concepts it is a good idea to get a solid understanding of the differences between presentation, application, and controller logic.

Presentation Logic

Presentation logic is the part of the application that deals with the presentation layer. It deals with the user interface and Web-based elements, such as HTML and XML. Presentation logic is concerned with displaying the information, not how the information was retrieved or how the application chose to display this information.

Presentation logic components can also contain logic about the direction the application will flow based on user input. When this happens there is no controller component. In other words, it handles not just displaying information to the user, but receiving information as well. In the case of JSP pages this means handling both the HTTP request as well as the response. When presentation logic contains logic to process the HTTP request, there is no separation of presentation logic from controller logic.

Controller Logic

Controller logic may or may not be present in the presentation logic, and this is the delineation between the different levels of JSP application component separation. Controller logic "controls" the application flow, and serves as the connector between the user interface and the application.

In the JSP application controller logic receives and interprets the HTTP request, deciding the next step of the application based on user input. When there is a separation of controller logic, the presentation layer simply concerns itself with the HTTP response.

A key function of the controller layer is the management of connections to the application layer. In the case of JavaBeans this means instantiating and connecting to the JavaBeans, as well as passing the results to the presentation layer.

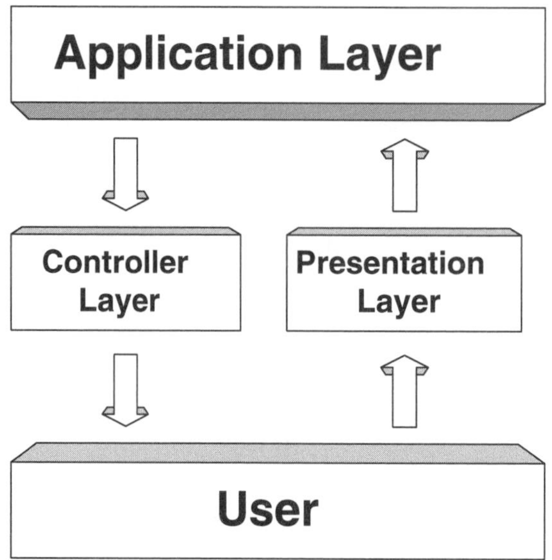

Figure 12–2 Separation of the Presentation and Controller Logic

Application Logic

Application logic is the center of the application. The application logic is responsible for the logic behind what the application is supposed to accomplish. For example, in a Web-based registration system the application logic would consist of taking the submitted name, checking it against the database, adding it to the database, and returning a result.

It is important to point out that there is no user interface logic in the application layer. This means that the application logic components can reside completely outside of the JSP application; in an Enterprise JavaBean or a CORBA API, for example.

One of the great benefits of a separate application logic layer is the ability to have multiple user interfaces to the same application. A Swing Java stand-alone application can connect to the same JavaBeans that a JSP application connects to and perform the same functionality through a different GUI.

Model 1: Separating Presentation and Application Logic

JSP Model 1 is what is though of as the traditional JSP architecture (see Figure 12.3). In Model 1 the browsers sends a request to the JSP page. The

JSP page connects to JavaBeans to process application logic and connect to data sources. The JSP page then connects to the JavaBean and sends a response to the browser. There is a separation of presentation and application logic.

JSP Model 1 is seen as a reasonable solution for fairly simple applications. Issues arise when the logic contained within the JSP page grows. With a large amount of logic there tends to be a lot of scriptlets or Java code within the JSP page. This is often the case with large applications. As a Java developer this may not seem a problem, but when designers maintain the JSP page an issue can arise from having large amounts of Java code on a JSP page.

In essence, the problem is that having two roles—application logic and presentation logic—is no longer sufficient to have a good separation of code. As more and more logic surrounds processing the HTTP request there is a greater need for separate "controller" logic to guide the flow of data and logic within the application. This idea gives birth to the JSP Model 2.

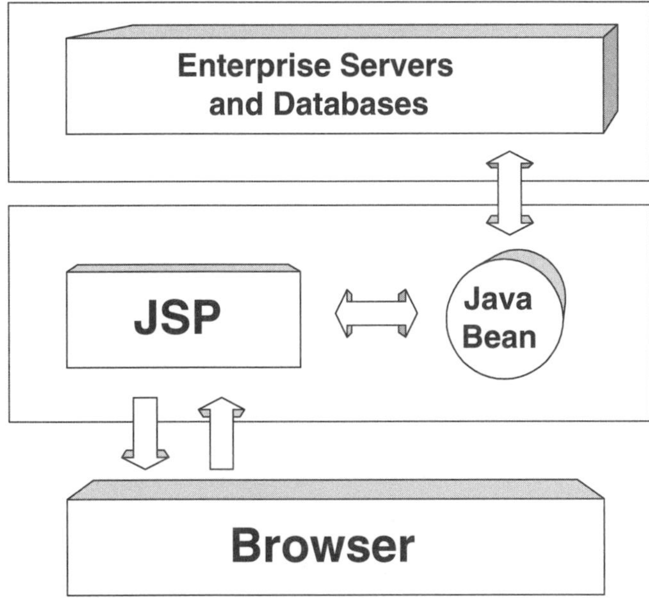

Figure 12–3 Model 1 JSP Architecture

Model 2: Separating Controller and Presentation Logic

JSP Model 2 adds a Java Servlet to the architecture to fulfill the role of processing the HTTP request and controlling data and logic flow. It decides what JSP page to forward to based on the request. It also is responsible for instantiating or connecting to any JavaBeans for application logic.

This model takes advantage of the strengths of both Servlets and JSP pages. Servlets are especially strong in processing-intensive tasks, and JSP pages are excellent for presenting data.

The three roles that make up the JSP Model 2 often mimic the roles of enterprise development projects. There is often a team for a core programming API represented by the JavaBeans or Enterprise JavaBeans. Another team might represent creating a Web-based front end for the API, much as another team might develop a Java Swing-based front end. This is represented by the Servlet or controller logic. Finally the JSP pages represent the designers or creative team of the development project. All in all, the Model 2 design pattern adds a new layer of abstraction to the JSP application development process, helping to scale the development of large, enterprise applications.

Listing 12.1 shows a simple controller servlet that determines which of three JSP pages to forward to, based on user input. It first handles new clients that do not have sessions by forwarding them to the login JSP page.

Then the Servlet determines the value of the request attribute "`action`". If action is equal to "`EDIT`", the page is forwarded onto `editData.jsp`, otherwise the page is forwarded on to `viewData.jsp`. Note that there are no JavaBeans instantiated inside on `ControllerServlet.java` as it is not necessary in this example. This is often the case in more complicated applications where more processing is needed to determine the appropriate course of action. `ControllerServlet.java` is a basic example of how controller logic is separated from presentation logic in JSP Model 2.

It is important to note that the ideas behind Model 2 are not new. They are based on a tried and tested programming pattern that predates Java itself. In fact, JSP Model 2 mirrors the ideas behind the Model-View-Controller (MVC) architecture developed for the SmallTalk programming environment.

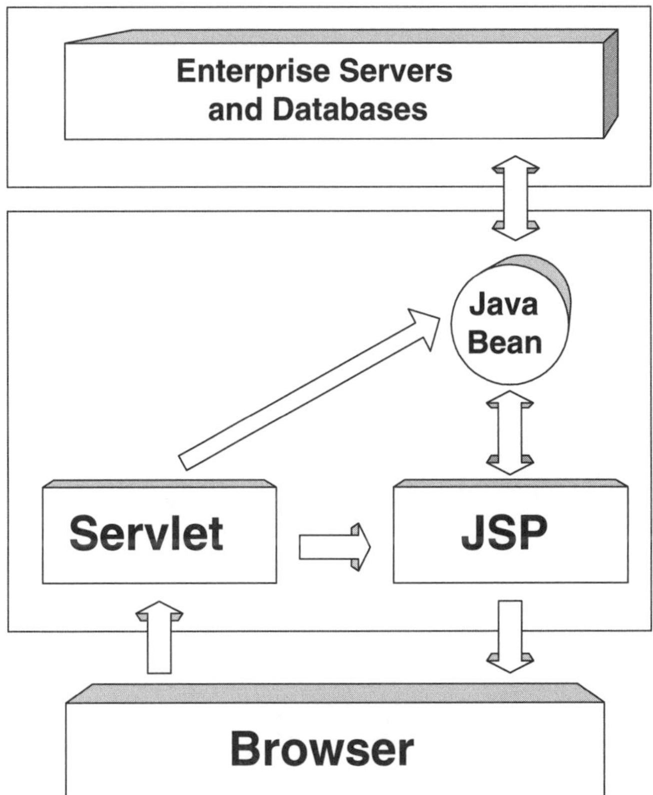

Figure 12–4 Model 2 JSP Architecture

Listing 12.1 ControllerServlet.java

```
import java.util.*;
import java.io.*;
import javax.servlet.*;
import javax.servlet.http.*;

public class ControllerServlet extends HttpServlet {

  public void doPost
       (HttpServletRequest req, HttpServletResponse res)
      throws ServletException, IOException {
```

Listing 12.1 ControllerServlet.java (continued)

```
    HttpSession session = req.getSession(false);
    if (session == null) {
      res.sendRedirect("/jsp/login.jsp");
    }

    ServletContext sc = getServletContext();
    String action = req.getParameter("action");

    if (!action.equals("EDIT")) {
      String url="/jsp/editData.jsp";
    } else {
      String url="/jsp/viewData.jsp";
    }

    RequestDispatcher rd = sc.getRequestDispatcher(url);
    rd.forward(req, res);

  }

  public void doGet
       (HttpServletRequest req, HttpServletResponse res)
      throws ServletException, IOException {
    doPost(req, res);
  }
}
```

Remember that both Model 1 and Model 2 are viable JSP application strategies. Only by carefully analyzing the size and scope of the application, the development environment, and the skill set of the development team can the right model be chosen for a particular application.

12.2 JSP Application Deployment

Even before an application is created, a deployment strategy should be developed for the incremental, test, quality control, and production releases of the application. This strategy should take into account the installation and configuration of files not only in the first installation, but with successive upgrades as well. A well-planned deployment strategy saves time during the software development life cycle.

There are two basic methods for deploying an application. The first method is to deploy the application by a custom method. This means creating an install script that correctly deploys the application files in the proper location and configures it appropriately. While this is a nonstandard method, it might be necessary for some complex or proprietary applications.

The second method is to use archive files. With archive files, such as .jar, .war, and .ear files, there is a standard location as well as configuration for a Web application, including all of its associated files. Created and maintained correctly, archives can be deployed across multiple standard application servers with ease.

ZIP, JAR, WAR, and EAR

Early on in the development of Java a need arose to package together files that compose Java applications. To resolve this problem there has been a series of different archive architectures developed to package files together into maintainable collections.

In the early stages this collection of files was maintained within a ZIP (.zip) file. By using Phillip Katz's standard data compression format, a series of Java classes could be packaged into a single file. Individual files could be read from this archive on an as-needed basis. But soon the Java framers realized that there was a fair amount of metadata that was required in packaging Java files together for deployment. This gave birth to the Java archive, or JAR (.jar) file.

Java archives are still a collection of files compressed into a single file, but in addition they contain specific information about how to deploy the files within the archive. This is most often implemented by creating a top-level directory in the archive titled `META-INF`. Inside the `META-INF` directory is a file called `manifest.mf`, which contains configuration information about the application, usually in colon delimited name/value pairs. In Chapter 8 a `manifest.mf` file entry of `Java-Bean: true` was necessary to let the application server know that the Java classes are to be considered a JavaBean. While Java archives files are still the most common types of archives used for distributing Java applications, the `manifest.mf` file has many limitations. It is a proprietary format, and the colon delimited name/value pair is limited in its ability to describe complex configurations. With complex Web application architectures the `manifest.mf` file simply would not suffice. This led to the development of the Web archive, or WAR (.war) file.

WAR files were introduced with the Java Servlet API, but due to the close relationship of Servlets and JSP pages they serve as an excellent method for distributing JSP applications. WAR files are JAR files with a .war extension, so they maintain the same file compression of previous archives. A WAR file can contain more than just Java class files. Some example files include Java Servlets, utility class files, JSP Pages, static HTML and XML documents, JavaBeans, Applets, and metainformation that ties the application together. The WAR file takes the idea of a `META-INF` directory and expands on its functionality. In a WAR file there is a top-level directory called `WEB-INF`. This directory holds classes and files within its directory tree. An important file to note is `web.xml`, which is commonly known as the deployment descriptor. This files expands on the `manifest.mf` file by providing an XML format for standard, extensible configurations.

But alas, once again the WAR archive format was great for its use for deploying Web-centric Java Servlet and JSP page applications, but did not scale to extremely large enterprise applications that extend outside of the Web platform. To resolve this issue a new Java archive format was created, called Enterprise archives or EAR (.ear) files.

Enterprise archives are a product of the Java 2 Enterprise Edition (J2EE). J2EE is a release of the Java Development Kit that contains the APIs for creating enterprise applications. EAR files are seen as a supercontainer for collecting multiple WAR and JAR files into a single application that is simple to deploy. For example, an application could have an HTML page to submit the user data, a servlet to process the data, and a JavaBean to store data in a database. The HTML page and Servlet are stored in a WAR file, the JavaBean is stored in a JAR file, and the WAR and JAR files are both stored in a EAR file, which is deployed to production.

Configuration of EAR files and their related WAR and JAR files can be complicated, so bundled with the J2EE SDK is the application deployment tool (DeployTool). This is a configuration tool for creating and editing JAR, WAR, and EAR files. Another powerful feature of DeployTool is its ability to connect directly to application servers to deploy EAR applications. DeployTool is a pure Java application and should run on any platform that supports the J2EE.

Support for WAR and EAR Files

It should be noted that both WAR and EAR files are relatively new technologies at the time this book was written. Care should be taken to ensure that the application server or JSP engine selected for production supports WAR or EAR files before selecting them for a deployment strategy.

WAR Files 101

Web archives, or WAR files, are the archive of choice for deploying JSP applications. Within the WAR files there is a directory structure that mimics the directory structure of a document root within a Web server. In addition there is a `WEB-INF` directory that contains information about the configuration of the application, as well as classes and JAR files containing Servlets, JavaBeans, and utility class files needed by the application.

The `WEB-INF` directory contains the `web.xml` file as well as two different directories: `classes` and `lib`. `classes` contains Servlet and utility classes needed by the application. `lib` contains JAR files that might contain Servlets, JavaBeans, and utility classes that might be useful to the application. Listing 12.2 gives an example of a WAR file that might be the output of a `jar tvf sample.war` command. Note that the real difference between the `lib` and `classes` directory is whether or not the included Java classes are maintained in a JAR or are simply in their package hierarchy.

Listing 12.2 A sample WAR file.

```
/index.html
/viewData.jsp
/editData.jsp
/images/logo.gif
/images/dot_clear.gif
/WEB-INF/web.xml
/WEB-INF/lib/editBean.jar
/WEB-INF/classes/com/javadesktop/servlets/viewServ-
let.class
/WEB-INF/classes/com/javadesktop/util/MyConversion.class
```

web.xml: The Deployment Descriptor

The `web.xml` file, commonly known as the deployment descriptor, contains configuration and deployment information about the Web application. It can contain information about the application in general, such as MIME type mappings, error pages, session configuration, and security. It can contain information about definitions and mappings to both JSP pages and Servlets. Another type of information that can be contained within the deployment descriptor is Servlet context initialization parameters.

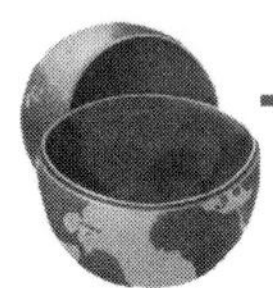

CORE Note: web.xml section sequence

It is important to note that the DTD of the web.xml file defines a particular sequence that entries can occur within the web.xml file.

Since many applications do not validate the XML of the web.xml file, an inappropriately setup web.xml file may be read without problems but may not behave as expected. Worse still in these cases the application will work until the required information from the web.xml file is needed.

Unfortunately there are too many potential attributes to a web.xml file to list them all here. If the sequence of the sample web.xml file shown here is followed then its fairly safe. Alternatively, finding out the exact details of the sequence would require examining the DTD itself.

Listing 12.3 is a simple `web.xml` file created around a servlet and a JSP page. It includes a good selection of the different parameters that can be configured in a WAR file.

Listing 12.3 A Simple web.xml Example

```
<!DOCTYPE web-app PUBLIC
  "-//Sun Microsystems, Inc.//DTD Web Application 2.2//EN"
  "http://java.sun.com/j2ee/dtds/web-app_2_2.dtd">
<web-app>
  <display-name>Sample Application</display-name>
  <context-param>
    <param-name>email</param-name>
    <param-value>webmaster@javadesktop.com</param-value>
  </context-param>
  <servlet>
    <servlet-name></servlet-name>
    <description>no description</description>
    <jsp-file>index.jsp</jsp-file>
  </servlet>
  <servlet>
    <servlet-name>ViewData</servlet-name>
    <servlet-class>com.javadesktop.ViewData</servlet-class>
    <init-param>
```

Listing 12.3 A Simple web.xml Example (continued)

```
      <param-name>Region</param-name>
      <param-value>North-East</param-value>
    </init-param>
  </servlet>
  <servlet-mapping>
    <servlet-name>ViewData</servlet-name>
    <url-pattern>/listing/*</url-pattern>
  </servlet-mapping>
  <session-config>
    <session-timeout>15</session-timeout>
  </session-config>
  <taglib>
    <taglib-uri>/taglib/mailtags</taglib-uri>
    <taglib-location>jsp/mailtags.tld</taglib-location>
  </taglib>
  <mime-mapping>
    <extension>pdf</extension>
    <mime-type>application/pdf</mime-type>
  </mime-mapping>
  <welcome-file-list>
    <welcome-file>index.jsp</welcome-file>
    <welcome-file>index.html</welcome-file>
    <welcome-file>main.htm</welcome-file>
  <welcome-file-list>
  <error-page>
    <error-code>404</error-code>
    <location>/error.html</location>
  </error-page>
</web-app>
```

As the deployment descriptor is an XML file, the first section is the DTD:

```
<!DOCTYPE web-app PUBLIC
  "-//Sun Microsystems, Inc.//DTD Web Application 2.2//EN"
  "http://java.sun.com/j2ee/dtds/web-app_2_2.dtd">
```

Next the `<web-app>` tag opens the definition of the Web application. The first entry within the `<web-app>` is the `<display-name>` tag, which represents a name for this particular Web application for GUI tools.

Next comes the parameters for the Servlet context of this Web application:

```
<context-param>
  <param-name>email</param-name>
  <param-value>webmaster@javadesktop.com</param-value>
</context-param>
```

Here a parameter with the name "email" is given a value of "webmaster@javadesktop.com". As all files in this Web application share the same Servlet context, this parameter will be available to any JSP page or Servlet contained within.

Following the Servlet context parameters is the Servlet definitions:

```
<servlet>
  <servlet-name></servlet-name>
  <jsp-file>index.jsp</jsp-file>
</servlet>
<servlet>
  <servlet-name>ViewData</servlet-name>
  <servlet-class>com.javadesktop.ViewData</servlet-class>
  <init-param>
    <param-name>Region</param-name>
    <param-value>North-East</param-value>
  </init-param>
</servlet>
```

There are two servlet definitions here, one being a JSP page and one being a traditional Servlet. `<servlet-name>` is the canonical name of the Servlet, and is referenced in other sections of the `web.xml` file. JSP pages do not require a `<servlet-name>` tag. `<jsp-file>` contains the full path to a JSP file within the Web application. `<servlet-class>` describes the fully qualified class name of the Servlet. Again, this is not necessary for a JSP page. `<init-param>` is used to describe parameters in name/value pairs, very similar to the `<context-param>` tag. In this case a parameter with the name "Region" is given a value of "North-East".

The next section of the deployment descriptor describes Servlet mappings, and is contained within `<servlet-mapping>` tags.

```
<servlet-mapping>
  <servlet-name>ViewData</servlet-name>
  <url-pattern>/listing/*</url-pattern>
</servlet-mapping>
```

Every Servlet must be mapped to a URL pattern on the Web server. Notice that there is a `<servlet-name>` parameter tag here that corresponds to a Servlet defined above in the `web.xml` file. The other tag contained within this section is the `<url-pattern>` tag, which signifies the URL pattern with which to map the Servlet. Also note that JSP pages do not require Servlet mapping.

Next comes the session configuration section:

```
<session-config>
  <session-timeout>15</session-timeout>
</session-config>
```

The `<session-config>` section currently contains only one element: `<session-timeout>`. This element describes the default number of whole minutes that should pass before a session times out. This setting is for the whole Web application.

Next comes the taglib configuration section:

```
<taglib>
  <taglib-uri>/taglib/mailtags</taglib-uri>
  <taglib-location>jsp/mailtags.tld</taglib-location>
</taglib>
```

The `<taglig>` section defines how the application should register tag libraries. This essentially creates an alias from the given URI into the TLD. When the engine reads a reference to the URI within a taglib directive tag, it is able to match it to the corresponding location.

The <taglib> section is followed by the <mime-mapping> section:

```
<mime-mapping>
    <extension>pdf</extension>
    <mime-type>application/pdf</mime-type>
  </mime-mapping>
```

The <mime-mapping> section defines mappings between file extensions and MIME types. In this example the Adobe Acrobat `pdf` file type is defined. After the MIME type section is the welcome page section:

```
<welcome-file-list>
  <welcome-file>index.jsp</welcome-file>
  <welcome-file>index.html</welcome-file>
  <welcome-file>main.htm</welcome-file>
<welcome-file-list>
```

The welcome page section defines an ordered list of file names to use for the default file in a directory URL. In this example there are three file types listed in order to be selected. The final section in Listing 12.3 is an `<error-page>` section:

```
<error-page>
  <error-code>404</error-code>
  <location>/error.html</location>
</error-page>
```

This section contains a mapping between an error code or exception type to the path of a resource in the Web application. In this example, the HTTP error code of 404 (File Not Found) is mapped to the URL `/error.html`.

In closing the Web application there is a `</web-app>` tag. While Listing 12.3 has a fair number of example tags used, deployment descriptors can be far more complex. For a detailed guide on the syntax of the `web.xml` file see the Java Servlet 2.2 specification, available at the Sun Java Web site: *http://www.java.sun.com/*

While an understanding of the capabilities and syntax of the `web.xml` file are important to understand, WAR files and `web.xml` files can be quickly created and edited utilizing the application deployment tool that is packaged with the J2EE development kit. This tool is commonly known as DeployTool.

Sun DeployTool

The Sun application deployment tool, or DeployTool, is an excellent cross-platform means for creating EAR, WAR, and JAR files. It is distributed with the J2EE Software Development Kit, which is available from Sun Microsystems without cost. It is distributed on Microsoft Windows and Sun Sparc platforms, but should be able to run on any Java 2 JVM.

To utilize the DeployTool to create WAR, JAR, and EAR files the application must first be installed. It is packaged with the J2EE SDK, and can be downloaded from the Sun Java Web site (*http://www.java.sun.com/*). Once installed, be sure that environmental variables for JAVA_HOME and J2EE_HOME are set. Next, DeployTool can be launched by executing the appropriate script for your system (usually `deploytool.bat` or `deploy-`

`tool.sh`). Once launched, DeployTool should display a screen similar to that of Figure 12.5.

DeployTool is an EAR file centric application, so before a WAR file can be created a new application object must be created. To do this choose "New Application..." from the File menu. If a WAR file is desired, the name of this application is unimportant. Next, a new Web application needs to be created. To do this, "New Web Component..." is selected from the File menu. This starts the WAR file wizard. After an informational screen the wizard should look like Figure 12.6. This screen allows configuration of the information that pertains to the entire WAR application.

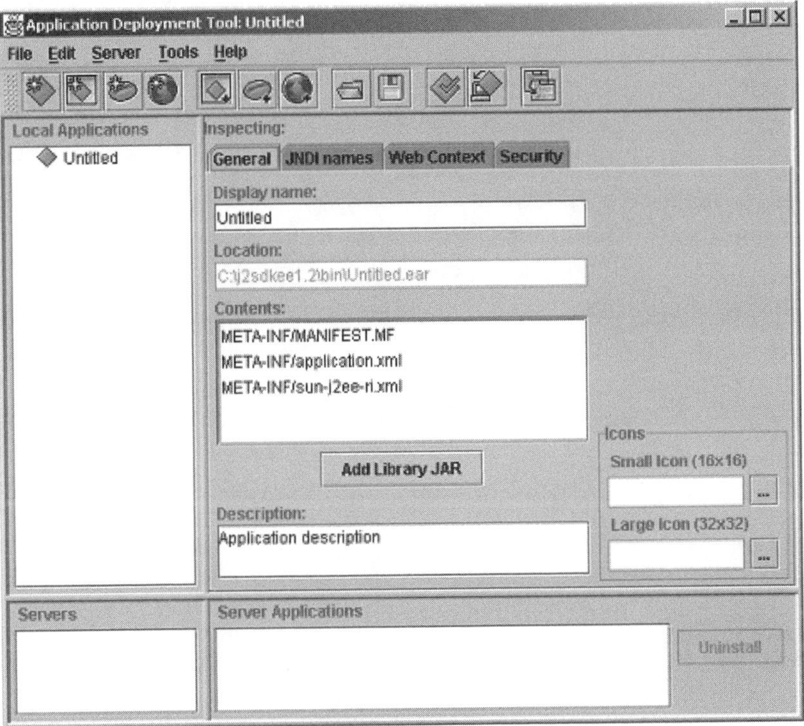

Figure 12–5 DeployTool Primary Interface

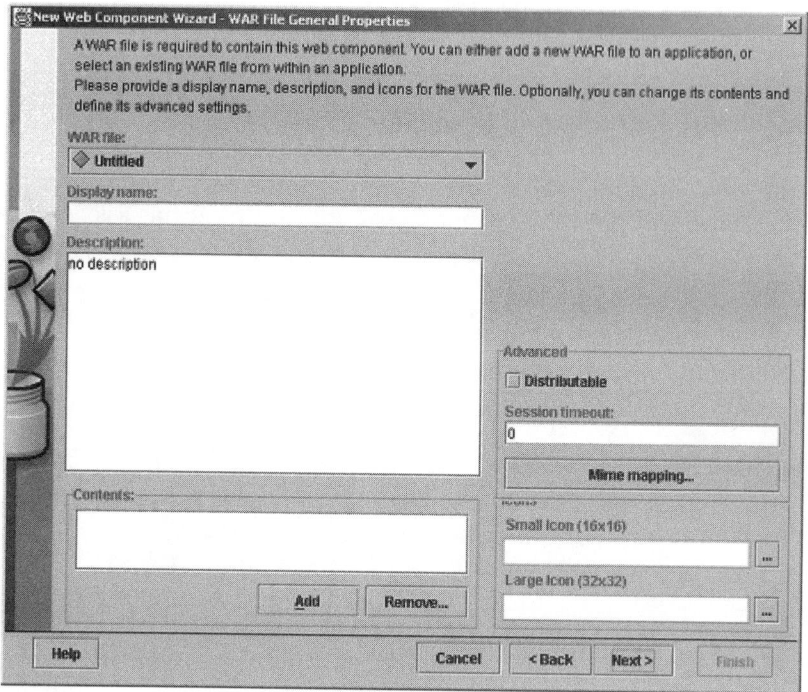

Figure 12–6 DeployTool War File Component Interface

The only information required on this page is to add contents to the WAR file. To do this click on the "Add..." button. A screen comes up looking like Figure 12.7.

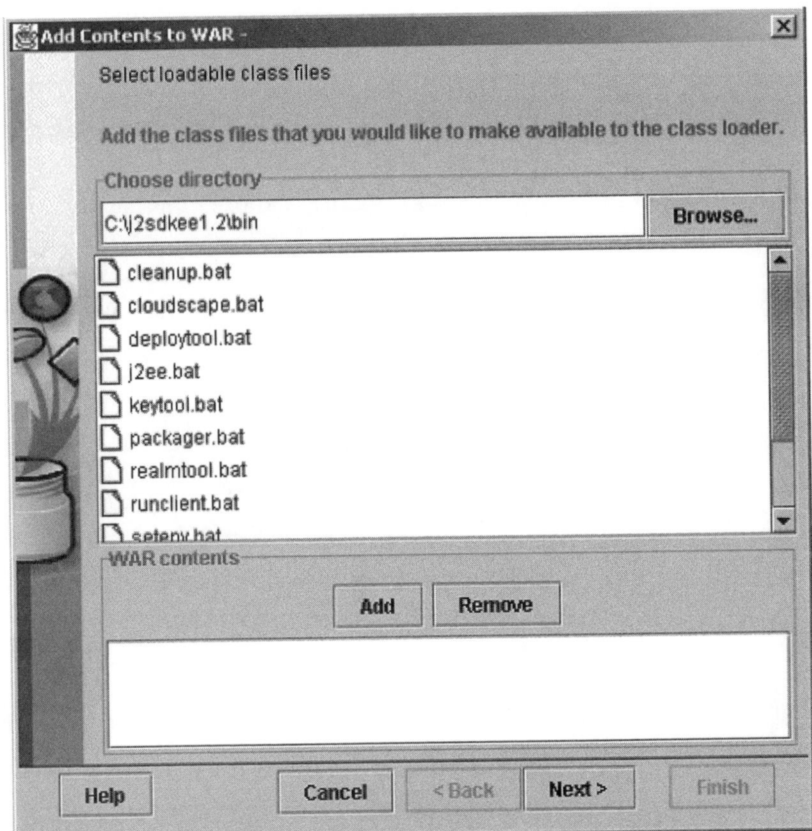

Figure 12–7 DeployTool Add Class File Interface

This is the first of two screens that allows files to be added to the WAR file. This first screen is for Java class files, including JAR files. In this section all Servlets, JavaBeans, and other utility class files should be added. When complete, the "Next" button should be selected. This brings up a similar page, this time for content files. The page should look like Figure 12.8. Content files include HTML pages, XML pages, image files, style sheets, and other Web-based components, as well as JSP pages.

After clicking "Next," a screen comes up asking weather the Web component will contain a Servlet, JSP page, or no Web component. Choose the correct choice, and then choose "Finish." While there are other configuration options, this is the default number of choices necessary to create a WAR file.

DeployTool should now be back at the original opening page. To save the WAR file select the "Web App" object in the Local Applications tree hierarchy. Then choose "Save As..." from the "File" menu. This will allow the WAR file to be saved. While this was only a quick run-through of DeployTool's capabilities, it should be obvious that it is a time-saving tool for creating WAR files.

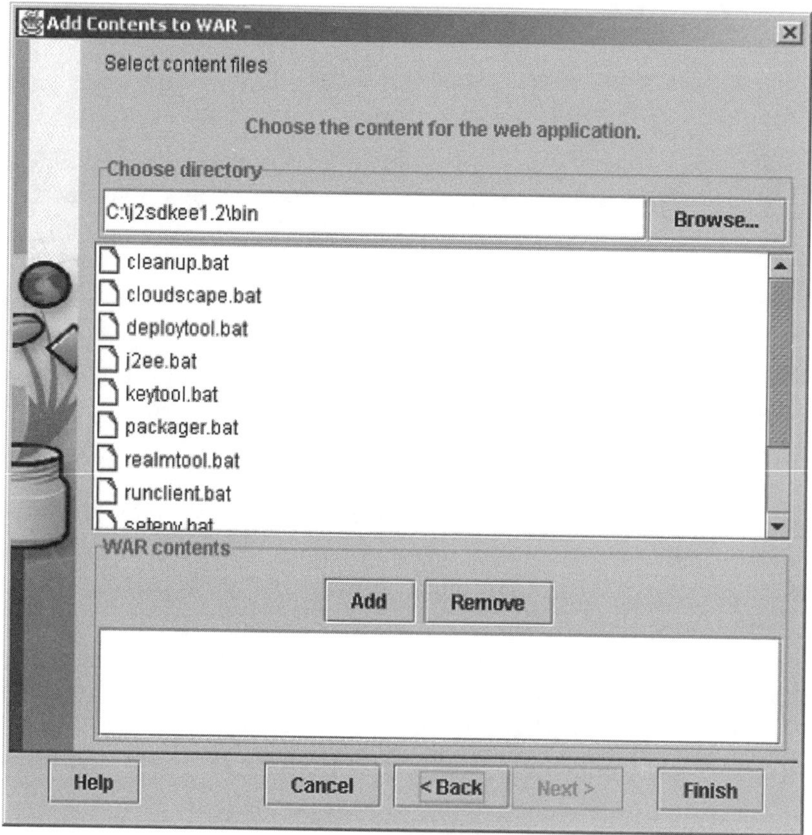

Figure 12-8 DeployTool Add Content File Interface

Which is the best strategy?

While the design and deployment options for JSP programs are somewhat new, they contain enterprise-class strategies for architecting and releasing applications. As there are several different options to choose from, the JSP author soon realizes that there is more than one way to create an application. The key is to use the versatility and options of JSP design and deployment options to develop an application that best suits its needs and requirements.

THE FUTURE

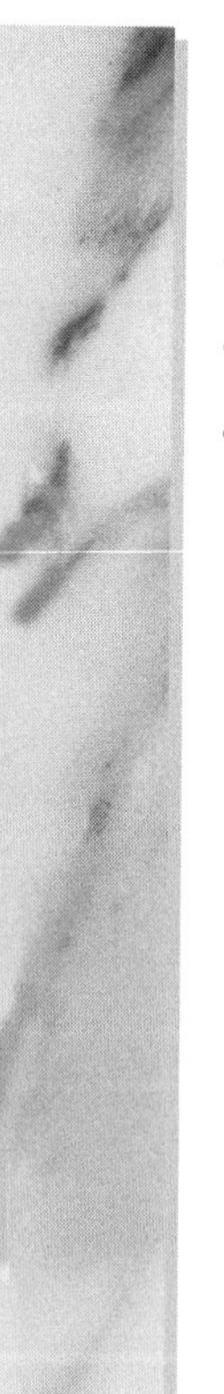

Topics in this Chapter:

- The Impact of the J2EE
- JSP and GUI Tools
- XML, XML, and more XML
- Where Do I Go From Here?

Chapter 13

It is obvious that JSP page development has a large future in Web application development. It is almost weekly that a new or existing application is released with JSP support. This is the testament to the flexibility of JSP.

It is also important to note that JSP is fairly new, so keep sharp eyes out for new specifications and enhancements.

The Impact of the J2EE

With the release of the J2EE edition of Java, a new world of standards-based Web applications has emerged. Developers of Web application servers are scrambling to write J2EE compliance into their servers. Java developers are excited about the ability to package and deploy their applications in a common format that can be transferred across servers and platforms.

Never before have Enterprise JavaBean, DCOM, and CORBA applications been so easy to integrate. J2EE provides the foundation for every part of designing, developing, and deploying Web applications.

With the widespread adoption of J2EE comes the integration of JSP pages. JSP provides the front end for enterprise Java applications on the Web, and plays a vital role in developing scaleable, cross-platform software. As Web applications become more sophisticated, the capabilities of JSP will grow.

JSP and GUI Tools

As the popularity of JSP pages increase, look for the integration of JSP page creation in HTML page-development tools to increase. JSP was built from the ground up to be easy to parse, thus making it easily editable in a development tool.

Already, many popular environments such as Macromedia Dreamweaver, Adobe GoLive, and Allaire Homesite have announced JSP integration. These are just the forefront of a wave of JSP/HTML tools to hit the market.

Also look for Java Integrated Development Environments (IDEs) to feature JSP integration and debugging. Sun's Forte for Java and IBM WebSphere Studio already feature these tools, and many of their competitors have announced future integration.

By far the most promising part of JSP pages is tag libraries, which are ripe for integration into both JSP/HTML editors as well as Java IDEs. With their portable framework, XML syntax, and advanced configuration features, they are perfect for packaging and deploying reusable JSP components.

In the future, different development environments with JSP support can share components in the form of tag libraries. With their ability to hide underlying logic they are perfect for software developers who want to develop tools that protect intellectual property while giving maximum flexibility.

All in all, JSP pages will play an important role in development environments. They allow for quick creation and deployment of Web applications, which is important in today's mindset of Internet time.

XML, XML, and more XML

In the future, XML will also play a major role in Web application development. JSP pages are perfect for both XML page generation as well as integration into XML tools. This is mostly due to the close relationship JSP has with Java, as well as the fact that Java hosts a comprehensive set of XML tools and libraries. The large set of tools available for manipulating XML is key here, as these tools can also be used to manipulate XML pages that are written to be XML-compliant.

While it is probably not true that XML will eventually replace HTML, it *is* probably true that HTML will become fully XML-compliant. In addition, XML is playing an ever-increasing role in applications beyond the Web. From application integration, to configuration management, to standardization, XML will play an important role in the future of enterprise applications.

While JSP pages are well integrated into XML, the JSP specification authors promise to add further integration in future releases of JSP. This is due to the integration of XML tools into the standard Java Development Kits (JDKs). You can be certain that the future of XML will play a vital role in the development of the JSP page specification.

Where do I go from here?

While JSP page applications are excellent tools on their own, they are only the tip of the iceberg for most enterprise Web applications—the icing on the cake, so to speak. They represent the final step of an application before data is presented to the user. Once JSP is mastered, a software developer should move his studies to the back office, learning the underlying core applications.

Relational and object-oriented database management systems are a good place to start, as they form the foundation for most Web applications. The next step would be to learn one or more of the distributed component environments, such as Enterprise JavaBeans, CORBA, or DCOM.

Another good area of study is Enterprise Application Integration (EAI). For the most part, the data needed in applications is out there, often in legacy or disparate systems. Connecting those systems to share data is often the biggest challenge.

Whatever area of study and development a developer chooses to follow, the techniques and models learned from JSP page development serve as a solid stepping-stone for keeping pace with the rapid evolution of today's software development.

Appendix A

JSP API QUICK REFERENCE

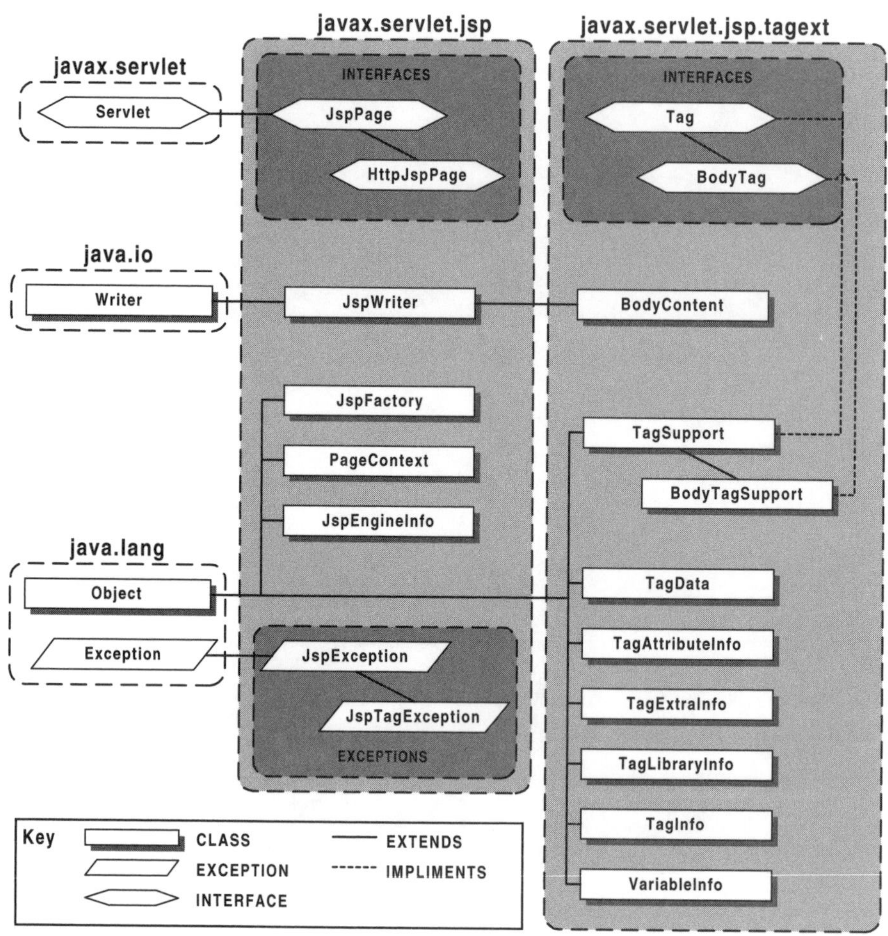
javax.servlet
Servlet
javax.servlet.jsp
INTERFACES
JspPage
HttpJspPage
javax.servlet.jsp.tagext
INTERFACES
Tag
BodyTag
java.io
Writer
JspWriter
BodyContent
JspFactory
PageContext
JspEngineInfo
TagSupport
BodyTagSupport
java.lang
Object
Exception
JspException
JspTagException
EXCEPTIONS
TagData
TagAttributeInfo
TagExtraInfo
TagLibraryInfo
TagInfo
VariableInfo
Key
CLASS
EXCEPTION
INTERFACE
EXTENDS
IMPLIMENTS

Classes in javax.servlet.jsp.*

The JSP 1.1 API package, javax.servlet.jsp, contains the following classes and interfaces:

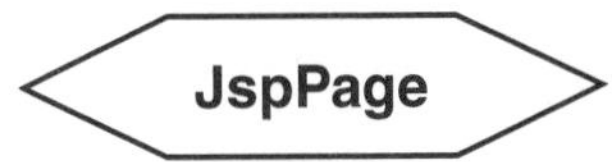

Interface:	**`javax.servlet.jsp.JspPage`**
SuperInterface:	`javax.servlet.Servlet`
SubInterfaces:	`javax.servlet.jsp.HttpJspPage`

This is the interface that a JSP engine will use to create classes from the JSP source code.

The interface defines a protocol with three methods; jspInit(), jspDestroy(), and _jspService(). The first two methods, jspInit() and jspDestroy(), can be defined by the JSP author.

The Third method _jspService depends on the specific protocol used and cannot be expressed in a generic way in Java. The _jspService() method should always be defined by the JSP processor based on the contents of the JSP page, and never manipulated by the JSP author. For these reasons it is not shown here.

Method:	**`jspInit`**
Parameters:	`none`
Returns:	`nothing (void)`

jspInit() is invoked when the JspPage is initialized.

Method:	`jspDestroy`
Parameters:	`none`
Returns:	`nothing (void)`

jsp_destroy() is invoked when the JspPage is about to be destroyed.

JspWriter

Class: **`javax.servlet.jsp.JspWriter`**
SuperClass: `java.io.Writer`
SubClasses: `javax.servlet.jsp.tagext.BodyContent`

This abstract class emulates some of the functionality found in the java.io.BufferedWriter and java.io.PrintWriter classes.

From a practical and functional standpoint, this class contains all the methods of the functions of PrintWriter and BufferedWriter (print, println, write, clear, et al). However it significantly differs in that it throws java.io.IOException from the print methods.

Since the methods directly reflect the methods of PrintWriter and BufferedWriter, they will not be listed here.

PageContext

Class: `javax.servlet.jsp.PageContext`
SuperClass: `java.lang.Object`
SubClasses: none

A PageContext instance provides access to all the namespaces associated with a JSP page, provides access to several page attributes, as well as creating the layer above the implementation details.

Field: **`static int PAGE_SCOPE`**
The named reference remains available in this PageContext until the return from the current Servlet.service() invocation.

Field: **`static int REQUEST_SCOPE`**
The named reference remains available from the ServletRequest associated with the Servlet until the current request is completed.

Field: **`static int SESSION_SCOPE`**
The named reference remains available from the HttpSession (if any) associated with the Servlet until the HttpSession is invalidated.

Field: **`static int APPLICATION_SCOPE`**
The named reference remains available in the ServletContext until it is reclaimed.

Field: **`static final String PAGE`**
Name used to store the Servlet in this PageContext's nametables.

Field: **`static final String PAGECONTEXT`**
Name used to store this PageContext in its own nametables.

Field: **`static final String REQUEST`**
Name used to store ServletRequest in PageContext nametable.

Field: **`static final String RESPONSE`**
Name used to store ServletResponse in PageContext nametable.

Field: **`static final String CONFIG`**
Name used to store ServletConfig in PageContext nametable.

Field: **`static final String SESSION`**
Name used to store HttpSession in PageContext nametable.

Field: **`static final String OUT`**
Name used to store current JspWriter in PageContext nametable.

Field: **`static final String APPLICATION`**
Name used to store ServletContext in PageContext nametable.

Field: **`static final String EXCEPTION`**
Name used to store any uncaught exception in ServletRequest attribute list and PageContext nametable.

Method: **`initialize`**
Parameters: `Servlet servlet,`
`ServletRequest request,`
`ServletResponse response,`
`String errorPageURL,`
`boolean needsSession,`
`int buffer,`
`boolean autoflush`
Returns: `nothing (void)`
Throws: `IOException,`
`IllegalStateException,`
`IllegalArgumentException`
The initialize method is called to initialize an uninitialized PageContext so that it may be used to service an incoming request and response within its _jspService() method. This method is required to create an initial JspWriter, and associate the "out" name in page scope with this newly created object.

Method: **`release`**
Parameters: `none`
Returns: `nothing (void)`
This resets the internal state of a PageContext, releasing all internal references, and preparing the PageContext for potential reuse by a later invocation of initialize().

Method: **`setAttribute`**
Parameters: `String name,`
`Object attribute`
Returns: `nothing (void)`
Register the name and object specified with page scope semantics.

Method: **`setAttribute`**
Parameters: `String name,`
`Object attribute,`
`int scope`
Returns: `nothing (void)`
Register the name and object specified with specified scope semantics.

Method: **`getAttribute`**
Parameters: `String name`
Returns: `Object`
Return the object associated with the name in the page scope or null.

Method: **`getAttribute`**
Parameters: `String name,`
`int scope`
Returns: `Object`

Return the object associated with the name in the specified scope or null.

Method: **`findAttribute`**
Parameters: `String name`
Returns: `Object`

Searches for the named attribute in page, request, session (if valid), and application scope(s) in order and returns the value associated or null.

Method: **`removeAttribute`**
Parameters: `String name`
Returns: `Object`

Remove the object reference associated with the specified name

Method: **`removeAttribute`**
Parameters: `String name,`
`int scope`
Returns: `Object`

Remove the object reference associated with the specified name from the specified scope.

Method: **`getAttributeScope`**
Parameters: `String name`
Returns: `int`

Returns the scope of the object associated with the name specified or 0.

Method: **`getAttributeNamesInScope`**
Parameters: `int scope`
Returns: `Enumeration`

Returns an enumeration of names of all the attributes the specified scope.

Method: **`getOut`**
Parameters: `none`
Returns: `JspWriter`

Returns the current JspWriter being used for client response.

Method: **`getSession`**
Parameters: `none`
Returns: `HttpSession`

Returns the HttpSession for this PageContext or null.

Method: **`getPage`**
Parameters: `none`
Returns: `Object`

Returns the Page implementation instance associated with this PageContext.

Method: **`getRequest`**
Parameters: `none`
Returns: `ServletRequest`

Returns the ServletRequest for this PageContext

Method: **`getResponse`**
Parameters: `none`
Returns: `ServletResponse`

Returns the ServletResponse for this PageContext.

Method: **`getException`**
Parameters: `none`
Returns: `Exception`

Returns any exception passed to this as an errorpage.

Method: **`getServletConfig`**
Parameters: `none`
Returns: `ServletConfig`

Returns the ServletConfig for this PageContext.

Method: **`getServletContext`**
Parameters: `none`
Returns: `ServletContext`

Returns the ServletContext for this PageContext.

Method: **`forward`**
Parameters: `String relativeUrlPath`
Returns: `nothing (void)`
Throws: `ServletException, IOException`

This method is used to redirect, or "forward," the current ServletRequest and ServletResponse to another active component in the application. The jsp tag `<jsp:forward ...>` calls this method.

Method: **`include`**
Parameters: `String relativeUrlPath`
Returns: `nothing (void)`
Throws: `ServletException, IOException`

Causes the resource specified to be processed as part of the current request being processed. The output of the request is written directly to the response output stream. The current JspWriter for this JSP is flushed as a side-effect of this call, prior to processing the include. The jsp tag `<jsp:include ...>` calls this method.

Method: **`handlePageException`**
Parameters: `Exception e`
Returns: `nothing (void)`
Throws: `ServletException,`
`IOException`

This method is intended to process an unhandled page level exception by redirecting the exception to either the specified error page for this JSP, or if none was specified, to perform some implementation dependent action.

Method: **`pushBody`**
Parameters: `nothing`
Returns: `BodyContent`

Return a new BodyContent object, save the current "out" JspWriter, and update the value of the "out" implicit object in the page scope attribute namespace of the PageContext.

Method: **`popBody`**
Parameters: `nothing`
Returns: `JspWriter`

Return the previous JspWriter "out" saved by the matching pushBody(), and update the value of "out" in the page scope attribute namespace of the PageConxtext.

JspEngineInfo

Class: **`javax.servlet.jsp.JspEngineInfo`**
SuperClass: `java.lang.Object`
SubClasses: `none`

The JspEngineInfo is an abstract class that provides information on the current JSP engine.

Method: **`getSpecificationVersion`**
Parameters: `nothing`
Returns: `String`

Specification version numbers use a "Dewey Decimal" syntax that consists of positive decimal integers separated by periods ".", for example, "2.0" or "1.2.3.4.5.6.7". This allows an extensible number to be used to represent major, minor, micro, (etc.) versions. The version number must begin with a number.

Other Classes and Interfaces

The HttpJspPage interface and the JspFactory Class, are both used exclusively by the JSP engine and do not offer any useful methods to the JSP developer. As such it doesn't make sense to present them here.

If you are attempting to build a JSP engine, there are several great resources available including the standard JavaDocs and the reference implementation of the JSP engine.

Classes in javax.servlet.jsp.tagext.*

The JSP Tag Extensions package, javax.servlet.jsp.tagext, is a subset of the JSP package. The package javax.servlet.jsp.tagext defines the following classes and interfaces:

Interface: **`javax.servlet.jsp.tagext.Tag`**
SuperInterface: `none`
SubInterfaces: `javax.servlet.jsp.tagext.BodyTag`

The tag interface defines the basic protocol between a tag handler and JSP page implementation class. It defines the life cycle and the methods to be invoked at start and end tag.

There are several methods that get invoked to set the state of a tag handler. The tag handler is required to keep this state so the page compiler can choose not to reinvoke some of the state setting.

The page compiler guarantees that setPageContext and setParent will all be invoked on the tag handler, in that order, before doStartTag() or doEndTag() are invoked on it. The page compiler also guarantees that release will be invoked on the tag handler before the end of the page.

Field: **`static int EVAL_BODY_INCLUDE`**

Constant to indicate that the body should be evaluated into the existing out stream.

Field: **`static int EVAL_PAGE`**

Constant to indicate to continue with the remainder of the page.

Field: **`static int SKIP_BODY`**

Constant to indicate to skip the body evaluation

Field: **`static final SKIP_PAGE`**

Constant to indicate to skip the remainder of the page

Method: **`doEndTag`**
Parameters: `nothing`
Returns: `int`
Throws: `JspException`

Process the end tag for this instance

Method: **`doStartTag`**

Parameters: `nothing`
Returns: `int`
Throws: `JspException`

Process the start tag for this instance

Method: **`getParent`**
Parameters: `nothing`
Returns: `Tag`

Retrieve the current nesting tag of this tag

Method: **`release`**
Parameters: `nothing`
Returns: `nothing (void)`

Called when a tag is being cleaned up, should clean up additional resources. The page compiler guarantees this method will be called on all tag handlers, but there may be multiple invocations on doStartTag and doEndTag in between.

Method: **`setPageContext`**
Parameters: `PageContext pc`
Returns: `nothing (void)`

Set the current PageContext. Called by the page implementation prior to doStartTag().

Method: **`setParent`**
Parameters: `Tag t`
Returns: `nothing (void)`

Set the current nesting tag of this tag. Called by the page implementation prior to doStartTag().

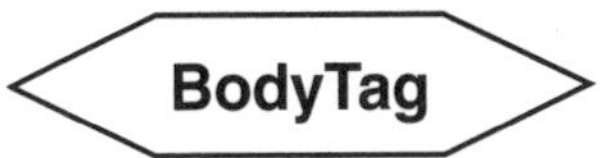

Interface: **`javax.servlet.jsp.tagext.BodyTag`**
SuperInterface: `javax.servlet.jsp.tagext.Tag`
SubInterfaces: `none`

The BodyTag interface extends tag by defining additional methods that let a tag handler access its body. The interface provides two new methods: one is to be invoked with the BodyContent for the evaluation of the body, the other is to be reevaluated after every body evaluation.

Field: **`static final EVAL_BODY_TAG`**

Request the creation of new BodyContent on which to evaluate the body of this tag. This is an illegal return value for doStartTag when the class does not implement BodyTag, since BodyTag is needed to manipulate the new writer.

Method: **`doAfterBody`**
Parameters: `nothing`
Returns: `int`
Throws: `JspException`

Actions after some body has been evaluated. Not invoked in empty tags or in tags returning SKIP_BODY in doStartTag() This method is invoked after every body evaluation. The pair "BODY -- doAfterBody()" is invoked initially if doStartTag() returned EVAL_BODY_TAG, and it is repeated as long as the doAfterBody() evaluation returns EVAL_BODY_TAG.

The method reinvocations may be lead to different actions because there might have been some changes to shared state, or because of external computation.

Method: **`doInitBody`**
Parameters: `nothing`
Returns: `nothing (void)`
Throws: `JspException`

Prepare for evaluation of the body. The method will be invoked once per action invocation by the page implementation after a new BodyContent has been obtained and set on the tag handler via the setBodyContent() method and before the evaluation of the tag's body into that BodyContent. This method will not be invoked if there is no body evaluation.

Method: **`setBodyContent`**
Parameters: `BodyContent b`
Returns: `nothing (void)`
Throws: `JspException`

Setter method for the bodyContent property. This method will not be invoked if there is no body evaluation.

BodyContent

Class: **javax.servlet.jsp.tagext.BodyContent**
SuperClass: javax.servlet.jsp.JspWriter
SubClasses: none

A JspWriter subclass that can be used to process body evaluations.

Method: **clearBody**
Parameters: none
Returns: nothing (void)

Clear the body.

Method: **flush**
Parameters: none
Returns: nothing (void)
Throws: IOException

flush() is not valid within a tag, so it has been redefined to throw an exception.

Method: **getEnclosingWriter**
Parameters: none
Returns: JspWriter

Returns the JspWriter that encloses the tag.

Method: **getReader**
Parameters: none
Returns: Reader

Return the value of the evaluated BodyContent as a writer.

Method: getString
Parameters: none
Returns: String

Return the value of the evaluated BodyContent as a string.

Method: **writeOut**
Parameters: Writer out
Returns: nothing (void)
Throws: IOException

Write the contents of this BodyContent into a writer.

TagSupport

Class: **`javax.servlet.jsp.tagext.TagSupport`**
SuperClass: `java.lang.Object`
SubClasses: `javax.servlet.jsp.tagext.BodyTagSupport`
Implements: `javax.servlet.jsp.tagext.Tag`

Actions in a tag library are defined through subclasses of tag.

Method: **`findAncestorWithClass`**
Parameters: `Tag from,`
`Class klass`
Returns: `Tag`

Find the instance of a given class type that is closest to the tag. This method allows coordination among cooperating tags.

Method: **`getId`**
Parameters: `none`
Returns: `String`

Retrieves the ID attribute of the tag.

Method: **`setId`**
Parameters: `String id`
Returns: `nothing (void)`

Sets the ID attribute of the tag.

Method: **`getValue`**
Parameters: `String key`
Returns: `Object`

Retrieves a value from the tag.

Method: **`getValues`**
Parameters: `none`
Returns: `Enumeration`

Returns an enumeration of the values set in the tag.

Method: **`setValue`**
Parameters: `String key,`
`Object value`
Returns: `nothing (void)`

Sets a value in the tag.

Method: **`removeValue`**
Parameters: `String key`
Returns: `nothing (void)`

Removes a value in the tag.

BodyTagSupport

Class: **`javax.servlet.jsp.tagext.BodyTagSupport`**
SuperClass: `javax.servlet.jsp.tagext.TagSupport`
SubClasses: `none`
Impliments: `javax.servlet.jsp.tagext.BodyTag`

Actions in a tag library are defined through subclasses of tag.

Method: **`getBodyContent`**
Parameters: `none`
Returns: `BodyContent`

Retrieve the current bodyContent

Method: **`getPreviousOut`**
Parameters: `none`
Returns: `JspWriter`

Retrieve the previous JspWriter. This could be a JspWriter from an enclosing tag or the JSP page itself.

TagExtraInfo

Class: **`javax.servlet.jsp.tagext.TagExtraInfo`**
Constructor: `TagExtraInfo()`
SuperClass: `java.lang.Object`
SubClasses: `none`

Extra tag information for a custom tag; this class is mentioned in the tag library descriptor file (TLD). This class must be used if the tag defines any scripting variables through VariableInfo or if the tag wants to provide translation-time validation of the tag attributes.

Method: **`getTagInfo`**
Parameters: `none`
Returns: `TagInfo`

Returns a TagInfo object from the tag.

Method: **`getVariableInfo`**
Parameters: `none`
Returns: `VariableInfo`

Returns a VariableInfo object from the tag.

Method: **`isValid`**
Parameters: `TagData`
Returns: `boolean`

Allows translation-time validation on tag syntax. Returns true if this tag matches the requirements shown in the TagData Object.

Method: **`setTagInfo`**
Parameters: `TagInfo`
Returns: `none`

Assign the TagInfo object.

VariableInfo

Class: **`javax.servlet.jsp.tagext.VariableInfo`**
Constructor: `VariableInfo(String varName, String className, boolean declare, int scope)`
SuperClass: `java.lang.Object`
SubClasses: `none`

This object contains information on the scripting variables that are created or modified by a tag at run-time. Once created these variables are accessible from outside the scope of the tag.

Field: **`static int NESTED`**

Constant that indicates that this variable exist only between the start and end tags.

Field: **`static int AT_BEGIN`**

Constant that indicates that this variable exist after the start tag.

Field: **`static int AT_END`**

Constant that indicates that this variable exist after the end tag.

Method: **`getVarName`**
Parameters: `none`
Returns: `String`

Retrieve the name of the scripting variable.

Method: **`getClassName`**
Parameters: `none`
Returns: `String`

Retrieve the class of the variable.

Method: **`getDeclare`**
Parameters: `none`
Returns: `boolean`

True if this was created as a new variable.

Method: **`getScope`**
Parameters: `none`
Returns: `int`

Returns the scope of this variable.

Other Classes and Interfaces

There are several other classes included in the tag extension API that are intended primary for use by the JSP engine itself. Because of their size and complexity they have not been included in this reference.

Again, if the intention is to create a JSP engine there are several great resources available including the standard JavaDocs and the reference JspEngine implementation.

Appendix B

JSP APPLICATIONS

The following list contains applications and tools that work with Java-Server Pages. Each listing conveys the JSP version supported, application type, company name, URL, pricing model, and a brief description. The JSP version will either be .91, .92, 1.0, or 1.1.

Application type is broken down into application server, Web server, development environment, embeddable, standalone, or both embeddable and standalone. Application server usually conveys an environment that supports Enterprise JavaBeans, DCOM, CORBA, or a combination of these technologies. Web server signifies an HTTP server with JSP support. Embeddable signifies that the product can be embedded into another application, such as a Web server. Standalone signifies a standalone JSP engine, often bundled with a Servlet engine.

Pricing model is broken down into commercial, GNU public license, or open source. These categories are generalizations. For example, many applications are commercial, but available free for development. See the specific product's Web site for further details.

This is by no means a comprehensive list, as new JSP applications appear weekly. In addition, as time passes this information will change. As always, for the latest information search the Web!

Allaire JRun 3.0

JSP Version: 1.1 **Application:** Embeddable or Standalone
Company: Allaire Corp.
URL: *http://www.allaire.com/products/jrun/*
Pricing Model: Commercial

Allaire JRun is a Servlet 2.2 and JSP 1.1 engine that can run as a standalone Web server or embedded into several different Web servers. JRun is offered free for development. It is also a fully compliant EJB 1.1 Server.

ATG Dynamo Application Server

JSP Version: 1.1 **Application:** Application Server
Company: Art Technology Group
URL: *http://www.atg.com/*
Pricing Model: Commercial

While the ATG Dynamo Application Server that natively supports JSP is not released as of this writing, it deserves mention here. The original Page Compilation technology that laid the foundation of the Sun Java Web Server and helped drive the development of JSP was licensed from ATG. ATG has announced full J2EE capability for its Dynamo Application Server suite.

BEA WebLogic 5.1

JSP Version: 1.1 **Application:** Application Server
Company: BEA Systems, Inc.
URL: *http://www.weblogic.com*
Pricing Model: Commercial

BEA WebLogic Server 5.1 is a full-featured Application Server with support for the Servlet 2.2 and JSP 1.1 specifications. It also supports EJB, JMS, JDBC, JNDI, CORBA, and XML. It is best known for its scaleable architecture, which features connection sharing, resource pooling and clustering of both dynamic Web pages and EJB components. It is certified on over 16 platforms.

Bluestone Sapphire/Web

JSP Version: 1.1 **Application:** Application Server

Company: Bluestone Software, Inc.

URL: *http://www.bluestone.com*

Pricing Model: Commercial

Bluestone Sapphire/Web is a full-featured J2EE Application Server with support for the Servlet 2.2 and JSP 1.1 APIs, as well as EJB 1.1. While it has support for many different IDEs, it has its own built-in IDE called Sapphire/Developer. It has support for most major databases, and while it is MS Windows centric for development, it can be deployed on many different Hardware/Software platforms.

Drumbeat 2000 JSP

JSP Version: .92 **Application:** Development Environment

Company: Macromedia, Inc.

URL: *http://www.macromedia.com*

Pricing Model: Commercial

Drumbeat 2000 is a Visual IDE for creating JSP pages with IBM WebSphere and DB2. It is a fast way to build JSP pages without coding. In late 2000, Macromedia plans to release UltraDev, a new development environment integrating its popular Dreamweaver HTML editor with Drumbeat 2000. Drumbeat 2000 JSP runs on Microsoft Windows 95/98/NT. It requires IBM WebSphere Application Server and IBM DB2 Universal Database 5.2 to build database-driven applications.

EasyThings Web Server

JSP Version: 1.0 **Application:** Web Server
Company: EasyThings Group
URL: *http://easythings.iwarp.com/*
Pricing Model: Commercial

The EasyThings Web server includes a JSP engine, as well as SAX based XML and HTML parsers. Additionally it includes a SSI engine.

Enhydra

JSP Version: 1.1 **Application:** Application Server
Company: Lutris Technologies
URL: *http://www.enhydra.com/*
Pricing Model: Open Source

Enhydra is an Open Source application server that facilitates the rapid development and deployment of Java and XML based applications. It supports distributed load on multiple servers, server fail over, and load balancing through session affinity and weighted round-robin distribution. It supports the Servlet 2.2 and JSP 1.1 APIs.

Forte for Java

JSP Version: 1.1 **Application:** Development Environment
Company: Sun Microsystems
URL: *http://www.sun.com/forte*
Pricing Model: Open Source

Sun's Forte for Java is a full-featured Java development environment, including design and debugging of Java Servlets and JSP pages. Forte for Java comes in three versions, the Community Edition, Internet Edition, and Enterprise Edition. The Community Edition is free for noncommercial development and is being released under the Mozilla Public License model. As it is open standards-based, it runs on many different environments, including Sun Solaris, Microsoft Windows, and Linux.

GemStone/J Application Server

JSP Version: 1.1 **Application:** Application Server
Company: GemStone Systems, Inc.
URL: *http://www.gemstone.com/*
Pricing Model: Commercial

GemStone/J Application Server is a J2EE compliant Application Server integrated into a CORBA ORB environment. One of its best features is the Persistent Cache Architecture (PCA), which allows quick access to data. The GemStone/J environment is available for both the Windows NT and Solaris platforms.

IBM WebSphere Application Server 3.0

JSP Version: 1.0 **Application:** Application Server
Company: IBM Corporation
URL: *http://www.ibm.com/websphere*
Pricing Model: Commercial

IBM WebSphere is a full-featured Web Application Server that supports the Servlet 2.1 and JSP 1.0 specifications. It includes pooled database access for DB2 and Oracle Relational Databases, and can support the EJB 1.0 specification. It has built-in support for load balancing and distributed transactions. It can run on AIX, Solaris, Windows, Linux, NetWare, and the IBM family of servers. WebSphere Studio is an integrated IDE for WebSphere that supports visual layout of JSP pages and multiplatform debugging.

Inprise Application Server 4.0

JSP Version: 1.0 **Application:** Application Server
Company: Inprise Corp.
URL: *http://www.inprise.com/appserver/*
Pricing Model: Commercial

IAS supports the Servlet 2.1 and JavaServer Pages 1.0 specifications. It is a full-featured application server with EJB 1.1, CORBA, JNDI, JMS, and Java Transaction Service support. It even integrates CORBA and EJB with RMI over IIOP and Java to IDL mapping. IAS also integrates well with the Inprise JBuilder IDE, with supports development of JSP pages. IAS 4.0 does not support tag libraries.

InstantOnline Basic for JSP

JSP Version: 1.1 **Application:** Embeddable
Company: Gefion Software
URL: *http://www.gefionsoftware.com/*
Pricing Model: Commercial

InstantOnline Basic for JSP is a set of JSP 1.1 custom actions, as defined by the JSP 1.1 specification.

Intalio Platform

JSP Version: 1.1 **Application:** Application Server
Company: exolab.org
URL: *http://www.exoffice.com/*
Pricing Model: Open Source

Intalio is an Open Source Application Server based on several different Open Source software packages, including Tomcat, JavaORB, Cocoon, Castor, PostgreSQL, and OpenLDAP. Intalio supports CORBA services and DCOM components, as well as Enterprise JavaBeans. It also makes use of XML and related technologies for deployment, management, graphical user interfaces, publishing, and data exchange.

iPlanet Application Server 6.0

JSP Version: 1.1 **Application:** Application Server
Company: iPlanet SUN / Netscape Alliance
URL: *http://www.iplanet.com/*
Pricing Model: Commercial

The iPlanet Application Server 6.0 is a high performance, high availability application server that provides the capabilities to build and deploy massively scalable, mission-critical Internet applications. It has many advanced features, such as real-time event and performance monitoring and system integration into several different types of legacy systems. It supports the Servlet 2.2 and JSP 1.1 APIs and is a fully compliant J2EE system.

iPlanet Web Server, Enterprise Edition 4.1

JSP Version: 1.1 **Application:** Web Server
Company: iPlanet SUN / Netscape Alliance
URL: *http://www.iplanet.com/*
Pricing Model: Commercial

The Netscape Web servers have always been some of the best commercially available. Their speed, reliability, and integration capabilities are renown. The enterprise-class runs on Windows NT, Solaris, and Linux. The 4.1 release of their enterprise-class server has native support for the Servlet 2.2 and JSP 1.1 APIs. The only piece lacking from their implementation is WAR file support.

iServer

JSP Version: 1.0 **Application:** Embeddable
Company: Servertec
URL: *http://www.servertec.com/*
Pricing Model: Commercial

iServer is a small, fast, platform independent Application/Web Server written entirely in Java. Besides JSP Pages and Servlets, it supports open standards such as HTTP, CGI, SSI, HTML, TCP/IP, RMI, IIOP, CORBA, JDBC and XML.

Jakarta Tomcat 3.1: JSP Reference Implementation

JSP Version: 1.1 **Application:** Embeddable or Standalone
Company: The Apache Group
URL: *http://jakarta.apache.org/tomcat/*
Pricing Model: Open Source

Tomcat is the official Reference Implementation for the Java Servlet 2.2 and JavaServer Pages 1.1 specifications. Developed under the Apache license in an open and participatory environment, Tomcat is intended to be a collaboration of the best-of-breed developers from around the world. Tomcat can function standalone or as an Apache module.

Jetty

JSP Version: 1.0 **Application:** Embeddable or Standalone
Company: Mort Bay Consulting
URL: *http://jetty.mortbay.com/*
Pricing Model: Open Source

Jetty is an Open Source HTTP Servlet Server written in 100% Java. It is designed to be lightweight, high performance, embeddable, extensible, and flexible. It supports SSL, SSI, and Server Push. Jetty has also been used in telephony and SmartCard applications.

jo!

JSP Version: 1.0 **Application:** Web Server
Company: Tagtraum Industries
URL: *http://www.tagtraum.com/*
Pricing Model: Open Source

jo! is a pure Java Web server that fully implements the Servlet 2.1 and JSP 1.0 APIs. In addition it features authentication using role abstraction, automatic compressed transfer of text or HTML files, and auto-internationalization. jo! is based on Java 2 Standard Edition (J2SE). It will not run under Java 1.1.x or lower.

JSPExecutor

JSP Version: 1.0 **Application: Standalone**

Company: Tagtraum Industries

URL: *http://www.tagtraum.com/*

Pricing Model: GNU Public License

JSPExecutor gives you the ability to execute JSP Pages either inside your application or from the command line. Theoretical uses could be to generate source code or reports.

LiteWebServer

JSP Version: 1.1 **Application:** Web Server

Company: Gefion Software

URL: *http://www.gefionsoftware.com/LiteWebServer/*

Pricing Model: Open Source

LiteWebServer is a pure Java Web server with native support for the Servlet 2.2 and JSP 1.1 specifications. LiteWebServer's very small size (420 KB complete) makes it ideal for embedded systems, for bundling with Web application demos sent to potential customers, and for running Web applications distributed on CD-ROMs. LiteWebServer is offered free of charge. If you want support or would like to bundle LiteWebServer with your own product you need to purchase an annual support license. With the support license you also get access to the complete source code.

Mercator Web and Commerce Broker

JSP Version: 1.0 **Application:** Application Server

Company: Mercator Software

URL: *http://www.mercator.com/*

Pricing Model: Commercial

Mercator Web and Commerce Brokers are integration suites that support JSP and Servlets as well as EDI, XML, EJB, CORBA, COM, and LDAP. They have advanced application server capabilities such as centralized control and single sign-on through LDAP directory servers. They also feature prebuilt adaptors for BEA Tuxedo, Candle ROMA, IBM MQSeries, Microsoft MSMQ, Oracle AQ and TIBCO Rendezvous.

New Atlanta ServletExec 2.2

JSP Version: 1.0 **Application:** Embeddable or Standalone
Company: New Atlanta Communications, LLC
URL: *http://www.newatlanta.com/*
Pricing Model: Commercial

ServletExec 2.2 implements the Java Servlet 2.1 specification, and the JSP 1.0 final specification. It boasts the ability to deployed on any major Web server and operating system. ServletExec 2.2 features a browser-based user interface for administration and configuration.

Oracle Application Server 4

JSP Version: 1.0 **Application:** Application Server
Company: Oracle Corporation
URL: *http://www.oracle.com/*
Pricing Model: Commercial

Besides having the best integration to Oracle Databases, Oracle Application Server (OAS) has support for Servlets, JSP pages, and Enterprise JavaBeans. At the heart of the OAS is a CORBA 2.x compliant ORB. One unique feature of the OAS is interoperability with Oracle8i at the EJB and CORBA levels. The OAS is available on all major UNIX platforms and Windows NT.

Oracle JDeveloper

JSP Version: 1.1 **Application:** Development Environment
Company: Oracle Corporation
URL: *http://www.oracle.com/*
Pricing Model: Commercial

Oracle JDeveloper is a J2EE Development Environment with full support for Servlets and JSP. It includes Wizards to develop JavaServer Pages and Servlet applications, as well as a built-in personal Web server to test and debug JSP and Servlet pages within the IDE. Included with JDeveloper are several JavaBeans for use with the Web called Web Beans. It also includes a built-in deployment tool to deploy Oracle Business Components as either EJB or CORBA applications.

Orion Application Server

JSP Version: 1.1 **Application:** Application Server

Company: OrionServer.com

URL: *http://www.orionserver.com/*

Pricing Model: Commercial

Orion is an Application Server with full EJB 1.1 support, including entity Beans with container-managed persistence. It supports JSP 1.1 and Servlet 2.2. Orion runs on any machine with a Java 2 compatible Java Virtual Machine. Currently it is a standalone application. Future plans include integration into IIS and Apache. It is free for development.

PolyJSP

JSP Version: .92 **Application:** Embeddable

Company: Plenix

URL: *http://www.plenix.org/polyjsp/*

Pricing Model: Open Source

PolyJsp is an extensible JSP implementation designed to support multiple scripting languages and multiple JSP versions. Completely based on XML and XSL, PolyJsp currently supports Java, JavaScript and WebL as scripting languages. It meets the JSP .92 specification. PolyJsp is a direct descendant of ESP (EcmaScript Pages), a Servlet used for authoring dynamic Web pages in EcmaScript. Installation of PolyJsp requires a Web server and Servlet engine.

PowerTier 6 for EJB

JSP Version: 1.0 **Application:** Application Server
Company: Persistence Software, Inc.
URL: *http://www.persistence.com/*
Pricing Model: Commercial

PowerTier is both an Application Server as well as a development environment for creating Servlet, JSP Page, and EJB Web-based applications. PowerTier generates end-to-end JSP to EJB code. This is done by changing object models from modeling tools like TogetherJ or Rational Rose into fully developed e-commerce applications through its PowerPage product. PowerPage then generates the JSP pages needed to access EJB 1.1 compliant objects.

Pramati Server for J2EE 1.0

JSP Version: 1.1 **Application:** Application Server
Company: Pramati Technologies
URL: *http://www.pramati.com/*
Pricing Model: Commercial

Pramati is an Application Server that boasts one of the smallest footprints available. Besides JSP 1.1 and Servlet 2.1 APIs, it also supports the EJB 1.1 API. It also has nice features such as concurrent project management, as well as bean generation, packaging, and deployment wizards.

Resin 1.1

JSP Version: 1.1 **Application:** Embeddable or Standalone
Company: Caucho Technology
URL: *http://www.caucho.com/*
Pricing Model: Open Source

Resin 1.1 is an Open Source implementation of the JSP 1.1 specification that supports both Java and JavaScript as scripting languages. Resin boasts the fastest Servlet and JSP engines, and has fully integrated support for XML and XSLT. Another nice feature is load balancing when integrated with Apache, IIS, and Netscape Web servers.

RocketJSP 1.0

JSP Version: 1.0 **Application:** Embeddable
Company: Mun Wai - Author
URL: *http://rocketjsp.homepage.com/*
Pricing Model: GNU Public License

RocketJSP is a JavaServer Pages (JSP) 1.0 Engine. It can be installed in any HTTP server with a Servlet 2.1 compliant Servlet Engine. It is released under the GNU General Public License and is part of the Giant Java Tree (*www.git.org*). At the time of this writing Rocket JSP was still in beta testing.

SilverStream Application Server

JSP Version: 1.0 **Application:** Application Server
Company: SILVERSTREAM Software, Inc.
URL: *http://www.silverstream.com/*
Pricing Model: Commercial

SilverStream Application Server supports the Servlet 2.1 and JSP 1.0 specifications. It is a full featured application server with support for J2EE and CORBA, as well as an integrated development environment. Currently it is distributed on Windows, Solaris, AIX, and HP-UX.

SJSP 1.1.5 (Sator JSP)

JSP Version: 1.1 **Application:** Embeddable
Company: Stepan Schejbal - Author
URL: *http://web.iol.cz/sator/projects/sjsp-1-1/*
Pricing Model: Commercial

SJSP is a JSP 1.1 implementation that is free for development or noncommercial use. It is designed to work as a plugin with all Servlet engines available today. SJSP boasts innovative memory management techniques with JSP templates, as well as translation-time Bean introspection to generate faster Java code.

SUN Java Web Server 2.0

JSP Version: 1.0 **Application:** Web Server
Company: Sun Microsystems
URL: *http://www.sun.com/software/jwebserver/*
Pricing Model: Commercial

The Java Web Server is a complete, robust Web server written completely in Java. It supports the Servlet 2.1 and JSP 1.0 specifications. One of the best features of JWS 2.0 is its security, which is derived from the Java platform security model.

Sybase Enterprise Application Server

JSP Version: 1.1 **Application:** Embeddable
Company: Sybase, Inc.
URL: *http://www.sybase.com/*
Pricing Model: Commercial

The Sybase Enterprise Application Server is a full-featured application server with extensive Java 2 Enterprise Edition (J2EE) support including Enterprise JavaBeans 1.1, Servlets 2.2, JSP 1.1, JNDI, JavaMail, JDBC, and JTA/JTS. It supports multiple platforms including Windows NT, Sun Solaris, HP UX, and IBM AIX.

Unify eWave Engine

JSP Version: 1.0 **Application:** Application Server
Company: Unify Corporation
URL: *http://www.unify.com/products/ewave/*
Pricing Model: Commercial

The Unify eWave Engine contains a Web server extension that supports the Java Servlet 2.1 and JSP 1.0 specifications. The unify eWave Engine is an Application Server that supports EJB, COM, DCOM, and RMI. It has nice features like EJB replication, which allows EJBs to be replicated across multiple servers and multiple machines for load balancing and high availability. The unify eWave Engine also features integrated database connection pooling, transaction management, and security management.

WAICoolRunner

JSP Version: 1.1 **Application:** Embeddable
Company: Gefion Software
URL: *http://www.gefionsoftware.com/WAICoolRunner/*
Pricing Model: Open Source

WAICoolRunner is a Servlet Engine for Netscape FastTrack Server 3.01 and Enterprise Server 3.0/3.5/3.6, with support for the Java Servlet 2.2 and JSP 1.1 specifications. WAICoolRunner is available free of charge. If you want support or like to bundle WAICoolRunner with your own product you need to purchase an annual support license.

zJSP 0.3

JSP Version: .91 **Application:** Embeddable
Company: David Creemer - Author
URL: *http://www.zachary.com/creemer/zjsp.html*
Pricing Model: GNU Public License

zJSP is an translator from JSP Pages to Java. It meets the JSP .91 specification. zJSP is really intended to be an experiment.

Appendix C

SAMPLE DATABASES

- SQL Scripts to Create Sample Database
- MS SQL Server
- MySQL
- Oracle 7/8

The following SQL scripts create the sample database tables for the examples in Chapter 9 and 10. Scripts are given for Microsoft's SQL Server (Listing C.2), Oracle 7 and 8 (Listing C.1), and MySQL server (Listing C.2). With minor edits, these scripts can be modified to be used with any SQL database.

Listing C.1 Oracle.sql

```
DROP TABLE system_users CASCADE CONSTRAINTS
/

CREATE TABLE system_users (system_id  VARCHAR2(6) NOT NULL,
                           first_name VARCHAR2(30),
                           last_name  VARCHAR2(30),
                           title      VARCHAR2(30),
                           phone      VARCHAR2(10),
                           building   VARCHAR2(3),
                           state_init VARCHAR2(2),
                           entry_date DATE,
CONSTRAINT PKsystem_users PRIMARY KEY (system_id))
/

DROP TABLE state CASCADE CONSTRAINTS
/

CREATE TABLE state (state_name VARCHAR2(30),
                    state_init VARCHAR2(2) NOT NULL,
CONSTRAINT PKstate PRIMARY KEY (state_init))
/


INSERT INTO system_users VALUES ('000121',
                                 'Damon',
                                 'Hougland',
                                 'Mattress Tester',
                                 '5557868945',
                                 '745',
                                 'TX',
                                 sysdate)
/

INSERT INTO system_users VALUES ('000333',
                                 'Aaron',
                                 'Tavistock',
                                 'Java Champion',
                                 '5557861234',
                                 '748',
                                 'CA',
                                 sysdate)
```

Listing C.1 Oracle.sql (continued)

```
/

INSERT INTO system_users VALUES ('000345',
                                 'Joseph',
                                 'Blow',
                                 'Mail Supervisor',
                                 '5557864567',
                                 '710',
                                 'CA',
                                 sysdate)
/

INSERT INTO system_users VALUES ('000234',
                                 'Bill',
                                 'Marketing',
                                 'Finance Engineer',
                                 '5559257440',
                                 '635',
                                 'TX',
                                 sysdate)
/

INSERT INTO system_users VALUES ('000235',
                                 'Lawrence',
                                 'Paydirt',
                                 'Company Nurse',
                                 '5559257777',
                                 '936',
                                 'CA',
                                 sysdate)
/

INSERT INTO system_users VALUES ('001847',
                                 'Nancy',
                                 'Jungle',
                                 'Recruiter',
                                 '5558472057',
                                 '145',
                                 'TX',
                                 sysdate)
/
```

Listing C.1 Oracle.sql (continued)

```
INSERT INTO system_users VALUES ('001848',
                                  'Kenny',
                                  'Hutchcraft',
                                  'Water Boy',
                                  '5558479987',
                                  '456',
                                  'AZ',
                                  sysdate)
/

INSERT INTO system_users VALUES ('001841',
                                  'Chip',
                                  'Circuit',
                                  'Legal Technician',
                                  '5553982648',
                                  '755',
                                  'CA',
                                  sysdate)
/

INSERT INTO system_users VALUES ('000124',
                                  'Shaoping',
                                  'Lee',
                                  'Master Chef',
                                  '5559551245',
                                  '756',
                                  'TX',
                                  sysdate)
/

INSERT INTO system_users VALUES ('000001',
                                  'Abigail',
                                  'Nora',
                                  'CEO',
                                  '5557560001',
                                  '700',
                                  'TX',
                                  sysdate)
/
```

Listing C.1 Oracle.sql (continued)

```
INSERT INTO system_users VALUES ('000002',
                                 'Gibson',
                                 'Charles',
                                 'COO',
                                 '5557560002',
                                 '700',
                                 'TX',
                                 sysdate)
/


INSERT INTO state VALUES ('ALABAMA', 'AL')
/

INSERT INTO state VALUES ('ALASKA', 'AK')
/

INSERT INTO state VALUES ('ARIZONA ', 'AZ')
/

INSERT INTO state VALUES ('ARKANSAS', 'AR')
/

INSERT INTO state VALUES ('CALIFORNIA ', 'CA')
/

INSERT INTO state VALUES ('COLORADO ', 'CO')
/

INSERT INTO state VALUES ('CONNECTICUT', 'CT')
/

INSERT INTO state VALUES ('DELAWARE', 'DE')
/

INSERT INTO state VALUES ('FLORIDA', 'FL')
/

INSERT INTO state VALUES ('GEORGIA', 'GA')
/

INSERT INTO state VALUES ('HAWAII', 'HI')
/
```

Listing C.1 Oracle.sql (continued)

```
INSERT INTO state VALUES ('IDAHO', 'ID')
/

INSERT INTO state VALUES ('ILLINOIS', 'IL')
/

INSERT INTO state VALUES ('INDIANA', 'IN')
/

INSERT INTO state VALUES ('IOWA', 'IA')
/

INSERT INTO state VALUES ('KANSAS', 'KS')
/

INSERT INTO state VALUES ('KENTUCKY', 'KY')
/

INSERT INTO state VALUES ('LOUISIANA', 'LA')
/

INSERT INTO state VALUES ('MAINE', 'ME')
/

INSERT INTO state VALUES ('MARYLAND', 'MD')
/

INSERT INTO state VALUES ('MASSACHUSETTS', 'MA')
/

INSERT INTO state VALUES ('MICHIGAN', 'MI')
/

INSERT INTO state VALUES ('MINNESOTA', 'MN')
/

INSERT INTO state VALUES ('MISSISSIPPI', 'MS')
/

INSERT INTO state VALUES ('MISSOURI', 'MO')
/
```

Listing C.1 Oracle.sql (continued)

```
INSERT INTO state VALUES ('MONTANA', 'MT')
/

INSERT INTO state VALUES ('NEBRASKA', 'NE')
/

INSERT INTO state VALUES ('NEVADA', 'NV')
/

INSERT INTO state VALUES ('NEW HAMPSHIRE', 'NH')
/

INSERT INTO state VALUES ('NEW JERSEY', 'NJ')
/

INSERT INTO state VALUES ('NEW MEXICO', 'NM')
/

INSERT INTO state VALUES ('NEW YORK', 'NY')
/

INSERT INTO state VALUES ('NORTH CAROLINA', 'NC')
/

INSERT INTO state VALUES ('NORTH DAKOTA', 'ND')
/

INSERT INTO state VALUES ('OHIO', 'OH')
/

INSERT INTO state VALUES ('OKLAHOMA', 'OK')
/

INSERT INTO state VALUES ('OREGON', 'OR')
/

INSERT INTO state VALUES ('PENNSYLVANIA', 'PA')
/
INSERT INTO state VALUES ('RHODE ISLAND', 'RI')
/
```

Listing C.1 Oracle.sql (continued)

```
INSERT INTO state VALUES ('SOUTH CAROLINA', 'SC')
/

INSERT INTO state VALUES ('SOUTH DAKOTA', 'SD')
/

INSERT INTO state VALUES ('TENNESSEE', 'TN')
/

INSERT INTO state VALUES ('TEXAS', 'TX')
/

INSERT INTO state VALUES ('UTAH', 'UT')
/

INSERT INTO state VALUES ('VERMONT', 'VT')
/

INSERT INTO state VALUES ('VIRGINIA ', 'VA')
/

INSERT INTO state VALUES ('WASHINGTON', 'WA')
/

INSERT INTO state VALUES ('WEST VIRGINIA', 'WV')
/

INSERT INTO state VALUES ('WISCONSIN', 'WI')
/

INSERT INTO state VALUES ('WYOMING', 'WY')
/
```

Listing C.2 MySQL.sql

```
DROP TABLE IF EXISTS system_users;

CREATE TABLE system_users (system_id  VARCHAR(6) NOT NULL,
                           first_name VARCHAR(30),
                           last_name  VARCHAR(30),
                           title      VARCHAR(30),
                           phone      VARCHAR(10),
                           building   VARCHAR(3),
                           state_init VARCHAR(2),
                           entry_date DATE,
               CONSTRAINT PKsystem_users PRIMARY KEY
(system_id));

DROP TABLE IF EXISTS state;

CREATE TABLE state (state_name VARCHAR(30) NOT NULL,
                    state_init VARCHAR(2) NOT NULL,
               CONSTRAINT PKstate PRIMARY KEY
(state_init));


INSERT INTO system_users VALUES ('000121',
                                 'Damon',
                                 'Hougland',
                                 'Mattress Tester',
                                 '5557868945',
                                 '745',
                                 'TX',
                                 NOW());

INSERT INTO system_users VALUES ('000333',
                                 'Aaron',
                                 'Tavistock',
                                 'Java Champion',
                                 '5557861234',
                                 '748',
                                 'CA',
                                 NOW());
```

Listing C.2 MySQL.sql (continued)

```
INSERT INTO system_users VALUES ('000345',
                                 'Joseph',
                                 'Blow',
                                 'Mail Supervisor',
                                 '5557864567',
                                 '710',
                                 'CA',
                                 NOW());

INSERT INTO system_users VALUES ('000234',
                                 'Bill',
                                 'Marketing',
                                 'Finance Engineer',
                                 '5559257440',
                                 '635',
                                 'TX',
                                 NOW());

INSERT INTO system_users VALUES ('000235',
                                 'Lawrence',
                                 'Paydirt',
                                 'Company Nurse',
                                 '5559257777',
                                 '936',
                                 'CA',
                                 NOW());

INSERT INTO system_users VALUES ('001847',
                                 'Nancy',
                                 'Jungle',
                                 'Recruiter',
                                 '5558472057',
                                 '145',
                                 'TX',
                                 NOW());

INSERT INTO system_users VALUES ('001848',
                                 'Kenny',
                                 'Hutchcraft',
                                 'Water Boy',
                                 '5558479987',
                                 '456',
```

Listing C.2 MySQL.sql (continued)

```
                                        'AZ',
                                        NOW());

INSERT INTO system_users VALUES ('001841',
                                        'Chip',
                                        'Circuit',
                                        'Legal Technician',
                                        '5553982648',
                                        '755',
                                        'CA',
                                        NOW());

INSERT INTO system_users VALUES ('000124',
                                        'Shaoping',
                                        'Lee',
                                        'Master Chef',
                                        '5559551245',
                                        '756',
                                        'TX',
                                        NOW());

INSERT INTO system_users VALUES ('000001',
                                        'Abigail',
                                        'Nora',
                                        'CEO',
                                        '5557560001',
                                        '700',
                                        'TX',
                                        NOW());

INSERT INTO system_users VALUES ('000002',
                                        'Gibson',
                                        'Charles',
                                        'COO',
                                        '5557560002',
                                        '700',
                                        'TX',
                                        NOW());
```

Listing C.2 MySQL.sql (continued)

```
INSERT INTO state VALUES ('ALABAMA', 'AL');
INSERT INTO state VALUES ('ALASKA', 'AK');
INSERT INTO state VALUES ('ARIZONA ', 'AZ');
INSERT INTO state VALUES ('ARKANSAS', 'AR');
INSERT INTO state VALUES ('CALIFORNIA ', 'CA');
INSERT INTO state VALUES ('COLORADO ', 'CO');
INSERT INTO state VALUES ('CONNECTICUT', 'CT');
INSERT INTO state VALUES ('DELAWARE', 'DE');
INSERT INTO state VALUES ('FLORIDA', 'FL');
INSERT INTO state VALUES ('GEORGIA', 'GA');
INSERT INTO state VALUES ('HAWAII', 'HI');
INSERT INTO state VALUES ('IDAHO', 'ID');
INSERT INTO state VALUES ('ILLINOIS', 'IL');
INSERT INTO state VALUES ('INDIANA', 'IN');
INSERT INTO state VALUES ('IOWA', 'IA');
INSERT INTO state VALUES ('KANSAS', 'KS');
INSERT INTO state VALUES ('KENTUCKY', 'KY');
INSERT INTO state VALUES ('LOUISIANA', 'LA');
INSERT INTO state VALUES ('MAINE', 'ME');
INSERT INTO state VALUES ('MARYLAND', 'MD');
INSERT INTO state VALUES ('MASSACHUSETTS', 'MA');
INSERT INTO state VALUES ('MICHIGAN', 'MI');
INSERT INTO state VALUES ('MINNESOTA', 'MN');
INSERT INTO state VALUES ('MISSISSIPPI', 'MS');
INSERT INTO state VALUES ('MISSOURI', 'MO');
INSERT INTO state VALUES ('MONTANA', 'MT');
INSERT INTO state VALUES ('NEBRASKA', 'NE');
INSERT INTO state VALUES ('NEVADA', 'NV');
INSERT INTO state VALUES ('NEW HAMPSHIRE', 'NH');
INSERT INTO state VALUES ('NEW JERSEY', 'NJ');
INSERT INTO state VALUES ('NEW MEXICO', 'NM');
INSERT INTO state VALUES ('NEW YORK', 'NY');
INSERT INTO state VALUES ('NORTH CAROLINA', 'NC');
INSERT INTO state VALUES ('NORTH DAKOTA', 'ND');
INSERT INTO state VALUES ('OHIO', 'OH');
INSERT INTO state VALUES ('OKLAHOMA', 'OK');
INSERT INTO state VALUES ('OREGON', 'OR');
INSERT INTO state VALUES ('PENNSYLVANIA', 'PA');
INSERT INTO state VALUES ('RHODE ISLAND', 'RI');
INSERT INTO state VALUES ('SOUTH CAROLINA', 'SC');
INSERT INTO state VALUES ('SOUTH DAKOTA', 'SD');
```

Listing C.2 MySQL.sql (continued)

```
INSERT INTO state VALUES ('TENNESSEE', 'TN');
INSERT INTO state VALUES ('TEXAS', 'TX');
INSERT INTO state VALUES ('UTAH', 'UT');
INSERT INTO state VALUES ('VERMONT', 'VT');
INSERT INTO state VALUES ('VIRGINIA ', 'VA');
INSERT INTO state VALUES ('WASHINGTON', 'WA');
INSERT INTO state VALUES ('WEST VIRGINIA', 'WV');
INSERT INTO state VALUES ('WISCONSIN', 'WI');
INSERT INTO state VALUES ('WYOMING', 'WY');
```

Listing C.3 SQLserver.sql

```
IF EXISTS (SELECT * FROM system_users
        WHERE system_id = object_id('system_users')
             and sysstat & 0xf = 3)
             DROP TABLE system_users
go

CREATE TABLE system_users(
    system_id      varchar(6)      NOT NULL,
    first_name     varchar(30)     NULL,
    last_name      varchar(30)     NULL,
    title          varchar(30)     NULL,
    phone          varchar(10)     NULL,
    building       varchar(3)      NULL,
    state_init     varchar(2)      NULL,
    entry_date     datetime        DEFAULT GETDATE(),
    CONSTRAINT PKsystem_users PRIMARY KEY NONCLUSTERED
(system_id)
)
go

IF EXISTS (SELECT * FROM state
        WHERE state_init = object_id('state')
             and sysstat & 0xf = 3)
             DROP TABLE state
go


CREATE TABLE state(
```

Listing C.3 SQLserver.sql (continued)

```
    state_name     varchar(30)     NOT NULL,
    state_init     varchar(2)      NOT NULL,
    CONSTRAINT PKstate PRIMARY KEY NONCLUSTERED
(state_init)
)
go


INSERT INTO system_users VALUES ('000121',
                                 'Damon',
                                 'Hougland',
                                 'Mattress Tester',
                                 '5557868945',
                                 '745',
                                 'TX',
                                 GETDATE())
go

INSERT INTO system_users VALUES ('000333',
                                 'Aaron',
                                 'Tavistock',
                                 'Java Champion',
                                 '5557861234',
                                 '748',
                                 'CA',
                                 GETDATE())
go

INSERT INTO system_users VALUES ('000345',
                                 'Joseph',
                                 'Blow',
                                 'Mail Supervisor',
                                 '5557864567',
                                 '710',
                                 'CA',
                                 GETDATE())
go

INSERT INTO system_users VALUES ('000234',
                                 'Bill',
```

Listing C.3 SQLserver.sql (continued)

```
                                   'Marketing',
                                   'Finance Engineer',
                                   '5559257440',
                                   '635',
                                   'TX',
                                   GETDATE())
go

INSERT INTO system_users VALUES ('000235',
                                   'Lawrence',
                                   'Paydirt',
                                   'Company Nurse',
                                   '5559257777',
                                   '936',
                                   'CA',
                                   GETDATE())
go

INSERT INTO system_users VALUES ('001847',
                                   'Nancy',
                                   'Jungle',
                                   'Recruiter',
                                   '5558472057',
                                   '145',
                                   'TX',
                                   GETDATE())
go

INSERT INTO system_users VALUES ('001848',
                                   'Kenny',
                                   'Hutchcraft',
                                   'Water Boy',
                                   '5558479987',
                                   '456',
                                   'AZ',
                                   GETDATE())
go

INSERT INTO system_users VALUES ('001841',
                                   'Chip',
                                   'Circuit',
```

Listing C.3 SQLserver.sql (continued)

```
                                          'Legal Technician',
                                          '5553982648',
                                          '755',
                                          'CA',
                                          GETDATE())
go

INSERT INTO system_users VALUES ('000124',
                                          'Shaoping',
                                          'Lee',
                                          'Master Chef',
                                          '5559551245',
                                          '756',
                                          'TX',
                                          GETDATE())
go

INSERT INTO system_users VALUES ('000001',
                                          'Abigail',
                                          'Nora',
                                          'CEO',
                                          '5557560001',
                                          '700',
                                          'TX',
                                          GETDATE())
go

INSERT INTO system_users VALUES ('000002',
                                          'Gibson',
                                          'Charles',
                                          'COO',
                                          '5557560002',
                                          '700',
                                          'TX',
                                          GETDATE())
go

INSERT INTO state VALUES ('ALABAMA', 'AL')
go

INSERT INTO state VALUES ('ALASKA', 'AK')
```

Listing C.3 SQLserver.sql (continued)

```
go

INSERT INTO state VALUES ('ARIZONA ', 'AZ')
go

INSERT INTO state VALUES ('ARKANSAS', 'AR')
go

INSERT INTO state VALUES ('CALIFORNIA ', 'CA')
go

INSERT INTO state VALUES ('COLORADO ', 'CO')
go

INSERT INTO state VALUES ('CONNECTICUT', 'CT')
go

INSERT INTO state VALUES ('DELAWARE', 'DE')
go

INSERT INTO state VALUES ('FLORIDA', 'FL')
go

INSERT INTO state VALUES ('GEORGIA', 'GA')
go

INSERT INTO state VALUES ('HAWAII', 'HI')
go

INSERT INTO state VALUES ('IDAHO', 'ID')
go

INSERT INTO state VALUES ('ILLINOIS', 'IL')
go

INSERT INTO state VALUES ('INDIANA', 'IN')
go

INSERT INTO state VALUES ('IOWA', 'IA')
go

INSERT INTO state VALUES ('KANSAS', 'KS')
```

Listing C.3 SQLserver.sql (continued)

```
go

INSERT INTO state VALUES ('KENTUCKY', 'KY')
go

INSERT INTO state VALUES ('LOUISIANA', 'LA')
go

INSERT INTO state VALUES ('MAINE', 'ME')
go

INSERT INTO state VALUES ('MARYLAND', 'MD')
go

INSERT INTO state VALUES ('MASSACHUSETTS', 'MA')
go

INSERT INTO state VALUES ('MICHIGAN', 'MI')
go

INSERT INTO state VALUES ('MINNESOTA', 'MN')
go

INSERT INTO state VALUES ('MISSISSIPPI', 'MS')
go

INSERT INTO state VALUES ('MISSOURI', 'MO')
go

INSERT INTO state VALUES ('MONTANA', 'MT')
go

INSERT INTO state VALUES ('NEBRASKA', 'NE')
go

INSERT INTO state VALUES ('NEVADA', 'NV')
go

INSERT INTO state VALUES ('NEW HAMPSHIRE', 'NH')
go

INSERT INTO state VALUES ('NEW JERSEY', 'NJ')
```

Listing C.3 SQLserver.sql (continued)

```
go

INSERT INTO state VALUES ('NEW MEXICO', 'NM')
go

INSERT INTO state VALUES ('NEW YORK', 'NY')
go

INSERT INTO state VALUES ('NORTH CAROLINA', 'NC')
go

INSERT INTO state VALUES ('NORTH DAKOTA', 'ND')
go

INSERT INTO state VALUES ('OHIO', 'OH')
go

INSERT INTO state VALUES ('OKLAHOMA', 'OK')
go

INSERT INTO state VALUES ('OREGON', 'OR')
go

INSERT INTO state VALUES ('PENNSYLVANIA', 'PA')
go

INSERT INTO state VALUES ('RHODE ISLAND', 'RI')
go

INSERT INTO state VALUES ('SOUTH CAROLINA', 'SC')
go

INSERT INTO state VALUES ('SOUTH DAKOTA', 'SD')
go

INSERT INTO state VALUES ('TENNESSEE', 'TN')
go

INSERT INTO state VALUES ('TEXAS', 'TX')
go

INSERT INTO state VALUES ('UTAH', 'UT')
```

Listing C.3 SQLserver.sql (continued)

```
go

INSERT INTO state VALUES ('VERMONT', 'VT')
go

INSERT INTO state VALUES ('VIRGINIA ', 'VA')
go

INSERT INTO state VALUES ('WASHINGTON', 'WA')
go

INSERT INTO state VALUES ('WEST VIRGINIA', 'WV')
go

INSERT INTO state VALUES ('WISCONSIN', 'WI')
go

INSERT INTO state VALUES ('WYOMING', 'WY')
go
```

Index

A

R

S

T

LICENSE AGREEMENT AND LIMITED WARRANTY

READ THE FOLLOWING TERMS AND CONDITIONS CAREFULLY BEFORE OPENING THIS CD PACKAGE. THIS LEGAL DOCUMENT IS AN AGREEMENT BETWEEN YOU AND PRENTICE-HALL, INC. (THE "COMPANY"). BY OPENING THIS SEALED CD PACKAGE, YOU ARE AGREEING TO BE BOUND BY THESE TERMS AND CONDITIONS. IF YOU DO NOT AGREE WITH THESE TERMS AND CONDITIONS, DO NOT OPEN THE CD PACKAGE. PROMPTLY RETURN THE UNOPENED CD PACKAGE AND ALL ACCOMPANYING ITEMS TO THE PLACE YOU OBTAINED THEM FOR A FULL REFUND OF ANY SUMS YOU HAVE PAID.

1. **GRANT OF LICENSE:** In consideration of your purchase of this book, and your agreement to abide by the terms and conditions of this Agreement, the Company grants to you a nonexclusive right to use and display the copy of the enclosed software program (hereinafter the "SOFTWARE") on a single computer (i.e., with a single CPU) at a single location so long as you comply with the terms of this Agreement. The Company reserves all rights not expressly granted to you under this Agreement.

2. **OWNERSHIP OF SOFTWARE:** You own only the magnetic or physical media (the enclosed CD) on which the SOFTWARE is recorded or fixed, but the Company and the software developers retain all the rights, title, and ownership to the SOFTWARE recorded on the original CD copy(ies) and all subsequent copies of the SOFTWARE, regardless of the form or media on which the original or other copies may exist. This license is not a sale of the original SOFTWARE or any copy to you.

3. **COPY RESTRICTIONS:** This SOFTWARE and the accompanying printed materials and user manual (the "Documentation") are the subject of copyright. The individual programs on the CD are copyrighted by the authors of each program. Some of the programs on the CD include separate licensing agreements. If you intend to use one of these programs, you must read and follow its accompanying license agreement. You may not copy the Documentation or the SOFTWARE, except that you may make a single copy of the SOFTWARE for backup or archival purposes only. You may be held legally responsible for any copying or copyright infringement which is caused or encouraged by your failure to abide by the terms of this restriction.

4. **USE RESTRICTIONS:** You may not network the SOFTWARE or otherwise use it on more than one computer or computer terminal at the same time. You may physically transfer the SOFTWARE from one computer to another provided that the SOFTWARE is used on only one computer at a time. You may not distribute copies of the SOFTWARE or Documentation to others. You may not reverse engineer, disassemble, decompile, modify, adapt, translate, or create derivative works based on the SOFTWARE or the Documentation without the prior written consent of the Company.

5. **TRANSFER RESTRICTIONS:** The enclosed SOFTWARE is licensed only to you and may not be transferred to any one else without the prior written consent of the Company. Any unauthorized transfer of the SOFTWARE shall result in the immediate termination of this Agreement.

6. **TERMINATION:** This license is effective until terminated. This license will terminate automatically without notice from the Company and become null and void if you fail to comply with any provisions or limitations of this license. Upon termination, you shall destroy the Documentation and all copies of the SOFTWARE. All provisions of this Agreement as to warranties, limitation of liability, remedies or damages, and our ownership rights shall survive termination.

7. **MISCELLANEOUS:** This Agreement shall be construed in accordance with the laws of the United States of America and the State of New York and shall benefit the Company, its affiliates, and assignees.

8. **LIMITED WARRANTY AND DISCLAIMER OF WARRANTY:** The Company warrants that the SOFTWARE, when properly used in accordance with the Documentation, will operate in substantial conformity with the description of the SOFTWARE set forth in the Documentation. The Company does not warrant that the SOFTWARE will meet your requirements or that the operation

of the SOFTWARE will be uninterrupted or error-free. The Company warrants that the media on which the SOFTWARE is delivered shall be free from defects in materials and workmanship under normal use for a period of thirty (30) days from the date of your purchase. Your only remedy and the Company's only obligation under these limited warranties is, at the Company's option, return of the warranted item for a refund of any amounts paid by you or replacement of the item. Any replacement of SOFTWARE or media under the warranties shall not extend the original warranty period. The limited warranty set forth above shall not apply to any SOFTWARE which the Company determines in good faith has been subject to misuse, neglect, improper installation, repair, alteration, or damage by you. EXCEPT FOR THE EXPRESSED WARRANTIES SET FORTH ABOVE, THE COMPANY DISCLAIMS ALL WARRANTIES, EXPRESS OR IMPLIED, INCLUDING WITHOUT LIMITATION, THE IMPLIED WARRANTIES OF MERCHANTABILITY AND FITNESS FOR A PARTICULAR PURPOSE. EXCEPT FOR THE EXPRESS WARRANTY SET FORTH ABOVE, THE COMPANY DOES NOT WARRANT, GUARANTEE, OR MAKE ANY REPRESENTATION REGARDING THE USE OR THE RESULTS OF THE USE OF THE SOFTWARE IN TERMS OF ITS CORRECTNESS, ACCURACY, RELIABILITY, CURRENTNESS, OR OTHERWISE.

IN NO EVENT, SHALL THE COMPANY OR ITS EMPLOYEES, AGENTS, SUPPLIERS, OR CONTRACTORS BE LIABLE FOR ANY INCIDENTAL, INDIRECT, SPECIAL, OR CONSEQUENTIAL DAMAGES ARISING OUT OF OR IN CONNECTION WITH THE LICENSE GRANTED UNDER THIS AGREEMENT, OR FOR LOSS OF USE, LOSS OF DATA, LOSS OF INCOME OR PROFIT, OR OTHER LOSSES, SUSTAINED AS A RESULT OF INJURY TO ANY PERSON, OR LOSS OF OR DAMAGE TO PROPERTY, OR CLAIMS OF THIRD PARTIES, EVEN IF THE COMPANY OR AN AUTHORIZED REPRESENTATIVE OF THE COMPANY HAS BEEN ADVISED OF THE POSSIBILITY OF SUCH DAMAGES. IN NO EVENT SHALL LIABILITY OF THE COMPANY FOR DAMAGES WITH RESPECT TO THE SOFTWARE EXCEED THE AMOUNTS ACTUALLY PAID BY YOU, IF ANY, FOR THE SOFTWARE.

SOME JURISDICTIONS DO NOT ALLOW THE LIMITATION OF IMPLIED WARRANTIES OR LIABILITY FOR INCIDENTAL, INDIRECT, SPECIAL, OR CONSEQUENTIAL DAMAGES, SO THE ABOVE LIMITATIONS MAY NOT ALWAYS APPLY. THE WARRANTIES IN THIS AGREEMENT GIVE YOU SPECIFIC LEGAL RIGHTS AND YOU MAY ALSO HAVE OTHER RIGHTS WHICH VARY IN ACCORDANCE WITH LOCAL LAW.

ACKNOWLEDGMENT

YOU ACKNOWLEDGE THAT YOU HAVE READ THIS AGREEMENT, UNDERSTAND IT, AND AGREE TO BE BOUND BY ITS TERMS AND CONDITIONS. YOU ALSO AGREE THAT THIS AGREEMENT IS THE COMPLETE AND EXCLUSIVE STATEMENT OF THE AGREEMENT BETWEEN YOU AND THE COMPANY AND SUPERSEDES ALL PROPOSALS OR PRIOR AGREEMENTS, ORAL, OR WRITTEN, AND ANY OTHER COMMUNICATIONS BETWEEN YOU AND THE COMPANY OR ANY REPRESENTATIVE OF THE COMPANY RELATING TO THE SUBJECT MATTER OF THIS AGREEMENT.

Should you have any questions concerning this Agreement or if you wish to contact the Company for any reason, please contact in writing at the address below.

Robin Short

Prentice Hall PTR

One Lake Street

Upper Saddle River, New Jersey 07458

ABOUT THE CD-ROM

The CD-ROM included with *Core JSP* contains the following:

- All example code used in *Core JSP*, including the sample Database creation scripts needed to test the examples.
- Links to other JSP resources on the Internet, as well as the *Core JSP* web site.
- Several JSP development tools, including:
    - Allaire HomeSite 4.51 Evaluation Version for Microsoft Windows 95/98/NT/2000.
    - Allaire JRun 3.0 Development Version for Linux 2.0 Kernel, HPUX, Sun Solaris, IBM AIX, Compaq Tru64, SGI IRIX, and Microsoft Windows.
    - Netscape Communicator 4.7 for Microsoft Windows, Solaris SPARC, Solaris x86, Linux 2.0 Kernel, SGI IRIX, HP-UX, Dec UNIX, and IBM AIX. Complete and minimal installation versions.
    - Forte for Java Community Edition for Linux, Sun SOLARIS, Windows 95/98/NT/2000, and any standard JRE.
    - Java Runtime Environment (JRE) for Windows 95/98/NT/2000, Solaris SPARC, Solaris x86, and Linux.
    - Apache Tomcat 3.1for Microsoft Windows and UNIX.

The CD-ROM can be used on Microsoft Windows 95/98/NT/2000, Linux, and many different versions of Unix.

License Agreement

Use of the software accompanying *Core JSP* is subject to the terms of the License Agreement and Limited Warranty, found on the previous two pages.

Technical Support

Prentice Hall does not offer technical support for any of the programs on the CD-ROM. However, if the CD-ROM is damaged, you may obtain a replacement copy by sending an email that describes the problem to: disc_exchange@prenhall.com